D1287920

EDITH BOLLING WILSON

First Lady Extraordinary

Also by Alden Hatch

THE DE GAULLE NOBODY KNOWS

CIRCUS KINGS *(with Henry Ringling North)*

THE WADSWORTHS OF THE GENESEE

CROWN OF GLORY: POPE PIUS XII

GENERAL IKE

REMINGTON ARMS IN AMERICAN HISTORY

EDITH
BOLLING
WILSON

First Lady Extraordinary

BY

ALDEN HATCH

DODD, MEAD & COMPANY

NEW YORK, 1961

ACKNOWLEDGMENTS

M Y MOST SINCERE THANKS are due to Mrs. Woodrow Wilson, not only for making her diary and private papers available to me and checking my manuscript for factual errors, but, especially, for the many hours of delightful conversation in the house on S Street when with rare intelligence and wit she reminisced about the great moments and great men she has known, and gave me fresh insight into the human side of the man she is sure was the greatest of them all, Woodrow Wilson.

Others to whom I am indebted for assistance include Mrs. Margaret C. Brown, Mrs. George L. Harrison, Mrs. James M. Helm, Mrs. Gilbert M. Hitchcock, Cary T. Grayson, Jr., and Sterling Bolling. I would also like to thank Chase, Ltd., for the use of the beautiful photograph of Mrs. Wilson that appears on the jacket.

Among the dozens of books which I read in the course of my research the following were particularly useful:

My Memoir by Edith Bolling Wilson; *Woodrow Wilson, Life and Letters,* by Ray Stannard Baker; *An American Chronicle* by

5

Ray Stannard Baker; *Woodrow Wilson—An Intimate Memoir* by
Cary T. Grayson; *Our Times* by Mark Sullivan; *Woodrow Wilson*
by William Allen White; *Memoirs* by Josephus Daniels; and *The
Captains and the Kings* by Edith Benham Helm.

ALDEN HATCH

"Somerleas"
Cedarhurst
Long Island

CONTENTS

EDITH BOLLING WILSON

First Lady Extraordinary

CHAPTER I

THE COURTSHIP OF A PRESIDENT

THE PRESIDENT OF THE UNITED STATES was playing golf. He was doing it with the dogged determination of his Presbyterian nature, for he disliked the game and had once described it as "an ineffectual attempt to put an illusive ball into an obscure hole with implements ill adapted to the purpose." But his doctor had ordered President Wilson to take this form of exercise.

Under the circumstances the least young Dr. Cary Grayson could do was to keep his eminent patient company. In the last two stressful years as the naval doctor attached to the White House he had become completely devoted to the President.

On this windy, brilliant afternoon in March 1915, the two men would normally have played eighteen holes. But for some reason they decided to stop at the twelfth hole. They climbed into a Pierce-Arrow landaulet with the presidential seal on the door. At the White House they walked through the marble hall and up the great staircase, leaving a trail of mud from their boots.

As they rounded the corner into the long second-floor corridor the door of the push-button elevator opened and one of the most

beautiful women he had ever seen stepped out of it almost into the
President's arms. She, too, was wind-blown and disheveled. Her
small walking shoes were covered with mud and her dark hair
escaping from under a small tricorn hat was flying about her lovely
face. Her large violet eyes were round with surprise, then crinkled
into laughter.

Behind her the President saw his young cousin Helen Woodrow
Bones. She had run the great house for him ever since the death of
his wife, Ellen Axson Wilson, seven months before.

"Cousin Woodrow," said Helen Bones, "I should like to present
Mrs. Norman Galt."

Edith Bolling Galt had never been to tea at the White House
before; in fact she had avoided it rather assiduously. Her husband,
Norman Galt, owner of Galt's, where fashionable Washington
bought its jewels, had died eight years before. Since then she had
lived rather quietly in her small house at 1308 Twentieth Street
N.W., seeing only her particular friends. For, though the Bollings
were one of the great families of Virginia, the fact that her husband
had been "in trade" made her suspect to the Cliff Dwellers, as old
Washingtonian society was called. Nor did she aspire to their
company.

Mrs. Galt cared even less about politics and politicians. Her
interests were in travel, the theater, good music and books, and her
friends were people of like tastes.

She had met the President once before at one of those gigantic
White House receptions which he gave early in his administration.
Asked if she felt any emotional impact when she first touched his
hand, she smiled and said, "No! He just gave me the push-along
handshake."

She had met Helen Bones through Dr. Grayson. The doctor
often came to her house to court her young friend Alice Gertrude
(Altrude) Gordon and afterwards married her. On one occasion
he had brought Helen with him, and the rather lonely young chate-

laine of the White House had struck up a close friendship with
the older woman.

On this particular afternoon Helen Bones and Mrs. Galt had
gone for a walk together and Helen had invited her back for tea.
Edith Galt said, "I couldn't do that. My shoes are a sight and I
look like a tramp."

Helen answered, "Yes you can, for not a soul's there. Cousin
Woodrow is playing golf with Dr. Grayson. We'll go straight up
in the elevator and have tea alone in my sitting room. Cousin
Woodrow often asks me why I never bring my friends here. He
really wishes I'd have someone in this lonely old house."

Thus, as Edith says, "I turned a corner and met my fate."

As they all stood there laughing in the corridor she admits that
she was thinking, "At least I'm disheveled in a suit by Worth." And
she noted that both the President's and Grayson's golfing knickers
and tweed Norfolk jackets were poorly cut. "They were *not* smart."

At the President's insistence tea was transferred to the Oval
Room on the second floor. The men changed. The ladies fresh-
ened up—with a good deal of care—and they met in front of a
crackling fire.

That was an enchanted hour. Everyone was suddenly at his very
best. Helen, tiny and dark, glowed with happiness. Young Dr.
Grayson, much smarter now in his naval officer's uniform, told
funny stories, his black eyes snapping with merriment. Edith Galt,
responding happily to the atmosphere, felt as if she were among
old friends. She was aware that the President could hardly take
his eyes off her.

Indeed, Woodrow Wilson for the first time in many weary
months of strain and sorrow, of war in Europe and trouble in
Mexico and death in his home, felt as happy as a boy. He laughed
out loud at Grayson's stories, recited some appropriate limericks
and talked such nonsense as the people who knew only his austere
public image would not have believed possible. And all the time
he was fixing in his mind the picture of Mrs. Galt's beauty.

At forty-three she was quite an impressive woman. She was

rather tall with a full-curved figure, had a round, radiant face distinguished by a fine aquiline nose, and straight dark brows over laughing eyes that changed from blue to violet. Her skin was the creamy white of the magnolias Wilson remembered in a South Carolina Spring. He had an impression of abounding vitality.

The hour passed too quickly. When Mrs. Galt rose to go, the President boyishly tried to prolong her stay by inviting her to dinner. But she declined from shyness or a sense of propriety, for she was a very proper lady indeed. When she had gone it occurred to Woodrow Wilson that he had not laughed so much since Ellen died.

A few days after this Helen Bones telephoned to ask if Mrs. Galt would like to take an automobile ride instead of their usual afternoon walk. Edith agreed; she loved driving and the little electric coupe she used in Washington would not take her very far. Helen said she would send a car to pick her up.

As she drove up to the shining portico of the White House in the big Pierce-Arrow touring car with the top down, Mrs. Galt was amazed to see the President in a golfing cap and overcoat standing beside Helen Bones. He wanted to ride in front beside Robinson the chauffeur. The lone Secret Service man sat on the jump seat and the two women had the big back seat all to themselves.

Mrs. Galt noted that the President's face looked drawn and exhausted, and that he hardly spoke at all as the big car rolled across the bridge over the Potomac and through the spring-fresh countryside. For the first time she was conscious of the burdens the Presidency put upon a man and felt a faint stirring of the maternal instinct to protect him. When they returned to the White House the President again asked her to stay for dinner. This time she did not refuse.

The three of them ate in the great gloomy state dining room with its dark paneled walls and heavy draperies. Candles in huge, ornate candelabra barely lightened the tenebrous gloom, and the Negro butler and two uniformed footmen silently waiting on them added to the oppressive atmosphere. For the second time that day Edith Galt was conscious of the liabilities of being President.

It was very different after dinner before the fire in the Oval Room. Woodrow Wilson looked suddenly young and vigorous and his unexpected gaiety lifted all their spirits. To entertain the ladies he read aloud from some of his favorite classics. No one could read more movingly than Woodrow Wilson, who by expression and emphasis added new meaning and beauty to familiar words. When a statement appeared confused he would discuss with the ladies what the author had intended to say. At one rather difficult passage he told Mrs. Galt, "If I had written that as a boy my father would have made me restate it."

That led him to talk about his youth and the close relationship with his minister father. The clear precise style for which Wilson had become famous was, he said, due to his father's training. Often when his son brought him a paper he had written, the Reverend Mr. Wilson would ask, "Did you mean so and so?"

If Woodrow said, "Yes," his father might reply, "Well, you did not say it. So suppose you try again and see if you can say what you mean this time. If not we'll have another talk and a third go at it."

Smiling, the President said, "Many times we had a fourth and fifth go at it before I got it precisely right."

The talk about his boyhood led Wilson and Edith Galt to find many things in common. They had both grown up in a South impoverished by the Civil War. They had known many of the same hardships and simple pleasures. In an hour or two they knew each other better than years of casual acquaintanceship might have made possible. Mrs. Wilson says, "For the first time I felt the warm personality of Woodrow Wilson. He had a boylike simplicity. . . . Thereafter I never thought of him as the President of the United States, but as a real friend. . . ."

The President was indeed boyish in his eagerness to be with his new friend. All that spring he constantly suggested expeditions for

the three of them to take, and when the increasing pressures of the
European war kept him in his office, they went for after-dinner
drives through the fragrant spring evenings. Mrs. Wilson records
that the President often discussed affairs of state with her. "From
the first," she writes, "he knew he could rely on my prudence, and
what he said went no further. When problems confronted him,
which they did in every hour of those tragic years, it seemed to
clarify things to talk to us as we sped along through the cool April
night. . . ."

Thus, even before the thought of marriage occurred to either of
them, Edith's education in the complexities of America's position
in a suddenly chaotic world began. If the President was a little
ingenuous in so freely discussing official secrets with a beautiful
woman, his confidence was not misplaced.

On April 28, 1915, Mrs. Galt received her first note from the
President. Because its stately phrasing is so typical of their relationship it is worth quoting:

MY DEAR MRS. GALT:

I have ordered a copy of Hamerton's "Round My House"
through the bookseller. . . . I hope it will give you a little
pleasure. I covet nothing more than to give you pleasure—
you have given me so much.
If it rains this evening would it be any fun for you to come
around and have a little reading—and, if it does not rain, are
you game for another ride? . . .

Your sincere and grateful friend
WOODROW WILSON

Only two days later Mrs. Galt was invited to dine at the White
House. That afternoon a corsage of golden roses arrived from the
President.

On May 3 Mrs. Galt dined again at the White House. She still
has the dress she wore that night—white satin with creamy lace and
a touch of emerald green velvet at the edge of its deep, square neck.

The dinner was quite a family gathering. Grayson was there, of course, and Helen Bones, the President's daughter Margaret, his sister Mrs. George Howe, and her daughter, Mrs. Cothran. Summer warmth had suddenly rolled up over Washington from the South and after dinner they sat in the columned oval of the south portico. Dr. Grayson left early and the ladies decided to stroll in the grounds.

When they had disappeared the President hitched his wicker chair close to Mrs. Galt's, and with his fine gray eyes searching her face said, "I asked Margaret and Helen to give me a chance to tell you something I have already told them."

Then in the shy, formal words of a very young man, but with a moving intensity of feeling, he told Edith Galt that he loved her deeply.

She was so surprised that for once her gracious poise deserted her and she said the first thing that came into her head, "Oh, you can't love me. You don't really know me and it's less than a year since your wife died."

The President said very seriously, "Yes, I know you must feel that, but, little girl, time in this place is not measured by weeks or months, but by deep human experience. Since Ellen's death I have lived a lifetime of loneliness and heartache. I was afraid, knowing you, that I would shock you, but I would be less than a gentleman if I continued to make opportunities to see you without telling you what I have told my daughters and Helen—that I want you to be my wife. In the spotlight that is always on this house and on me, whoever comes here is immediately observed and discussed; and do what I can to protect you from gossip, it will inevitably begin. If you care for me as I do for you we will brave this. . . . As for the girls, they have been wonderful about it. They tell me they love you for your own sake, but would anyway for mine."

This long declaration set Mrs. Galt's head whirling but did not stampede her. She felt she must have time—a long time—to know herself, to distinguish between the glamour of the great office Wilson held and the hypnotic effect of his brilliant mind, and her true feelings for the man himself. They talked for at least an hour. In the end they agreed that he would wait, and in the meantime they would continue their friendship.

The next morning a very distraught Helen Bones went walking with Edith in Rock Creek Park. After a little she sat down on a rock and burst into tears. "Cousin Woodrow looks really ill this morning," she said, "just as I thought some happiness was coming into his life. And now you are breaking his heart."

Right then Grayson inopportunely galloped up on his big horse, Kelly, and of course wanted to know what was wrong. The ladies got rid of him with a rather flimsy excuse. But the interruption gave Mrs. Galt time to pull herself together. She admits that she felt like an ogre. But she explained very carefully to Helen that no one, least of all the President, would want to be married for pity; that she must have time to know her own heart. "To do this I must continue to see him," she said, "and I am honest enough to say I want to see him. Now that my eyes are open it may seem unwomanly [her exact phrase] to go on with these informal dinners and long rides. But as in the circumstances he can't come to me, I will go to him. This must satisfy even you."

Just four days after the President proposed to Mrs. Galt he received a terrible shock. The American people were jarred out of their secure serenity by what, in that comparatively innocent era seemed the most barbarous act man's inhumanity had ever perpetrated. The great Cunarder *Lusitania* was torpedoed without warning by a German submarine a few miles off the Irish coast, and sank in twenty minutes. Eleven hundred and ninety-eight men, women and children were drowned, of whom 114 were American citizens.

To understand the impact of shock and horror on this country we must return mentally to a less savage world, a world that did not yet know about poison gas or genocide, Buchenwald or Hiroshima; a world that was a little naïve. In their incredulous anger the American people were ready to go to war to avenge that infamy. Had the President so much as nodded they would have done so.

The pressures bearing down on Woodrow Wilson were enormous. First was his own disgust at the deed and his deep compassion for the victims—tears came into his eyes as the cabled reports mounted. He had a human impulse to avenge it. Then there were all the people shouting about the honor of America and the cowardice of doing nothing. Finally for the first time in history the entire world was looking to America for leadership.

But the President was no coward and he believed that to yield his conviction that war was too terrible to contemplate as anything but a last resort would be moral cowardice. At Philadelphia, on May 10, he dampened the fires of American anger by the famous speech, so often misrepresented, in which he said, "The example of America must be a special example . . . not merely of peace because it will not fight, but of peace because peace is the healing and elevating influence of the world and strife is not. There is such a thing as being too proud to fight. . . ."

However, Wilson could not let German ruthlessness go unrebuked. However much he wanted peace, another *Lusitania* would surely hurl America into war by a sort of popular explosion. So he wrote a note to the imperial German government—on his own typewriter without consulting the State Department—calling them to "strict accountability" and stating his expectation that "they will make reparation as far as reparation is possible . . . and that they will take immediate steps to prevent the recurrence of anything so subversive of the principles of warfare. . . ."

He read the note to the Cabinet with great emotion. They all applauded except Secretary of State William Jennings Bryan, who signed it with avowed reluctance. This dedicated pacifist considered this a step toward war.

On May 14, the day after the dispatch of the first *Lusitania* note, Wilson sailed in the presidential yacht *Mayflower* to review the Atlantic Fleet in New York Harbor. With him went Mrs. Howe, her daughter and small granddaughter, Helen Bones; Margaret Wilson; his secretary, Joseph Tumulty; Dr. Grayson; and Mrs. Norman Galt and her friend Altrude Gordon. Edith told herself that the expedition had been planned so long before the President's proposal that to drop out would "cause comment." Actually she was as eager as a schoolgirl for the treat.

Of all the perquisites of the Presidency, Woodrow Wilson liked the *Mayflower* best. Though he had never been to sea until he was a grown man, he loved it now and was an excellent sailor. To such a man the yacht was a delight. She was one of those extravagant, lovely things that have vanished with the era of the great tycoons. Her graceful, curving hull and superstructure were painted white and picked out in gold. Two high masts and a very tall funnel related her distantly to the age of sail.

Her interior was as elaborate as a fine mansion. Indeed, the white Corinthian columns supporting the ceiling of the main saloon and the elaborate paneling and woodwork made her resemble the White House and, also, a Mississippi steamboat. The principal rooms were furnished with Chippendale chairs and settees, Oriental rugs, pictures and the bric-a-brac so dear to Edwardian taste. The sleeping cabins were equally luxurious with twin beds, dressing tables and fine big windows looking out on the promenade deck, which was as long as that of a small ocean liner.

As the huge white yacht hummed softly down the Potomac River the war receded like the lights of Washington. It was a very merry party. They sat on the circular sweep of the fantail looking over moon-lacquered water until the ship's bell tolled for Mount Vernon. Then the others drifted tactfully off to less comfortable parts of the boat, leaving the President alone with Mrs. Galt. "Let's lean on the rail instead of walking," he said to her. "I want to talk to you, ask your advice."

So they stood close together looking along the foaming wake while the President continued. "I am terribly distressed by a letter I had late today from the Secretary of State. He says that his pacifist beliefs make it impossible for him to go on in the Department. He cannot follow me in wishing to warn our country and Germany that we may be forced to take up arms if they continue submarine warfare, and therefore he feels it is his duty to resign."

The President paused to let her consider this. Then he asked, "What do you think the effect would be?"

"Good," said Mrs. Galt bluntly. "For I hope you can replace him with someone who is able, and who would in himself command respect for the office both at home and abroad."

They talked for a long time after that about the worsening situation. In the end they came back to Bryan's offer to resign. Quoting a line from a play she had seen years before, Edith said, "My advice is, 'Take it, sir, and thank God for the chance.' "

Thus for the first time Edith Galt laid her feather on the scales of history. That she was wrong to dismiss so great a man so flippantly she admitted in mellow later years. But she was instinctively right about the act itself. For with all his noble qualities William Jennings Bryan, by his beliefs, his education and his moral code, was among the least fitted of American politicians for the post of Secretary of State. As Franklin K. Lane put it, "He is too good a Christian to run a naughty world." Yielding to his views would have been disastrous.

That quiet sail down the Potomac turned into a shambles the next morning as the *Mayflower,* groaning and squeaking with every heave and pitch rounded Cape Charles to the open sea in a violent storm. Edith recorded, not too unhappily, that all the ladies except herself were laid low. She came on the windy deck to find Altrude Gordon lying flat on her back with devoted Dr. Grayson sitting beside her. He, too, looked ghastly. "Why don't you get a rug for poor Altrude?" she suggested.

Grayson gave her a look like a hound dog kicked in the ribs. Then, "like the gentleman he was," he gathered himself in a desperate leap and disappeared below before anything could happen.

The President came along obviously feeling fine and said he would send up his valet, Brooks, with some brandy for Altrude. After a long wait Mrs. Galt decided to go for the brandy herself.

She found poor Brooks in the dining saloon hanging to the side-
board with one hand, and a silver tray with brandy and a glass in
the other, completely immobilized by his chaotic interior. "I'll take
the brandy, Brooks," she said kindly. "You go and lie down."

When she was halfway through the main saloon the *Mayflower*
leaped like a harpooned whale and Mrs. Galt knew that her time
had finally come. She lay down on her back in the middle of the
floor carefully holding the brandy bottle upright on her chest and
closed her eyes.

She opened them to find the President bending over her saying
anxiously, "Are you hurt, Mrs. Galt?"

"No, Mr. President," she replied formally, "I'm only sick, but
I'll be all right in a minute or two."

Suddenly the absurdity of the situation struck them both and
they roared with laughter.

Edith Galt had seen the pressures and loneliness of the Presidency; now for the first time she took part in its pageantry. She
stood beside the President on the bridge of the *Mayflower* as she
sailed slowly up the Hudson between the long double line of battleships, cruisers and destroyers. Every gray ship was bright with
flags, her decks filled by ranks of sailors in whites; every band
played "The Star-Spangled Banner" as the *Mayflower* came abreast
and the guns banged out the twenty-one-gun salute to the Commander-in-Chief, repeated half a hundred times as ship after ship
joined in. The reports of the cannon echoed back from the Pali-
sades and the white smoke haze half hid the saluting crews and
curled up the tall, basket-type masts of the battleships.

A stirring scene calculated to make any man's—or woman's—
blood run hot with pride and lust of glory. But Wilson was not
carried away. Afterward he drove through tremendous, cheering
crowds to the Biltmore Hotel where he spoke again of peace, saying, "Those quiet ships lying in the river have no suggestion of
bluster about them. . . . The force of America is the force of moral

principle. . . . There is nothing else she loves, and there is nothing else for which she will contend."

In the days before air conditioning everyone who possibly could left Washington in summer. President Wilson as usual rented a house in Cornish, New Hampshire. Harlakenden House, which belonged to Winston Churchill, the American novelist, was a big comfortable rambling old place on a hill overlooking the winding Connecticut River. It was the custom for Wilson's whole family to join him there, and in the summer of 1915 Helen Bones and Margaret Wilson invited Mrs. Galt to come as well.

Edith thought it rather daring to accept, but she wanted to very much. Looking back, she expresses amazement that she had not yet made up her mind. How anyone who knew Woodrow Wilson could possibly *not* love him defeats her imagination now. She hesitated because he was President of the United States, honestly afraid that she might not measure up to the responsibilities of being his wife. Despite her apparent poise, she was really shy about the social obligations since she had so little training to meet them.

The few week ends and one stretch of ten days that the President managed to spend in Cornish, between tense exchanges with the imperial German government, settled one thing forever. Edith no longer doubted her love for the man. But she still feared the office.

"If you are defeated for election next year I'll marry you," she promised.

That was as far as she would go.

She spent the remaining two months of summer with friends in Geneva, New York, and came back to Washington in September. It seemed to her that she had been away a very long time.

The first night she was home, September 3, 1915, she was invited to dinner at the White House. Helen and Margaret welcomed her in the marble hall under the big brass lantern and said that the President was with the Secretary of War. As they sat in the Red Room waiting for him, both girls leaped to attack her. They said that the strain of the last two months had been almost unbearable for Wilson and they insisted it was her fault—more so than the Kaiser's.

Just as Edith began to bristle defensively, the President came quickly in from the Blue Room. One look at the deep new lines in his face told her that, whatever the reason, he was under intense strain.

Wilson strode straight across the room holding out both his hands to Edith. She put her hands in his and looked into his eyes —"unlike any others in the world"—and all her defenses went down.

Of course nothing happened right then. There was the usual meal in that cavernous state dining room—no one has ever known why Wilson always ate dinner there instead of in the cheerful break-fast room. After dinner Margaret rushed off to keep an engage-ment. The open car came up to the door with Robinson at the wheel and Mr. Murphy of the Secret Service beside him. The President, Helen Bones and Mrs. Galt went out for a drive as usual, except that it was not usual.

The President was in a somber mood. He could not shake off the thoughts that crowded his brain. While they drove slowly through the familiar streets and on to the dark country lanes of Bethesda, Maryland, Wilson talked steadily about the worsening state of the nation. The impact of Allied purchases of munitions had started a wild industrial boom that he feared would end in an awful crash. Our relations with Mexico were strained to the ut-most by the chaotic revolutionary conditions there. Finally the German government, after a period of restraint, was baring its fangs again. "I doubt if anything I can in honor do will keep us out of war," the President said.

He sat for a while with his troubled eyes contemplating the un-certain future. Then he sadly made the sacrifice he had planned. "And so, little girl," he said, "I have no right to ask you to help me by sharing this load that is almost breaking my back, for I know your nature and you might do it out of sheer pity."

Edith Galt had listened in anxiety and pride, deep understanding and wonder at the greatness of this simple man, her emotions rising to a pitch of violence. Now the torrent of her love burst the veneer of prudery. She flung her arms around the President's neck. Then with a final attempt to stave off tears and save her pride she said humorously, "Well, if you won't ask me, I'll volunteer, and be ready to be mustered in as soon as can be."

CHAPTER II

A VERY SMALL WEDDING

DESPITE MRS. GALT'S MAIDENLY HESITATIONS, love's course so far had been pretty smooth. But storms were gathering unknown to the dwellers in that House, at once so exposed to public observation and so insulated from public opinion.

The trouble did not, as could have been expected, come from the President's family. He had three daughters who might have resented the advent of a stepmother so soon after their own mother's death. Jessie, the gentlest, had been married in the White House to Francis Sayre in 1913. Eleanor (Nell), by far the prettiest and most vivacious, had also been married in the White House, to Wilson's Secretary of the Treasury, William Gibbs McAdoo. Margaret, the oldest, lived partly at the White House and partly in New York, where she was studying singing. She was a rather strange young woman who looked exactly like her father even to his long straight nose, jutting chin and rimless pince-nez. Margaret had an almost masculine mind of her own.

All three girls abetted their father's romance. They honestly liked Mrs. Galt and they realized that their high-strung, sensitive

father, whose spirit was as volatile as his high purpose was resolute, desperately needed feminine companionship and love. Perhaps they were glad to drop the responsibility on other shoulders.
Mrs. Galt's were very capable.

Other members of the first Mrs. Wilson's family were equally
enthusiastic. For example, her brother, Stockton Axson, wrote:
"We are all thoroughly thankful that the great man doesn't have
to keep on being a *lonely* great man. . . . Isn't she [Mrs. Galt] a
vivid person? And with all that, most sweet and lovely."

But if the President's own family were serene, his official family
were tearing their hair out in handfuls. As Wilson had warned his
fiancée, she had become the subject of malicious gossip. Practically every member of the Cabinet was getting letters from influ-
ential constituents asking if the President intended to marry Mrs.
Galt. Most of the letters warned that if he did, so soon after his
first wife's death, the repercussion in the country might ruin his
chance of re-election in 1916.

The gentlemen of the Cabinet took these warnings very seriously. So did the President's secretary, Joseph Tumulty. That
exuberant young Irish politician, who had joined the President
when he became Governor of New Jersey and had helped to advise
him ever since, was not only worried, he may also have been jealous
of Mrs. Galt's ascending influence.

The various Cabinet members conferred with each other and
with Tumulty as to how far this "terrible business" had gone and
how to stop it. Finally they decided to see what Secretary of the
Navy Josephus Daniels—who was, perhaps, closest to the President
—could do.

Daniels was a wise, warm southern gentleman. And although
he knew nothing about ships and habitually went to sea wearing a
yachting cap and a frock coat, he did know a great deal about the
human heart. In his autobiography he tells how one day in September Postmaster General Albert Burleson, "the Political Generalis-
simo of the Wilson Administration," asked to see him "on a very
important matter."

Burleson, looking like a worried banker in his dark suit, winged collar and rimless eyeglasses, carefully closed all the doors and said almost in a whisper, "What do you think of the gossip that the President is deeply interested in Mrs. Galt?"

"In my judgment," Daniels said cheerfully, "we'll have a new boss before Christmas."

"Are you certain of that?" Burleson quavered.

"Just as certain as that you're sitting in that chair. Nobody has told me anything. The President has not asked my advice or consent. But the sails are set. I predict that by New Year's Day Mrs. Galt will change her name to Mrs. Woodrow Wilson."

"It's because I feared this that I've come to see you," said Burleson.

"Why to see me?" Daniels asked with affected innocence.

Burleson explained that scores, yes hundreds, of prominent Democrats from all parts of the country had been coming to see him and writing him letters—senators, congressmen, national committeemen, journalists. . . . And he added, "It's unanimous that if the President remarries before November, 1916, we might as well give up the fight right now."

"Oh, it's not as bad as that," Daniels soothed, "though in a close election it might be injurious."

"Something has to be done to postpone the marriage," Burleson moaned.

"What do you suggest?"

Burleson said that the bigwigs of the party had held a conference. "We unanimously agreed that someone should go to the President and lay the matter before him, appeal to his party loyalty, his patriotism."

Daniels writes, "Then came the shock of my life." Burleson told him that the conference had unanimously decided that he was the man to carry out the mission.

Though he seemed so amiable, Josephus Daniels was a downy old bird who was not about to jeopardize his friendship with Wilson and bring the fury of a future first lady down on his head.

Grasping the arms of the chair of the Secretary of the Navy, which he liked very much, he drawled, "I am honored by your confidence, but I do not feel inclined to exchange this seat for the difficult and perhaps dangerous, high and exalted position of Minister Plenipotentiary and Envoy Extraordinary to the Court of Cupid on a mission in which neither my heart nor my head is enlisted and in the performance of which I may well suffer official decapitation."

To this day when asked which of Wilson's Cabinet she liked best Edith Wilson says "Secretary Daniels."

Other men were not so wise. While they conspired and the storm of gossip raged, the principals happily made plans for the future. Mrs. Galt herself felt that the engagement should not be announced until after the election of 1916. She says that she was convinced the Republicans would win it and that "a sort of stubborn pride" made her want to show the world she was marrying the man, not the President. In view of Wilson's anxiety to marry her, his real need of her, this shows a certain egotism which, as her love for him grew, was swept away. For eventually she submerged her interests, her convenience and her personality totally in his.

It also shows how innocent of the world she really was to suppose that for a whole year she could continue to be with the President so often without causing a nation-rocking scandal.

She was soon disillusioned. On the evening of September 18 she was sitting in the library on the second floor of her small house waiting for the President and Dr. Grayson to pick her up for an evening's drive. The little doctor came in alone, his face white and wretched, his long nose pinched, his eyes black with misery. He told her an extraordinary story.

It seemed that Colonel E. M. House, Wilson's closest friend and adviser who because of his mousy appearance and supposed influence was known as "the Gray Eminence of the Administration," had just been to see the President. He and Wilson's son-in-law McAdoo had been told of the engagement in confidence. They had immediately sounded out some of their newspaper friends on an off-the-record basis. What they had learned had turned the little Colonel from gray to green.

One of the scurrilous features of the presidential campaign of 1912 had been a whispered scandal about Wilson's relations with Mrs. Thomas Peck of Bermuda. The truth was that Wilson had met Mrs. Peck on a vacation he had taken alone in Bermuda in 1908. He had enjoyed her brilliant conversation and the interesting people he met in her pretty, white coral villa. Later she came to visit the Wilsons in Princeton where his first wife formed a great friendship with her. For several years after that Wilson and Mrs. Peck wrote each other long intellectual letters about the state of Princeton University, the nation and the world.

During the campaign this rather cerebral friendship had been distorted into an impassioned love affair by the whisperers. They had Wilson neglecting his wife to dally with the siren of the islands. Those philosophical letters were said to be warmer than the correspondence of Chopin and George Sand. In view of Wilson's character and in the light of reason the whole thing was ridiculous. But in a political campaign the heat dims the light. A lot of people believed the libel.

Now, three years later, Colonel House had told the President that if his engagement to Mrs. Galt were announced the whole scandal would be revived. There was even a rumor that Mrs. Peck herself was going to publish the letters.

Poor Dr. Grayson, the most sensitive, shy man who ever packed a stethoscope, had a terrible time explaining these things to Mrs. Galt. It was the most horrible night of his whole life, as it was of hers.

"The President told Colonel House that it was his duty as a gentleman to protect you from such backstairs gossip," said Dr. Grayson. "He said he did not care about his own political fortunes and he did not think they would be affected. But the publicity would hurt and involve you in a way he had no right to ask."

"When House left," Grayson continued, "the President sat down to write you. He went white to the lips and his hand shook as I sat watching him try to write. His jaw was set, determined no matter what it cost him to spare you. Finally—a long time later— he put his pen down and said, 'I cannot bring myself to write this. You go, Grayson, and tell her everything, and say that my only alternative is to release her from any promise.' "

Grayson was in tears when he finished. He could hardly speak the last words. He got to his feet and said desperately, "What shall I tell him?"

Edith Galt was literally stunned. "Tell him I'll write," she whispered.

To understand a little of Edith Galt's feelings after Dr. Grayson left that night, one must move back mentally into the almost incomprehensible world of Victorian mores. It was a world of hypocrisy if you like, but the hypocrisy was based on real virtues, on belief in God, and in absolute good and evil; on the sacredness of womanhood and, above all, on the necessity of avoiding even the appearance of wrongdoing. A "lady," bred in the traditions of southern womanhood and surrounded all her life by the restrictions and protection of the code of southern chivalry, as Mrs. Galt had been, was more truly innocent than almost any adult now living. For such a one to be suddenly confronted with dark innuendo and scandal was a tremendous psychological shock. To brave it, she must be courageous indeed.

So Edith sat in her library through the whole night. To her credit never once did she think that there was any truth in the Peck scandal. Knowing Wilson so well she found the idea simply incredible and never gave it a thought. What did trouble her was the apprehension of being personally besmirched, the vulgar smear of a dirty business. She struggled all night with that fear and repulsion—almost physically as Luther fought with the devil. But she was too real a person to capitulate to false standards. Toward morning she got stiffly out of her chair and going to her desk sat down and wrote:

1308 TWENTIETH STREET
Sept. 19—1915

DEAREST—

The dawn has come . . . and all the hurt selfish feeling has
gone with the darkness—and I now see straight—straight into
the heart of things—and am ready to follow the road "Where
love leads."

How many times I have told you I wanted to help—and
now when the first test has come I faltered—But the falter-
ing was for love, not lack of love. I am not afraid of gossip
or threat with your love as my shield. . . .

This is my pledge, my dearest one, I will stand by you—
not for duty, not for honour—but for love-trusting, protecting comprehending love. . . .

I am so tired I could put my head down on the desk and
go to sleep but nothing could bring me real rest until I had
pledged you my love and allegiance.

Your own
EDITH

She sent the letter by hand to the White House early that morning. There was no answer from the President. All that day she
waited expectantly; and the next day and into the next. At first
she was worried, then angry and finally frightened. Her racing
mind pictured a gigantic conspiracy whose members had somehow
managed to intercept her letter; who would stop at nothing to part
her from the President. Two dozen times her hand reached for the
telephone and was pulled back by pride. Perhaps the President
was making this an excuse to break with her. . . . The hours passed
like years.

About noon of the third day Grayson suddenly appeared again.
He looked even more haggard than before. Standing stiffly in the
doorway of the room he said, "I beg that you will come with me to
the White House. The President is very ill. I can do nothing. You
are the only person who can help."

Then, typically careful of the delicate code by which they lived, he warned her, "Neither Miss Margaret nor Miss Bones is there, so I shall have to act as chaperone."

"Did the President ask you to come?" Edith asked.

"No," said Grayson. "I told him I was coming and he said it would be unfair to you and weak of him to ask it." Then the Doctor burst out emotionally, "If you could see him you would not hesitate. He does not speak or sleep or eat."

Edith said, "Wait!" and fled to her bedroom. Not unnaturally, she was confused and frantic. She was almost sure, now, that her letter had been intercepted. Even so, how could Wilson doubt her? She records her emotions in the flowery phrases of a nineteenth-century novelist, but they were as real as Steinbeck's brutal prose. Then she remembered she had written, "I'll stand by you." Jamming a hat on any which way and grabbing a coat she joined Grayson.

The White House seemed hushed; the servants looked scared. They went up in the elevator. Grayson silently opened the door of the President's bedroom and beckoned to her.

All the curtains were drawn and Edith could barely see in the dim light. Brooks, who had been sitting beside the bed, moved away like a shadow. She saw the President's face turn toward her, "white and drawn with pain." Then she ran toward him, and took the hand he stretched out to her. It was icy cold, and clung to hers like a frightened child.

The mystery of the missing letter was not cleared up until the day after their marriage. Then rather shamefacedly the President drew it from his pocket, dog-eared but still sealed. "I was afraid to open it," he confessed.

To this day Mrs. Wilson believes that the whole episode was made up by House and Tumulty, with McAdoo as an accessory before the fact, to stop her from marrying the President. This is not true. There were, in fact, a lot of scandalous rumors flying around the newspaper offices. Wilson's official biographer, Ray Stannard

Baker, writes, "Political enemies who dared not attack [Wilson] in the open took this vile means of besmirching the President's character. Lying innuendos regarding his relationship with Mrs. Peck circulated everywhere. . . ."

The "panicky Democrats," as Baker calls them, were doing only what they thought was their duty for the party and the President himself. But, though Mrs. Wilson soon restored McAdoo to her good graces, she never forgave Colonel House and Joseph Tumulty.

The result of their intervention had the reverse effect from what these gentlemen had intended. Edith Galt agreed to an immediate announcement of the engagement. On the evening of October 6, 1915, she joined the President in his study just after Tumulty had left. Wilson sat down at the huge flat-topped desk and by the light of the old oil student lamp, brought by him all the way from Princeton, slipped a piece of paper in his battered typewriter, also a cherished relic of his academic days, and began to type. Edith leaned over his shoulder making occasional suggestions or supplying details.

The result was the following press release:

> The engagement was announced today of Mrs. Norman Galt and President Woodrow Wilson.
> Mrs. Galt is the widow of a well-known Washington business man who died some eight years ago. . . . She was Miss Edith Bolling and was born in Wytheville, Virginia . . . where her father, the Hon. William H. Bolling, a man of remarkable character and charm, won distinction as one of the ablest lawyers . . . of a State famous for its lawyers. In the circle of cultivated and interesting people who have had the privilege of knowing her, Mrs. Galt has enjoyed an enviable distinction, not only because of unusual beauty and charm, but also because of her unusual character and gifts. She has always been sought out as a delightful friend, and her thoughtfulness and quick capacity for anything she chose to undertake have made her friendship invaluable to those who were fortunate enough to win it.
> It was Miss Margaret Wilson and her cousin Miss Bones

who drew Mrs. Galt into the White House circle. . . . It is, indeed, the most interesting circumstance connected with the engagement just announced that the President's daughters should have picked Mrs. Galt out for their special admiration before their father did.

The President's announcement knocked the war in Europe right out of the headlines. The entire front page of virtually every newspaper in the country was devoted to the engagement. Banner headlines screamed the news in gigantic black, red or blue type. There were complete biographies of the President lifted from the newspaper morgues and hastily inaccurate accounts of Mrs. Galt's little-known life. They all made a great play of the fact that she was descended from Pocahontas. A headline in the Washington *Times* is typical:

MRS. GALT IS A REAL AMERICAN PRINCESS OF INDIAN LINEAGE. President's Fiancee is a Descendant, Ninth Generation, of Pocahontas.

All the papers carried the same beautiful picture of Mrs. Galt.

It was pure chance that she happened to have a good one, for she hated publicity. Only a few weeks before, Altrude Gordon had asked Mrs. Galt to go with her to the studio of Arnold Genthe, the Cecil Beaton of American society, where she had a hard-to-get appointment. As they came in, Genthe looked at Mrs. Galt with widening eyes and said, "Oh *yes*, come with me."

"I'm not the one who has the appointment," Edith said, smiling. "It is this young lady."

Genthe said crossly, "All right, I'll take her later, but I refuse to do anything until I photograph you."

The picture turned out to be the only one that ever did her complete justice. It became as familiar to Americans as George Washington on a dollar bill.

Beginning at dawn on October 7, Mrs. Galt was inundated by telegrams, letters and phone calls of congratulations as well as hundreds of invitations. The Cliff Dwellers suddenly realized that they had overlooked a good bet and made frantic efforts to rectify the error. They got nowhere.

With all the hoopla in the papers and the gossip columnists giving all they had, no one even mentioned Mrs. Peck.

There was a merry family dinner at the White House that night. All the Bollings then in Washington were there and all the Wilsons too. Edith's mother, Mrs. William H. Bolling, sat on the President's right and Edith on his left. For once the cavernous state dining room could not dim the gaiety.

In the course of dinner Edith once wanted to attract the President's attention. She said, "Woodrow . . ." Then a crimson blush spread from her forehead down her throat and bosom. Everyone there suddenly realized that it was the first time she had ever called him by his first name.

A crash of laughter, in which the President and his fiancée joined, made the chandeliers tinkle.

The next two months were filled with gay incidents. One of the few invitations they accepted was a New York dinner which Colonel and Mrs. House gave in their honor. That afternoon Wilson dropped into Dreicer and Co. to buy an engagement ring. In the car on the way to the Colonel's dinner he slipped on Edith's finger a great solitaire diamond set in platinum. Its extravagance was the measure of his love, for aside from his presidential salary he had only the meager savings of his academic career.

The President and his fiancée made their first public appearance at a Philadelphia World's Series game between the Boston Red Sox and the Phillies. Long afterward Edith wrote, "No matter how accustomed one grows to the deference paid the great office of the Presidency, it never ceases to be a thrilling experience to have all traffic stopped, the way cleared and hear acclaims from thousands of throats. So, in my first experience of sharing that acclaim, I was excited as any child."

During the first few innings the engaged couple took the crowd's

mind off the play. Then they were forgotten in the excitement of
a close game. Mrs. Galt was rooting for the Red Sox, the President
for the Phillies, and they teased each other at each turn of the
play. Like the old fans they both were they stood up for the traditional seventh-inning stretch. When an aide pointed out that it
was time to return to their train for Washington, Wilson took one
look at Edith's excited face and insisted that the train be held.
The couple stayed until the very end.

Now that they were officially engaged the President felt it was
comme il faut to go to Edith's house. He dined alone there with
her for the first time on October 10. No. 1308 Twentieth Street
was a narrow brick house with a high stoop, only two rooms deep.
The first floor consisted of a tiny entrance hall, a dining room and,
in front, a drawing room with a bay window. On the second floor
were a fine, comfortable library and Mrs. Galt's bedroom. The
third floor had a guest room, frequently occupied by Altrude Gordon, and an austere room with a full-size pool table. The Negro
servants slept on the fourth floor.

Since the drawing room, furnished with delicate French pieces
and a multitude of bibelots, was gay but uncomfortable, they always sat in the library after dinner. Once he began going there
the President went often. On fine nights he liked to walk swinging
along at a great pace through the empty streets of the small town
Washington then was, whistling a musical comedy tune while his
single Secret Service man trotted to keep up with him.

But of course there were many times they could not be together,
so the President had a telephone line installed that did not go
through the exchange but ran directly from his study in the White
House. Over that telephone he talked with Edith about all the
problems, international and domestic, that confronted him, which
he now faced with new strength and buoyancy.

It became his custom to send her inside information on these
matters by special messenger with a little note of comment or explanation. Then he would either call her to get her opinion or else
she would reply by letter. She says, "In this way I followed day

by day every phase of the mosaic which he was shaping into a pattern of statecraft, and we continued this partnership of thought and comradeship unbroken to the last day of his life. It was a rare privilege, and except for formal interviews with officials, I always 'sat in' when one or two people we knew came to discuss policies. In that way I was never a stranger to any subject, and often able in small ways to be of help."

The wedding day was set for December 18, 1915. Woodrow Wilson and Edith Galt were completely agreed that it should be a small and simple ceremony. To her friends who said, "You should be married in the White House," Edith replied that she thought this would be in bad taste and that furthermore a large wedding would bring many gifts, some of which might put an unfair financial strain on government officials. Other presents would embarrass the President because they would be the magnificent offerings of favor-seekers.

One present, however, they liked too much to refuse. It was a nugget of gold from the State of California. The wedding ring was fashioned from it—by Galt's of course. There was enough gold left over to make a scarf pin for Wilson enameled with the presidential seal, and a heavy seal ring with "Woodrow Wilson" engraved in the characters of his own peculiar shorthand.

Because her house was so tiny and her family so large, Edith Galt and the President agreed that only close relatives could be asked. Practically the only exceptions were Dr. Grayson and Altrude Gordon and a few of their old servants.

It was extremely difficult to maintain this rule under the tremendous pressure of Washington society and the newspapers, but in spite of her soft, sweet manner Edith Galt had a chrome-steel will. At the time of the wedding she even refused to bend it for the President himself.

It seems that the Episcopal bishop who was supposed to marry them had a wife. However, in making the arrangements with the bishop Mrs. Galt explained that since she was asking no one outside the immediate families and since his wife did not live in Washington, it would be no discourtesy if she were not invited. The bishop replied that they both understood.

However, two days before the wedding the bishop wrote Mrs. Wilson that his wife had come to Washington after all. They were sailing soon for England and it would cause her much "chagrin to acknowledge to her titled friends that she had not been asked to the marriage of the President." So he was going to bring her and he assumed that she would be welcome. He assumed too much.

With sparks of violet fire shooting out of her eyes Mrs. Galt plumped herself down at her desk and wrote an icy note to the unfortunate prelate informing him that she understood his wife's embarrassment and since it was now impossible to add to the list, "my only course is to excuse you from performing the ceremony." Then she called the President on the private telephone and read him both letters.

There was considerable amusement in the President's voice as he tried to calm his irate fiancée. He agreed that it was a preposterous thing for the bishop to have done, but he urged respect for his office as a reason for letting him get away with it. Also, he said, "There will be more gossip. Don't send your letter now. Wait a bit and think it over."

"No," said Mrs. Galt. "This letter goes right now. I will postpone our wedding rather than be bludgeoned into a thing like this."

"Yes," said the President, "I was afraid of that. But after all this poor fellow has enough to stand with a wife like that. . . ."

The letter went, nevertheless. Mrs. Galt's own pastor, Dr. Herbert Scott Smith of St. Margaret's Episcopal Church, was hurriedly asked to substitute for the bishop, and since Wilson was an elder of the Presbyterian Church, he was reinforced by Dr. James H. Taylor of the Central Presbyterian Church of Washington.

There were no more ructions. Edith's wedding day dawned crisply bright with a powder of fresh snow. Here is her record of how she spent the day:

Arose at 7:30 A.M.
Talked with the President over the private wire at 8:00 A.M.
Breakfasted with mother and sisters 8:10 A.M.
Read mail 8:45 to 9:00 A.M.
Received call from President 9:30 A.M.
Modiste and milliner's 10:00 A.M.
Inspected decorations 11:00 A.M.
Received calls from members of our family in town 11:30 A.M.
Dictated answers to notes of congratulations. Wrote thanks for wedding gifts 12 noon.
Luncheon 1:00 P.M.
Rested 1:30 P.M.
Went for automobile ride with President 4:30 P.M. [Evidently not even superstitious custom could swerve Edith.]
Returned home 6:00 P.M.
Married to President Wilson 8:30 P.M.
Cut bride's cake 8:45 P.M.

At the White House Ike Hoover reported to the President for the customary orders of the day. As he was leaving he said, "Mr. President, I will be on hand tonight as usual to tell you when it is time for the ceremony."

Grinning broadly the President asked, "Do you think I will need that, Hoover?"

Wilson arrived at 1308 Twentieth Street at eight o'clock and ran lightly upstairs to the familiar library where Edith was waiting for him. She looked lovely in a plain black velvet gown with a great splash of orchids at her waist and a large black velvet hat graced by an exotic sweep of rare feathers. Under it her face was rosy with excitement and her eyes were like black opals.

For once tension constricted their conversation until there was a knock on the door and Hoover said, "It is eight-thirty, Mr. President."

As they came out of the door the cathedral chimes of the clock in the hall were ringing the half hour. The President, pale with emotion, offered Edith his arm and they walked down the stairs in complete silence. The little drawing room was like a rain forest of ferns, white orchids and American beauty roses. Doctor Smith in the colorful vestments of his church and Doctor Taylor in a Covenanter's black robe were waiting behind a white satin *prie-dieu.*

And Mrs. Galt and Woodrow Wilson were married. Mrs. Bolling gave her daughter away and when the last words of blessing had been spoken the President reverently kissed his bride.

The cake was cut only fifteen minutes after the ceremony began, and the buffet supper was gay but brief. The President's three daughters kissed them both, his sons-in-law offered congratulations which even McAdoo really meant. They were followed by the hearty good wishes of Stockton Axson and Norman Galt's brother and sister. The last words were spoken by old "Aunt" Mathilda, who had belonged to Edith's grandfather in another world. "Goodbye, Miss Ether," she quavered. "Take Jesus with you for your doctor and your friend."

The White House Pierce-Arrow was waiting in the roped-off street. The bride and groom got away so quickly that the distant crowd had no time to raise a cheer. They drove to Alexandria where the President's private car, also named *Mayflower,* was waiting attached to a train bound for Hot Springs, Virginia. The press and the public were for once circumvented as they waited hopefully at Washington's Union Station.

There has been only one break in the security that all parties maintained. Mr. Starling of the Secret Service said many years later that as he reported for duty in the private car the following morning he was astounded to see the President of the United States, all dressed up in a cutaway and high silk hat, dancing a buck-and-wing while he sang at the top of his voice:

> "Oh you beautiful doll,
> "You great big beautiful doll!"

CHAPTER III

A VIRGINIAN FAMILY

IN THEIR BIOGRAPHIES of the new Mrs. Woodrow Wilson the newspapers were accurate about one thing—she was descended from Pocahontas, the daughter of King Powhatan, who married one John Rolfe, Gent. Rolfe said his purpose was to improve English-Indian relations.

Pocahontas' granddaughter, Jane Rolfe, married Colonel Robert Bolling and from them the line runs straight down the ladder of generations to Edith. The Bollings were very proud of their Indian blood, and it is a fact that the Bolling men were mostly tall and dark with aquiline noses, straight black brows and high cheekbones—they called it "that Indian look." Whether it was due to their faint infusion of red man's blood or mind over biology is a question for the geneticists.

Like so many southern families who were stripped of everything but their gentility by the Civil War, the Bollings still loved to talk about The Plantation. It was located near Lynchburg in Campbell County, Virginia, a lovely upland region of good tobacco and grazing land. Appomattox Courthouse was about twenty-five miles to

42

the southeast. Edith's grandfather, Dr. Archibald Bolling, lived there with a hundred slaves to work the land. Her father, William Holcombe Bolling, was raised there. Like most of the planters' children he was given a little Negro boy his own age to grow up with him and be his body servant. Ambrose even accompanied his young master to the University of Virginia where he went to study law.

After graduating from the university, William Bolling came home to The Plantation. Shortly before the war he married Sallie White. They made a remarkably handsome young couple. A full black beard gave an air of virility to William's delicate aquiline profile, strong arched eyebrows and gentle, intelligent eyes. Edith's mother was a tall young woman with a slightly uptilted nose and lovely sloping shoulders. She wore her dark brown hair parted in the middle and gathered in wings over each ear. Their first two children were born at The Plantation.

The Civil War smashed this pleasant existence as no other in our whole history has done. William joined the Army of Northern Virginia and Dr. Bolling, who was too old to serve, turned his house into a hospital. His wife, daughters and young Mrs. William nursed the Confederate wounded who came in ever-increasing streams. Since there were no anesthetics to be had, it was an inferno of pain. Among the patients was a young German named Rudolph Teusler who had surprisingly elected to fight for the South —there were thousands of Germans in the Union Army. Edith's aunt, Mary Jefferson Bolling, fell in love with the sympathetic young man, and after the war she married him and went to live in Germany.

Campbell County was in the heartland of Virginia, which General Robert E. Lee successfully defended almost to the end, so at first the enemy was only a distant terror. But in the last desperate months the Union armies closed in. The Yankees swept the place bare of food but left the buildings intact. A few weeks later General Lee surrendered the Army of Northern Virginia at Appomattox. William Bolling had not far to walk home.

It was impossible to live on The Plantation with no help and no animals—all their beautiful horses had gone with the Yankees and only the mule remained. However, Mrs. Bolling senior had inherited a house in Wytheville in western Virginia, near the North Carolina line. William's one hope was to set up a law practice there, and earn enough to support his family. Fortunately he found an excellent partner in General William Terry, C.S.A.

In the post-bellum South there was no drawing card like a brave Confederate general. Besides, William Bolling was an excellent lawyer. The firm of Terry and Bolling prospered moderately. At least they ate.

The Bollings were very happy in Wytheville. Their house stood on the unpaved main street which was a sea of red mud in winter, and a desert of red dust in summer. On the corner was an old-fashioned drugstore with tall vials of mysterious liquids, ruby and emerald and deep blue, in the window. Right against it was the Bolling residence, which was really three small houses joined as one. Built of warm rose-colored brick, it had three gabled roofs, three chimneys, and each of the three principal upstairs bedrooms had a separate staircase. A wooden veranda ran along the whole front.

The pleasantest room was the upstairs library, which had a tall round-arched window opening on a small balcony. The Bolling girls used to entertain their beaux there. "I remember two very dull young men who called one evening," Mrs. Wilson says. "We had to receive them because they were the sons of the Episcopal minister. We thought they would never go home. Finally I said, 'I'll bet you can't jump from that balcony to the ground!'

"They took the dare and climbed over the rail and carefully let themselves down until they were hanging from the floor by their hands. I ran out and stomped on their fingers.

"I was terrible," she adds unrepentantly.

In a strait-laced era the Bolling children were, in fact a rather uninhibited family. There were nine of them in all—Rolfe, Gertrude, Annie Lee, William Archibald, Bertha, Charles, Edith, Randolph, Wilmer, Julian and Geraldine; Charles and Geraldine, however, died as infants. Edith was born in 1872, the seventh child.

Her first appearance was not encouraging. When Mrs. Bolling showed her new baby to her sister, the latter exclaimed in horror, "Oh, Sister, that's the ugliest child you ever had."

"She's no such thing," Sallie Bolling said indignantly. "And even if she were, she is so sweet and good you forget it."

Their two grandmothers, Mrs. Bolling and Mrs. Logwood, lived with them in Wytheville. The household revolved around Grandmother Bolling, a wisp of a little old lady, always dressed in a black silk hoop skirt, a tight bodice with full bishop sleeves and a starched white cap on her head. She sat enthroned in a rocking chair, with a well-cured dogskin thrown over it, in the big square room that was her realm. Her back had been injured by a fall from a horse and she could not even climb into her big four-poster bed, but she never stopped working, making clothes for the children or, when it got too dark to see, knitting stockings of silk or wool. Her creed, which Edith inherited was, "I hate can'ts. Anyone can do anything they try to."

Another trait the grandmother and granddaughter shared was their strong likes and dislikes. If they liked you they were forever loyal. If they did not, you were forever out. Grandmother Bolling disliked several of her grandchildren, but she liked Edith.

This meant that from the time she was about six years old Edith had to share the four-poster or sleep in a trundle bed alongside. She had to clean and feed the old lady's twenty-six canaries and wash and iron her white cap in a most particular way. Edith says that the only fun she got out of the canaries was giving the occasional casualties a bang-up funeral.

As Grandmother Bolling grew older and more feeble she slept only the cat naps of age. Sometimes she would wake Edith thirty or forty times in a night to help her turn over or get her something.

The compensations for this semislavery were that Grandmother Bolling poured out for Edith's benefit the extraordinary vitality of her mind and spirit, teaching her more than any school could attempt.

Though Grandmother Logwood was less dominating she was quite as much a person. Very tall, with a poker-straight back and a "queenly air," she was a great romantic. Edith loved to sit in front of her big wood fire in the evenings while she sang the pseudo-Gothic ballads that Sir Walter Scott had made the rage in her youth. Edith's favorite was the sad tale of "Lord Ullin's Daughter."

So the emotional side of Edith's character was formed; her idealization of love and marriage, and her way of thinking about and expressing these emotions which appears in her letters to Woodrow Wilson. Even as long ago as 1915 it was anachronistic.

But if the Bolling household was in one sense tied to a vanishing era, there was also a healthy edge of wit and realism. They liked to put on impromptu plays and tableaux, which was great fun, as they were always sure of a large captive audience. Edith recalls herself as a chubby little girl of six posing as "The Soldier's Bride" with a lace curtain over her straight brown hair while her brother Will played the soldier with a toy gun and an old Confederate forage cap.

Edith's formal education was limited to two years in school. A modern pedagogue would say she had none at all. But she ended up with more real learning than most college graduates. Grandmother Bolling taught her to read and write and figure. She even had a go at teaching her French. Since the old lady had taught the language to herself and pronounced it as spelled in English, the result was weird, but Edith could read it.

These lessons were supplemented by Edith's father. William Bolling was now a judge of the County Court. His duties kept him riding around the countryside on his black horse a good deal, but when he was home he was the friend and confidant of his children. Whenever the girls went out to parties he waited up for them until two or three in the morning—after coping all day, their mother was too exhausted. He'd have a roaring fire to welcome them, and they would sit around it telling him all about the party.

Mrs. Wilson has an almost photographic memory. She can recall the hat and dress someone wore at a party sixty years ago, or the exact conversation of Lord Balfour, for example, when he sat next to her at dinner in 1917. She attributes this to her father's training. When she went out he would say, "Now be sure to remember everything that happened so you can tell your grandmother. It's the only pleasure she has. She lives vicariously through you children."

On the evenings they did not go out, Judge Bolling gathered the children around him and read the classics to them in his beautiful, flexible voice—Dickens, Shakespeare, Milton, and even some of the racy seventeenth-century playwrights. "He was one of the few good readers I have ever heard," Mrs. Wilson writes. Woodrow Wilson was another.

Though the crowded cheerful life in Wytheville seemed to Edith to stretch on for ages, it did not in fact last very long. Inevitably members of the household drifted off. The first to go was Aunt Lizzie Logwood, who married General James G. Field. He had lost a leg in the war; with his white hair and scraggily white beard he looked "like Methuselah" to Edith. But with or without a leg, in law or in love, a Confederate general was a catch. At least the romantic Miss Logwood thought so.

Soon after their marriage Grandmother Logwood went to live with them in Albemarle County. Then Rolfe, the oldest son, married and went to work at Abingdon. The next to go was Gertrude, who married Mr. Alexander H. Galt of Washington in 1885.

Edith went to school when she was fifteen at Martha Washington College in Abingdon, Virginia. She chose Martha Washington because it had a fine music teacher who was a friend of her brother Rolfe. This was a bad mistake.

The headmaster was a bigoted old miser who seemed to Edith a combination of Dickens' less lovable characters, like Scrooge or the Master of Dotheboys Hall. The girls were starved and frozen. The music room was so cold that their stiff fingers could not strike the piano keys. But this regime may also have had its value. Edith shot up to her full height of five feet nine and lost her little-girl fat in a hurry. She was so thin that the girls called her the Gray Spider. But her brilliant eyes and fine bone structure promised authentic beauty.

She spent the next year recuperating at home. As she gained a little weight and her color returned, the promise of beauty was kept. The proof of it was that an "older man," aged thirty-eight, fell desperately in love with her.

So young and innocent was she at sixteen that she thought his attentions—the flowers and the candy, the expeditions and picnics he arranged, carefully chaperoned of course—were merely kind-nesses to a child. Her heart was quite untouched.

However, this "affair" may have been the reason why Judge Bolling managed to get together enough money to send his daugh-ter to Powell's School in Richmond, Virginia, the following winter. It was as different as possible from Martha Washington. There were only about thirty girls, all of them congenial. Edith loved Powell's and she loved Richmond. The former capital of the Con-federacy was a very small, bankrupt city just beginning to reassert its vitality. But to her it seemed "a seething mass of humanity and distractions."

That was Edith's last year in school. Randolph, Wilmer and Julian Bolling were growing up and, of course, it was far more important to educate boys than girls. Judge Bolling's budget could stretch no further. So instead of going back to Powell's, Edith went to visit her sister Gertrude Galt in Washington the winter she was eighteen.

The Alexander Galts lived in a pleasant little brick house on G Street between Nineteenth and Twentieth, five blocks west of the White House. It was like a broad village street paved with cobblestones and shaded by trees. Transportation to the center of town was provided by a vehicle called "the herdic," a long, two-horse omnibus that looked a little like a hearse.

Wearing her old school uniform, Edith went for a long walk

all by herself one bright September day. When she came home at seven-thirty she found a message from a woman friend of the Galts inviting her to Adelina Patti's concert that evening if she could reach the theater by eight o'clock. At the time Patti was the toast of three continents.

As Edith dashed to get her coat, her sister said, "You certainly can't go in that old green wool dress. Everybody will be in evening clothes."

"I certainly can," said Edith, gaily. "Nobody knows me and I don't care how I look if I can hear Patti."

"Well, come on," said Alexander Galt, who planned to escort her as far as the theater.

It seemed as though the herdic would never come. And when it did, it crept along at a slow trot of spavined nags with long stops at every corner while the driver fumbled through tiers of pockets making change. Galt and Edith got out and ran the last two blocks.

In the jam at the entrance they luckily found Edith's hostess—it was her lucky night. Leaving Galt, the two women crashed into the crowd like football players, and finally arrived breathless at their front-row seats. The house was ablaze with jewels and fine feathers, every man in a white tie and tails, the women in extravagant creations from Paris and flashing tiaras, filets and circlets. Edith had a sinking moment in her green plaid dress.

Then Patti came on and began to sing her classic arias as no one has sung them since. In the "Jewel Song" each sparkling note was truly like a jewel from Marguerite's casket. At the end the artist sang a touching English folk song that Grandmother Logwood had sung in her firelit room in Wytheville—"Comin' Thro' the Rye." Blinded by tears of happiness, Edith could have been no more ecstatic if a fairy godmother had clothed her in a dress by Worth and diamonds by Cartier.

When she got back to the Galts' house she was still walking in remembered beauty. Her cheeks were flushed, her eyes afire with emotion, sparkling with the mist of tears. She must have been a sight to stir the blood of any man.

The scene in her sister's dining room seemed very pedestrian to her. Alexander and Gertrude Galt were cooking oysters in a chafing dish, while a tall, dark, impeccably dressed young man, whom Alexander introduced as his cousin, watched them. Though Edith says she could not see how people could eat when there was such beauty in the world, she managed to tuck away a few oysters —after all she had had no dinner. Between mouthfuls she gave them a minutely detailed account of the evening, as her father had taught her to do. She was so wrapped up in it that no one else got a word in. And she scarcely even noticed the young man whose intense gray eyes never left her face.

His name was Norman Galt.

Norman Galt lived alone with his father in a big brownstone house on fashionable H Street between Fourteenth and Fifteenth Streets. The family fortune was based on Galt's, the finest jewelry store in the city. It was founded in 1802 and established its reputation almost immediately. President Thomas Jefferson bought a silver service for the White House from Galt's. Its reputation for integrity was absolute. Mrs. Wilson says proudly, "Galt's name on a piece of paper was considered as good as a government bond."

Norman, the youngest and ablest of Mr. Galt's four children— three sons and a daughter—was a worthy heir to this tradition— honorable, agreeable and discreet. He was very tall and dark, with gray-blue eyes and a small black mustache. A most immaculate person, he never wore the same suit two consecutive days. He took two baths and wore at least two clean shirts every day. Mrs. Wilson says, "He was much neater than I."

At the very moment of their first meeting Norman Galt fell in love with Edith Bolling. He was nine years her senior but he seemed much older than that with his precise manners and business cares, so she did not take him seriously at first. The attentions he paid her were only what she expected from men in general.

Galt courted Edith for four years before she gave in. "He finally wore me down," she says. It was certainly not the great love of her life; that was reserved for her maturity. But she was very fond of him. "Norman Galt was a lovely person. He was wonderfully kind to all my family."

At first they lived for a while in the big, old house with Mr. Galt. Edith had a sweet, thoughtful way with older people that won the old gentleman's heart. She in turn was genuinely devoted to him.

Though the Galts had their prosperous store, Norman and Edith were not well off at first. He and his brothers had arranged to buy Galt's from their father and went quite heavily into debt to do it. So the first house Norman and Edith bought was very tiny. Mr. Galt laughingly called it "The Palace." They moved in the evening before Thanksgiving Day. Judge and Mrs. Bolling, who happened to be in Washington, came to dinner that very night. Edith and Norman proudly showed them over it, bright with chintzes and the inexpensive but pretty furniture still "with the *new* on it."

That was only the first of many parties they gave in their little house in which they lived for six years. They had a great many friends, "all sorts of people, except politicians," and, of course, the Cliff Dwellers.

Two years after her marriage Edith lost a baby and with it her chance of ever having children of her own. Her thwarted maternal instinct thereafter flowed over her family and the remaining Galts and any lonely young people who appealed to her. Eventually it concentrated on Woodrow Wilson.

The roster of calamity continued. Old Mr. Galt died. Then in quick succession came two more shocks. Norman's bachelor brother, Charles, became a hopeless invalid, entirely dependent on him. Then Judge Bolling died suddenly. He had been, perhaps, both closer to Edith than any other person, and at the same time on a pedestal as her ideal of manhood. He was, in truth, both dynamic and gentle, and as handsome as the devil. His death was the first great heartbreak she suffered.

With his invariable kindness Norman Galt invited young Julian Bolling, who was only fifteen, to live with them in Washington and sent him to a good private school. He also gave Randolph and Wilmer jobs in the store.

The casualties in the Galt family threw the full responsibility for the store on Norman's shoulders. But he was quite equal to it. His management was so successful that in a very short time the young Galts' finances were greatly improved. One sign of this was the electric automobile he gave Edith in 1904, when cars were a rarity and hardly another woman in Washington drove one. It was exquisitely appointed with silver fittings and a cut glass vase that usually held one perfect orchid. In that elegant showcase with its big, clear glass windows, rolling down Pennsylvania Avenue on her rounds of shopping or paying her afternoon calls on Connecticut, she was as lovely a sight as the town might see.

Another pleasant by-product of prosperity was their trips abroad. They made two in the early 1900's and Edith lost her heart forever to Paris. The little girl in the green wool dress with whom Norman Galt had fallen in love could now buy her clothes at the great couturiers, of which the greatest was still Worth's. Its proprietor was an extraordinarily sensitive artist who loved beauty, whether of fabric, line or female form. M. Worth once said to Edith, "Ah, if I could hire you as a mannequin my fortune would be made."

On another occasion when he was helping Edith choose materials for a dress, a careless salesgirl put a piece of bright cerise silk beside something in maroon. M. Worth gave a cry of anguish and fainted. When he came to he went home with a violent sick headache and was not seen again for two days.

In 1906 the Galts planned a third trip to Europe. In the spring Edith had an attack of appendicitis. She stayed in bed for six weeks hoping it would subside so she could make the trip. But instead of going to Europe she had to have her appendix out.

The dread and terror Edith felt was less of the knife, or even death, than of the hospital. She had that revulsion all her life though she bravely overcame it for the wounded of World War I. By now the Galts had moved to the house at 1308 Twentieth Street and Norman, ready to spare her any anguish, arranged for her to be operated on there. No reputable doctor would agree to such a thing today, but, though unusual, it was not unheard of in a time that was only learning about asepis and had never heard of a blood bank.

The library was fitted out as an operating room with clean sheets covering the floor and furniture, and an operating table brought in. The anesthetist required no more paraphernalia than a gauze cone and a bottle of ether; and the instruments were boiled in dishpans. The surgeon and nurses wore white but no face masks. Luck was with them. Edith came through nicely.

However, she had a long convalescence. Soon after she was really on her feet again Norman was taken ill. He was only forty-five, but he was one of those people who age quickly. The doctors diagnosed his case as a liver infection, which may or may not have been correct. He died in 1908, after a short illness.

The death of her husband left a great void in Edith's life but did not change it materially. She continued to live in the house on Twentieth Street and surrounded herself with the family, both Galts and Bollings, to fill the gap. Norman had left her the sole owner of Galt's. This assured her financial independence but was also a responsibility which she took seriously. For underneath her soft southern manner was a strong character and a very acute mind.

She made no attempt to run Galt's herself. Mr. Bergheimer, the manager, who had been with the store for nearly fifty years, was both capable and trustworthy. However, she made a point of going to Norman's office at least once a week and examining the books—sales, costs, profits and losses—and discussing the business with Mr. Bergheimer.

Eventually Mr. Bergheimer also died and the less competent

Mr. Wright succeeded to the management. Since Edith saw no way of replacing her manager she decided to part with the business. Rather than bring in alien ownership she sold Galt's to its employees for "a very low figure," which nevertheless left her a comparatively rich woman.

Alone and solvent, Edith could indulge her love of travel. In 1910 she took her sister Bertha on a trip to Europe which included many little towns off the beaten path in Holland and the friendly countryside of prewar Germany.

In 1911, Edith was planning another trip to Europe when she heard of the death of her close friend James Gordon, a Scottish mining engineer who had married a Virginian. His wife had died the year before and Mr. Gordon had said to Edith, "If anything happens to me, please keep an eye on 'Altrude.' "

Alice Gertrude Gordon was his only child. Edith immediately went to see her in the big house at 1600 Sixteenth Street, which Altrude's father had left her. She found a pretty, softly rounded girl of seventeen with big brown eyes, and brown hair hanging in braids down her back, sitting forlornly in the stiffly formal drawing room. Edith was so moved that she did an impulsively foolish thing. Altrude herself has described it: "I had known Mrs. Galt only casually as a young person knows a friend of her parents. I remembered her best one Sunday in church, a very tall woman with violet-blue eyes, dark hair and a lovely, clear skin. She was wearing a bunch of violets that almost matched her eyes.

"After we had talked a few moments that day in my house she said, 'What are you going to do, child?'

"Of course, I didn't know. I was adrift.

"Mrs. Galt said, 'I'm going to Europe in a few weeks. Would you like to come with me?'

"Almost without thinking, I said, 'I'd love to.'

"It was just like her. She had such a compassionate, kind nature. Of course she was taking an awful chance. We hardly knew each other. As soon as her magic presence was gone, I bitterly regretted accepting her invitation, and I am sure she had dismal second thoughts about it."

Edith's thoughts were, in fact, dismal. She called herself all kinds of a fool for saddling herself with an unknown teenager. But they were both too polite to back out.

Their worst fears were unrealized. In both their memories that trip to Europe remains a sort of golden interim in their lives. The following year they went to Europe again. This time they went through the chateau country and on to Biarritz and Spain, where they saw a bullfight, which they hated, and met President Raymond Poincaré of France, whom Edith rather disliked.

In Washington Altrude lived in her own house, at first with an aunt and then with paid companions, for an unmarried girl did not live alone even with a houseful of servants. But she saw Edith Galt almost every day, and relied on her heavily.

They took one more trip together in 1914. That was the year their world—all our serene American worlds—cracked down the middle. In the White House the President of the United States grieved for his dying wife while he watched with horror the collapse of European civilization.

Edith and Altrude did not realize what was happening; they were not politically conscious. They just happened not to go to Europe that year. Instead they went on a canoe trip through the Rangeley Lakes in Maine. Such a trip seems decidedly arduous for two women (one of them forty-two), even by today's standards. But though Edith looked as softly feminine as any southern belle she was a remarkably rugged woman.

The trip started at a primitive hotel in Jackman, Maine. Torrential rain tattooing on the tin roof kept them awake most of the first night. In a wet and howling dawn they rolled out of bed and suggested they might postpone the start. "Naw," said the guide, "you're going to get wet anyway. Might as well start right."

So they hiked the first ten miles through wind-whipped rain, that trickled down their necks, carrying their duffel bags while the guides carried the canoes. By noon they reached a lake and the sun came out. Edith and Altrude caught a mess of fish for lunch, and dried out while the guides cooked the fish.

For the next two weeks they journeyed through the wilderness, traveling by canoe over the forest-ringed lakes, and down swift rivers running through canyons of tall black-green pines. On portages they walked through waist-high blueberry thickets where "the fruit was ripe, cool and covered with the bloom of frost." Every night they camped, sleeping on pine boughs in a pup tent before a roaring fire. Apparently they had a wonderful time, for when they returned to civilization scratched, muddy and in tatters, Edith wrote, "We were sorry it was over. . . ."

Altrude Gordon had a beau named Dr. Cary Grayson, whom she had met at one of the numerous balls which the great hostesses of Washington, like Evalyn Walsh McLean, gave almost nightly during the season. Altrude was much more of a social butterfly than Mrs. Galt, and so was Grayson; the two young people saw each other often after that. Grayson soon fell deeply in love.

Naturally Altrude wanted her older friend's opinion of her conquest and asked, "May I bring my new beau to tea?"

When they came in Edith saw that Altrude towered over her little doctor, who was only about five feet three. But he was so handsome and so vital that this made no difference. He had a strong face with a long, sharply chiseled nose, dark, lively eyes under straight brows and black curly hair. His slim, straight body in a lieutenant commander's uniform was like a steel spring or a rapier, and he carried it with a cocky air that Edith realized was intended to conceal his shyness.

She soon found that he was a delightful conversationalist, full of laughter and good stories. There was no malice in him; his brand of humor was drollery rather than wit.

Edith, who had more than a touch of malice in her own wit, nevertheless appreciated Grayson's humor. She immediately took one of her irreversible likings to him. Altrude says, "From then on she was always on his side."

Soon after their return from Maine, Altrude left for New York where she had rented an apartment for the winter. While Edith recuperated from an attack of ptomaine poisoning, Dr. Grayson formed the habit of dropping in for tea two or three times a week, ostensibly to cheer her up, but really to talk about his absent love, as Edith knew very well.

It was on one of these occasions that the doctor told her how lonely the President's young cousin, Helen Bones, was in the White House since Mrs. Wilson's death. The Wilsons had brought her up and educated her as they did so many of their young kinfolks. Now she was the only woman in that great house except the servants. "Miss Margaret [Wilson] does not like the life there," he said, "and is away most of the time. The little lady is starving for companionship. I know you would like her and I feel sure you could help her. I can't get her to take any exercise. After you know her you could take her out walking. It would do her worlds of good."

Edith was not enthusiastic. "My dear Doctor," she said. "You know I'm not a society person. I have never had any contacts with official Washington and I don't want any. So I'm the last person in the world to help you. Wait till Altrude gets back."

But Dr. Grayson could be a stubborn man. A few days later he telephoned to ask Edith if she would be at home. He arrived in an open White House car with Helen Bones and the President's daughter, Nell McAdoo. They invited Edith to go for a drive with them. She never could resist "a ride," as she called it, and besides she was much too well bred to refuse the President's daughter even if she had wanted to.

They had a delightful ride. It was a perfect day and Edith found both young women "full of charm and completely unspoiled." She liked them very much.

They took another drive a couple of days later, and as Grayson had predicted, a fine friendship grew up between Helen Bones and

Edith Galt. The latter was always at her best with very young or very old people who needed mothering. She formed the habit of taking Helen to Rock Creek Park in her little electric. They would park the car on the grass under the trees and go for a long walk on the wooded bridle paths. Then they would drive back to 1308 and have tea in front of the fire in the library.

But Edith refused to go near the White House.

There is something almost psychic about the effort Edith Galt made to avoid meeting President Wilson. It went far beyond her ordinary distaste for official Washington, even on one occasion to the point of rudeness. Though she disclaims any such feeling and says that Wilson meant absolutely nothing to her until the day they had tea in the Oval Room, it is almost as though her subconscious was afraid that he might mean too much.

Actually she had already seen him several times. The first time was in 1909 when she had peeked into the ballroom of the Belle-vue-Stratford Hotel in Philadelphia to see the President of Princeton University addressing the alumni. She did not, however, see his inauguration. Mrs. Rolfe Bolling, a dedicated Wilson fan, who had come to stay with her, was horrified when Edith announced that she was not going. "I saw McKinley's and Roosevelt's inaugurations. They're all alike," Edith insisted.

"All alike—the idea!" Annie gasped. "This is a *Democrat* and a great man. I'd stand in the crowd on the sidewalk to see him. And you won't even go to your own comfortable balcony at Galt's!"

Though she felt she was losing caste in her sister-in-law's eyes Edith stubbornly refused. She was, in fact, bored by Annie's political talk. It even made her a little hostile to Wilson's liberalism. She got a copy of his book *The New Freedom* and read passages aloud to Annie, asking rather sharply how she thought her hero was going to put his utopian ideas into effect.

Then she relented, and reading in the paper that the President was going to see Billie Burke at the National Theatre, wangled two seats for the performance. Annie got a crick in her neck looking up at the presidential box while Edith concentrated on the stage. But she noted that the President looked very tired.

In return for this favor Annie planned a great surprise. She came in one morning waving a letter and saying triumphantly, "Now see what I've done for my skeptical hostess. I've arranged for you to meet the President."

It appeared that she had written to Wilson telling him how hard she had worked for him during the campaign and asking if he would receive her and her Washington hostess. The letter was from the President's secretary, Joseph Tumulty, giving them an appointment at two o'clock that day. "I'm going to take you with me," she said.

"Not if I know it," Edith said briskly. "I've lived in Washington for seventeen years and never been to the White House. Why should I bother a tired man? I'd feel like an idiot going there."

"Are you serious?" Annie gasped.

Edith was serious. She took Annie to the White House in the electric and drove around the block until it was time to pick her up. Such conduct was not only a little rude, since the appointment had been made, it was unlike her.

However, she did go to a White House reception, probably to please her mother, and got that "push-along handshake." Also to please Mrs. Bolling, she got seats for Wilson's State of the Nation Address to the Congress. His closely reasoned, brilliant speech shook her skepticism about his program, but did not incline her to further encounters.

The only reason she went to tea with Helen on that fateful day in March 1915, was that the girl had promised that "Cousin Woodrow will be out playing golf."

CHAPTER IV

FIRST DAYS AS FIRST LADY

ON JANUARY 1, 1916, Mrs. Woodrow Wilson began to keep a diary. In Hot Springs, Virginia, she wrote, "Today I received all the guests at the hotel and many of the country people. I wore a blue azure afternoon dress and a blue hat . . . we left for Washington after dinner." That was the end of their honeymoon. It had been an idyllic interlude.

The Wilsons had arrived at Hot Springs the morning after their wedding, and after brief formalities at the railroad station, they drove through the snowy mountains in the fresh dry air that reminded Edith of her childhood near the Blue Ridge Mountains, to the sprawling wooden hotel. She wrote, "The whole place justified its name, 'The Homestead,' and the management did everything to promote our comfort and insure us privacy."

They had a charming suite bright with chintz-covered furniture. A wood fire sweetened the air with the nostalgic smell of burning pine logs; there were flowers everywhere. In addition to the sitting room, two bedrooms and baths, there was a private dining room where they ate the hearty country meals for which The Homestead was famous.

Almost every day they took long automobile rides over the narrow dirt roads through the wooded mountains, and every morning, except Sunday, they played golf come rain or even snow. In the latter case they used black golf balls which the President had especially made for him.

Fortunately Edith Wilson was already an excellent golfer. Every so often during the next two years the gleeful entry appears in her diary, "Played golf with W and Grayson. Beat them both."

At Hot Springs Edith played both the worst hole and the best of her life. The former was a short, uphill, par-four. It was a cold drizzly day and the turf had turned soggy. She topped the ball on the second shot, driving it into the mud. At that time they did not play winter rules at The Homestead, so Edith flailed away, mud flying in all directions. It took her seventeen strokes to dig that ball out.

Her best hole was also a par-four hole. There was a road with rail fences on each side of it across the fairway that one was supposed to carry on one's drive. The President's drive sailed across it, but Edith's was short—right in front of the fence. It looked like an impossible lie. Mr. Jervis of the Secret Service, who always caddied for her, came up and studied the situation with her. "What club would you like, ma'm?" he asked.

"A putter," she said decisively.

The man shook his head and she had the feeling that if she had still been plain Mrs. Galt he would have said, "You're crazy!"

She squared up to the ball and took a mighty swipe at it. It shot under the fence, across the road, scuttled along the intervening ground and rolled die-straight across the green into the cup for an eagle. Seldom in a life filled with triumphant moments did the President and Mrs. Wilson enjoy anything so much as the expression on Mr. Jervis' face.

To arrive at the White House as its mistress in the midst of a presidential term is a situation few women have had to face. Inevitably everyone is nervous. The staff, grown accustomed to a certain schedule, regards the "new boss" as an interloper who will probably destroy their pleasant routine and turn everything topsy-turvy. The President's official family tries to assess what impression the new first lady will make on the public and how it will affect his popularity and their personal fortunes. His private family could be expected to be equally uneasy. The new first lady, suddenly faced with national responsibilities, should be the most nervous of all. Edith Wilson was not like that.

Now that she had taken the plunge she accepted her position with poise. Her birth, her fortune and her beauty were great assets. However, she took her duties seriously, for she was passionately determined to help her husband. Loving him so greatly she knew she must not, could not, fail.

The fact that she had already won the friendship of Wilson's daughters eliminated one hazard. They were all gathered at the White House when the honeymooners returned, and gave them a wonderfully warm welcome.

The Wilsons occupied the usual presidential suite at the southwest corner of the building. It consisted of two bedrooms, two baths and a small dressing room. In those days the second-floor corridor ran right to the end of the house, stopping at an ugly fanlight. This end of it is now a sitting room. The Wilsons used the Oval Room as their sitting room. The President's study was in what is now called the Lincoln Room where the Emancipation Proclamation was signed. The enormous heavily carved double bed that had been made especially for Lincoln was in the President's bedroom.

Edith's room was decorated in blue and gold. Its walls were hung with pale blue brocaded satin and Victorian paintings. The floor was covered with Oriental rugs and the furniture was a hodge-podge of Chinese ebony cabinets and mahogany chairs and tables "covered with dainty bric-a-brac." To make herself feel more at home, Edith had her own bedroom furniture brought over from

1308 Twentieth Street—"my room in the White House was so enormous that it easily accommodated them."

She also brought a great many books, her piano, and her trusty Singer sewing machine. Margaret Wilson and Helen Bones hooted as they saw it being carried in. "What are you going to do with that?"

"It may come in handy," Edith answered.

It did come in handy during the war when they all used it to sew pajamas and hospital shirts for the Red Cross.

The new Mrs. Wilson slipped so smoothly into the White House routine that the staff found their fears foolish. "The housekeeper was a wonderful woman named Mrs. Jaffrey," she says. "She was very capable and strict with the staff. She had a suite on the third floor. All the men servants had to report there to be inspected before they went on duty. Mrs. Jaffrey would dine alone in her suite and every night she dressed in formal evening clothes."

Edith Wilson left the housekeeping pretty much in Mrs. Jaffrey's hands. She came up every morning with the menus for the day, which were usually approved without many changes.

The person most important to Edith was the social secretary, Miss Edith Benham. She was a tall vital woman about forty years old, though she looked younger, with brown hair and eyes and a strong face with a large mouth made for smiling. The French called her *belle-laide* (beautiful-ugly). The daughter of an admiral, Miss Benham had worked in several embassies and knew the intricate protocol of diplomacy as a good gamester knows Hoyle. She had succeeded Miss Belle Hagner as social secretary only a few weeks before the President's marriage.

Luckily she and her new boss took an immediate liking to each other. Miss Benham, who is now Mrs. James Helm, says, "I remember very clearly the first time I saw Mrs. Wilson. She had a radiant smile, beautiful teeth and a skin like magnolias. Those of us who admired the President were made happy by the wonderful care she took of him. She used all sorts of persuasions and ruses to make him exercise and to get him away from his problems.

"When she first came to the White House she accepted all the arrangements. Everything."

In the primitive organization of that simple time, poor Miss Benham had no office. Her desk was in the long corridor just outside the Wilsons' suite. She wrote almost all the social communications in longhand because typewritten notes were considered "common," and besides she could not type. However, she could call on a male stenographer named Mr. McGee to help her. The President also had a stenographer named Charles Swem. "He was a crackerjack," Mrs. Helm says, "a court reporter type. McGee was not that good, but between us we worked things out."

The Negro servants who staffed the White House adored their new mistress. Having been served by colored people all her life, Edith knew how to establish the kindly relationship between master and servant which was typical of the best of the old South. Mayes, the dignified old Negro who still guarded the front door in President Truman's time, said of her, "She was a blessing and a delight to President Wilson. He was so lonely before she came. I remember him and Dr. Grayson sitting back to back every evening in the study reading by the light of that little old oil lamp."

Mrs. Wilson returned Mayes' esteem. "He was a fine gentleman," she says, "and I liked him very much. Mayes was a professional barber and shaved Woodrow every day and always cut his hair.

"Brooks was also a mighty nice man and very reliable. When we arrived at the Paris Peace Conference we were invited to lunch at the Elysée palace the first day. The protocol officer said, 'Tell the President everyone wears a frock coat.'

"I said, 'My goodness, I don't believe he has one.'

"Brooks, beaming, said, 'It's all right, Mrs. Wilson, I brought two.' "

In addition to the regular White House staff, Edith retained her own Negro maid, Susan, who was also her friend. Susan was awed and a little confused by it all at first but soon settled down. She always referred to Wilson and the Secret Service as "the President and his silver service." When Edith finally explained that the word was *secret,* Susan changed to "the President and his secretive servants."

Edith ordered one change in White House routine which made things difficult for the staff. She decreed that she and the President would have breakfast upstairs in her room every morning at six o'clock so that they could get in Grayson's prescription of a round of golf before the pressures of the day began. "I suggested that the servants leave things ready," she says, "and that I would cook the eggs so they would not have to get up so early. But they insisted on serving us."

Edith's relations with the Secret Service men and ushers were equally friendly. Ike Hoover, the Chief Usher, would do anything for her. In fact the only member of the staff whom she did not like was Joseph Tumulty. He was a blond, blue-eyed, flamboyant Irishman, who loved Wilson with all his Celtic heart, and did in truth regard the President's second wife as an interloper. She in turn never forgave him for intriguing against her marriage. Their relationship was a kind of armistice. "I never liked Tumulty," Mrs. Wilson says. "But I got along with him in spite of that. One thing that made me nervous was that he could copy the President's signature so even I could not tell the difference. I told my husband that I thought it a very dangerous accomplishment but Woodrow said, 'I know he'll never do anything wrong. It's all right.' "

Without any doubt Tumulty would have committed hara-kiri with a carving knife before he would do anything he thought would injure his President. But he was not always wise.

Edith gave her first White House dinner on January 3, 1916, her mother's birthday. It was strictly a family affair, the guests, besides Mrs. Bolling, being Randolph and Bertha Bolling, Mr. and Mrs. Julian Bolling, Mr. and Mrs. Wilmer Bolling, and Mr. and Mrs. Alexander Galt. Edith still thought of the Galts as her family too. It was very informal and gay. Wilson was in high spirits and told his favorite story on himself, about a reporter covering a Mark

Twain Festival in Hannibal, Missouri. The reporter was questioning a Hannibalian who had never heard of Mark Twain.

"Have you heard of *Huckleberry Finn?*" the reporter asked.

"No suh, reckon I ain't."

"*Tom Sawyer?*"

"Not him either."

"How about *Pudd'nhead Wilson?*"

"*Yes suh!* Couple of years ago I voted for him."

The first lady's real baptism of fire came on January 9. It nearly killed her. The Pan-American Conference was being entertained at an evening reception at the White House. "In those days there was no control over invitations," Mrs. Helm explained. "Every member of the staff sent them out. The result was chaos."

That evening before they went downstairs, the President taught Edith how to shake hands without getting hurt. "You put your middle finger down and join the index and ring finger above it. In that way people can't get a grip. Your hand just slides through theirs."

After the lesson the President and his wife greeted the members of the Cabinet in the Oval Room and then led them in procession down the marble stairway while the Marine Band played "Hail to the Chief." As the crowd in the great entrance hall saw the first lady for the first time a subdued roar of exclamations rose toward her. She was wearing a white gown brocaded in silver with a train, and flowing white tulle draperies over her arms which she called "angel sleeves." She carried a large bouquet of glowing orchids which the President had sent her, and wore no jewelry—oddly enough, she never cared for it—her eyes shining with excitement were jewels enough.

She and the President moved slowly into the Blue Room and then to the glittering East Room where they formed the receiving line. They shook hands with 3,328 guests that evening. However, on a later occasion they shook hands with 8,000 people in one day.

That first reception was only the beginning for the lady who had lived quietly for so long. On January 11 they gave their first state dinner to the Cabinet. And on January 14 the Vice-President and Mrs. Thomas R. Marshall gave a large dinner for them at the Willard Hotel. Next came a great ball held in their honor by the Pan-American Union in their beautiful new marble building.

Though Edith had thought she would hate the formal entertaining, she found herself enjoying it immensely, especially the Pan-American Ball. She writes, "I still like to pause and remember that scene—the tropical beauty of the table laid in a great room . . . the many lights . . . exquisite beauty of form and coloring . . . orchids of every variety and shade massed like a garden abloom [around] a miniature pool reflecting their flaunting glory . . . the Diplomatic Corps in court uniforms with orders blazing . . . women in trailing gowns and many jewels, the Marine Band splendid in scarlet coats, and everyone smiling a welcome as we were escorted through the crowded rooms."

Edith's days were as busy as her evenings. When she and the President came in from golf about ten o'clock every morning, he went to the Executive Offices and she to Miss Benham's desk to answer her mail. They lunched together and she always walked back to the office with him, through the garden if the weather was fine, under the arcade if it were not.

Her afternoons were devoted to receiving the wives of ambassadors. Edith worked out a system of having each one to tea before a fire in the Red Room at thirty-minute intervals all afternoon until five-thirty or six. Then she tried to get the President to go out for a short ride. In the evenings when they were alone, they either worked on affairs of state together, or read, or played pool in a basement room.

This new routine was interrupted on January 27, when the Wilsons left for a speaking tour in the private car *Mayflower*. With war moving ever closer—only he knew how close—and the United States Army numbering only 80,000 men, the President was determined to show the Midwest the necessity of arming America for defense—"preparedness," he called it. It is almost impossible now to recall the utter horror of a majority of the American people, particularly those beyond the Alleghenies, at the very thought of war. Even arming for their own self-preservation seemed to many of them an immoral act. The hit song, "I Didn't Raise My Boy To Be a Soldier" was the lowest expression of this sentiment. Its highest was Bryan's noble letter of resignation. Wilson, sharing their feelings in the depths of his soul, was impelled by the awful responsibility of his office to lead or drive them to build the means of assuring their own survival in a world they did not comprehend.

On the other hand a large minority of Americans, led by vociferous Theodore Roosevelt, was trying to push the President into war and branding his preparedness program as "woefully inadequate." Wilson's Secretary of War, Lindley M. Garrison, belonged to this faction and resigned in the middle of the controversy. He was replaced with Newton D. Baker, who loved peace but became a great Secretary of War. Edith admired and liked Baker immensely.

Wilson, trying to hold the balance between these extremes, decided on the speaking tour to acquaint Americans with the real facts and his own position. He called it "taking counsel with the people."

The trip was a new challenge to Edith. Now she, who had hated politics, must learn to be a good political wife. It proved to be an inspiring experience.

The tour opened in New York where Wilson met head on the charge that he was inconsistent because he had opposed preparedness the year before. "The minute I stop changing my mind with the change of all the circumstances in the world I will be a back number," he said. . . . "What I am trying to impress on you now is that the circumstances of the world today are not what they were yesterday, or any of our yesterdays. . . . America will never be an aggressor . . . but America does not control the circumstances of the world, and we must be sure that we are faithful servants of those things which we love, and are ready to defend them against every contingency that may affect or impair them. . . ."

From New York the train rolled out through the Midwest— Pittsburgh on January 29; Cleveland that same evening; Milwaukee and Chicago, January 31; Des Moines, February 1; Topeka at noon February 2; Kansas City that night and St. Louis the next day.

In each of these cities the President made a long, thoughtful speech, explaining in his clear, precise English some phase of his preparedness program and the necessity for it. The reason mid-westerners opposed preparedness was largely lack of information. The President took them into his confidence and made them think. Most of his closely reasoned orations were extemporaneous. No one ever wrote a speech for Woodrow Wilson, because no man could do it as well as he.

In all those cities, and at the whistle-stops between, the presidential couple were mobbed by politicians, social leaders and plain admirers. On the car, in hotel suites, at luncheons, banquets and receptions they were always in the center of a milling throng offering them homage, affection and trust. From the first Edith understood that the crowds pressing about them, sometimes endangering them by their enthusiasm, were paying tribute to her husband. So no matter how charged with punishment the occasion, she never lost her poise. The warmth of her welcoming smile was as real at midnight of a grueling day as at its beginning. She never let herself seem tired. When she wanted to, Edith Wilson could make people love her on sight.

The strenuous trip was made easy for her by the success her beloved husband was clearly having. The crowds kept getting larger and more enthusiastic at every stop. To her delight, the President got more vigorous by the hour. Enkindled by the wonderful response of the people, he never got tired at all, but actually seemed to grow younger and more forceful.

He said, "I expected to meet quiet audiences and explain to them the issues of the day, and what did I meet? At every stop of the train multitudes of my fellow citizens crowded out, not to see the President of the United States, merely—he is not much to look at —but to declare their ardent belief in the majesty of the government which he stands for . . . and to declare . . . that they stood ready to do their duty in the hour of need."

The climax came at Kansas City in the flat heart of the Republican Midwest. Eighteen thousand shouting people were jammed into the great auditorium and as many more stood in the wind outside to catch a glimpse of him. Wilson's speech that night was incomparably brilliant. For once he allowed his deep emotion full expression.

He told them that he was asking for 500,000 citizen soldiers to be trained for their defense and they shouted, "We're with you! You can raise 500,000 men in Missouri!"

Then he said, "We are witnessing a cataclysm, and God only knows what the issue will be.

"See therefore the noble part that is assigned to America—to stand ready and cool, to keep alive all the wholesome processes of peace—and we who are trustees to repair this world . . . must take counsel with one another [for] the efficacious performance of that task. . . . I would not draw a passionate breath for fear I might disturb the nice equipoise of the peace of this part of the world. But, ladies and gentlemen, one cannot help seeing visions, one cannot help realizing what it means to stand for the honor of a great nation like this. . . .

"If America suffers all the world loses its equipoise. . . . That serene flag which we have thrown to the breeze upon so many occasions as the beckoning finger of hope to those who believe in the rights of mankind, will itself be stained by the blood of battle and staggering here and there among its foes . . . when America might have carried that standard forward serenely to the redemption of the affairs of mankind. I beg of you to stand by your government with your minds as well as your hearts. . . ."

A great crash of cheers assured the President that they would. Edith, watching the slim, beloved figure on the platform, uplifting that great crowd to heights of idealistic patriotism they had never known, felt a passion of love and reverence for her husband that amounted to adoration, almost in the religious sense of the word.

Even Wilson himself in the excitement of those days went beyond his intention. At St. Louis the next day he called for a Navy "incomparably the greatest in the world."

That had an unintended warlike ring. In the quiet of the private car rolling toward Washington, someone asked Wilson if he had really meant to go so far. With a humorous, rueful smile he answered, "No. I was intoxicated by the exuberance of my own verbosity."

However, the trip was an enormous success. The resulting pressure from the grass roots on the reluctant Midwestern congressmen assured the passage of the great naval construction bill and a beginning of training an adequate national army.

Wilson never forgot that trip. He became convinced that he had only to go to the people to win them to his way of thinking, and thus pressure Congress into following his recommendations. Edith became equally sure that her husband could always persuade the American people to follow his leadership.

After the excitement of the swing through the West, life in the White House seemed almost peaceful to Edith. The Wilsons settled into a routine in which formal entertainments alternated with quiet evenings or family dinners. Almost every week end, even in midwinter, they cruised down the Potomac to the Chesapeake in the *Mayflower* to anchor in some quiet cove and explore an oysterman's settlement or an almost forgotten tidewater village.

About once a week they went to the theater, either to Keith's vaudeville house, where a special box was held for the President, or to see the road company of a Broadway play. On other evenings they sometimes motored out to the country to have dinner in a quiet inn.

The family meals at the White House were always fun. Mrs. Wilson describes one occasion when the McAdoos came for lunch. Except at formal dinners grace was always said before the meal. This day the President said, "Mac, will you ask the blessing?"

McAdoo rose, tall and lank, and stood for a long moment swaying in acute embarrassment. Then he said, "Jesus." And abruptly sat down.

His wife privately told Edith of her chagrin. "Please have Father ask Mac again," she said. "I have coached him and he will do better next time."

McAdoo was indeed prepared next time, though he did not make Nell any happier. When the President asked him to say grace, he rose confidently, shot out the stiff cuff of his white shirt and read the blessing from it.

The evenings the Wilsons spent alone were not idle. During February, 1915, Wilson taught his wife how to use the private secret code in which he communicated with his personal emissaries abroad. Like all strong Presidents from Theodore Roosevelt to Franklin D., Wilson kept the conduct of foreign affairs in his own hands and never told the State Department any more than he could help. In Bryan's day the President had informed his Secretary of State *outside* of regular channels. But Secretary of State Lansing, whom Edith regarded as little more than a clerk, often had to guess what was going on.

The one man Wilson thoroughly trusted in foreign affairs was Colonel House, who held no official position. To communicate with the Colonel on his missions abroad Wilson used a comparatively simple cipher consisting of numbers based on a master key. Any good cryptographer could crack it quickly now, but it was never broken in World War I.

Edith soon learned how to use it. From that time the President would write his highly secret messages in longhand. Edith would encode them in her own handwriting, and the President would type the code numbers out on his typewriter. Thus no one else in the government had an inkling of what was in them.

Since Edith also decoded the incoming message she was the only person beside the President who saw the whole picture of American foreign relations and knew precisely what Wilson intended during all the tremendous years until he left the White House on March 4, 1921.

CHAPTER V

WILSON BY A WHISKER

S ERENITY AT THE WHITE HOUSE was always an illusion. It became less than illusory on March 9, 1915. That was the day
when Pancho Villa, the Mexican bandit chieftain, led his mounted
horde across the border and raided Columbus, New Mexico, killing
eight American soldiers and nine peaceful American citizens.

In the overshadow of World War I it is often forgotten that
throughout the spring and early summer of 1916 we balanced pre-
cariously on the brink of war with Mexico. Relations with the
revolutionary government of President Venustiano Carranza had
steadily worsened all that winter. Villa's raid almost blew the lid
off, as the bandit intended. Half of America was howling for
revenge. Even the people who had no stomach for fighting Germany favored marching on Mexico.

Only the most self-disciplined restraint and diplomatic ingenuity
on the part of Woodrow Wilson prevented war. Public clamor
forced him to send an expedition under General John J. Pershing
on a hopeless chase after Villa through the desert mountains of
Mexico's Chihuahua Province. But at the same time Wilson man-

aged to concoct a face-saving formula for President Carranza, who was also being pushed by his own people toward war.

At the peak of the crisis Wilson called the National Guard into the Federal service and sent them to guard the Mexican border. This necessary precaution turned out to be a stroke of pure luck, for when World War I became inevitable the National Guard formed a nucleus of trained men around which to build our four-million-man citizen army. Thus Wilson got his preparedness partly by chance.

The days of the Mexican crisis, to which was added the continuing menace of German intransigence and political pulling and hauling at home, were a terrible strain on the President. It was then, for the first time, that the people around him, Miss Benham, Dr. Grayson, Mayes and Brooks, and even Tumulty, realized how much he owed to Edith Wilson. No matter how she worried about the President or how ill she felt—she was subject to severe colds and neuralgic headaches—she always appeared bubbling with gaiety, suggesting new hideaways to motor to for dinner or a game of golf or insisting on a week end on the *Mayflower*.

Next to Edith, the yacht was Wilson's salvation, for when he was aboard, his edgy nerves seemed to lie down and his tired brain to draw new vigor from the salt wind. It seems extraordinary now that no criticism of the President's weekly cruises and daily golf ever appeared in the press. Apparently the newspapermen of that time were more considerate and more understanding of the needs of a Chief Executive upon whom the terrible weight of national life—and death—decisions rests, than they have been in recent years.

One of the greatest trials that Edith faced then was the Preparedness Parade of June 14, 1916. Wilson had announced that he would lead the march up Pennsylvania Avenue as an example to the nation. On the evening before the parade, the chief of the Secret Service came to the Oval Room where the President and his wife were sitting. "The Secret Service has uncovered a plot to assassinate you," said the man. "I beg you not to march. It would be a terrible thing for the country if its President were killed!"

Edith, searching her husband's face, saw his jaw set, his eyes harden. "It would be a terrible thing for the country," Wilson said, "to have a President who was a coward."

That sunny morning Edith drove her husband down to the Peace Monument where he joined the line of march. Then, filled with fear and pride, she went back to her box in the reviewing stand in front of the White House. Her description of the parade shows the measure of her love:

"How young and vital he looked as the line of marchers swung around Fifteenth Street where we could see them! He wore white flannel trousers, a blue sack coat, white shoes, a white straw hat, and carried an American flag about a yard and a half long. What a picture as the breeze caught and carried out the Stars and Stripes!"

Of all those thousands of marching men and women she saw only one.

Shortly before this the Wilsons had at least one utterly carefree, happy day. One wedding often promotes another, so, perhaps, Edith's radiant happiness led Altrude Gordon to yield at last to Dr. Grayson's suit. They were married on May 24, 1916, at St. George's Chapel in New York. The White House contingent went there for the wedding, including Helen Bones and Randolph Bolling. Nell McAdoo met them in New York.

With the independence she had acquired by necessity, Altrude herself gave the wedding, and planned to have no attendants. But just before the ceremony she asked Edith to stand beside her at the altar. Mrs. Wilson says, "Fortunately I had worn a pale gray taffeta and a big gray hat of tulle so I did not spoil the effect of the white decorations and the bride's white loveliness."

The small reception at Altrude's own apartment was gay indeed, enlivened as it was by little Grayson's jubilation at the successful

conclusion of his long courtship. Edith could not have been more
pleased. After all, she had always been "on his side."

The President was also very much on Grayson's side. The only
time he ever exercised the powers of the Presidency for a friend
was to send the name of the young doctor to the Senate for promo-
tion to rear admiral. This caused an unholy row that took Wilson
completely by surprise. No one had any complaint about Grayson,
but a group of Republican senators, led by Henry Cabot Lodge of
Massachusetts, vented their spleen against the President by trying
to block the nomination of his friend.

It was also good politics in an election year to accuse the President of favoritism. Seeing the way things were going, it would
have been good politics on Wilson's part to withdraw Grayson's
name. But one of the strengths of his character—and also a weakness of his relations with the Senate—was his stubbornness in the
face of opposition. In this case stubbornness was reinforced by personal loyalty. Regardless of consequences Wilson used every bit
of the leverage of the Presidency to force the issue. Grayson's
nomination was confirmed.

The summer of 1916 was, as Mrs. Wilson says, "crowded with
every sort of thing." In addition to the danger of two wars, it was
an election year. There were not enough hours for all the things
that had to be done so the Wilsons decided to start their days at
5:00 A.M. in order, as the President said, "to sneak up on them
in the dark."

There was no vacation for the President that year. He was, of
course, renominated by acclamation at the Democratic National
Convention in St. Louis in June, where William Jennings Bryan
coined the campaign slogan, "He kept—and will keep us—out of
war!"

Wilson was troubled and angry when he heard that phrase, which
seemed to him a false promise. To Edith and Josephus Daniels, he
said, "They talk of me as though I were a god. Any little German

lieutenant can put us into war at any time by some calculated out-
rage."

Meanwhile the Republicans nominated Associate Justice of the
Supreme Court Charles Evans Hughes of New York. Theodore
Roosevelt's distaste for Wilson was even stronger than his dislike
of the conservative Republican leader. Before the nomination he
called Hughes "a whiskered Wilson." Later, he supported him.
With the Republican Party reunited it looked like a losing fight
for Wilson.

The President was so meticulous about using his office for personal advantage that he refused to campaign from the White House
because it belonged to the nation. Instead he rented a house called
Shadow Lawn at Spring Lake on the Jersey shore. But he stayed
in Washington all summer. The heavy program of legislation and
the sparring for political advantage kept Congress in session until
September 8, a record for an election year. Wilson felt he could
not leave until they adjourned.

Democratic National Chairman Vance McCormick, whom Wilson called "a steam engine in boots," was frantic at the delay in
starting the campaign, but Wilson told him, "Don't worry, McCormick. This is exactly what the people want. They want the President to stay on the job at a time like this."

Meanwhile Wilson did not know officially that he had been
nominated. The notification ceremony was set for September 2.
At three o'clock on September 1, the Wilsons, Helen Bones, the
Graysons and Tumulty finally left Washington for Spring Lake,
arriving there in the evening. The house was absolutely black because of a power failure. Margaret Wilson and some friends from
New York stumbled out of the darkness laughing, to greet them.
Just then all the lights came on and Edith got her first view of the
house she had rented sight unseen.

Shadow Lawn was the final grotesque flowering of Victorian
resort architecture—the white dinosaur of summer "cottages." It
was a gigantic white wooden house with a templelike oval of fluted
pillars in front and piazzas running all around it supplied with set

after set of porch furniture. "I felt as though I were walking through Macy's furniture department," Mrs. Wilson says.

The main feature of the interior was a huge, paneled two-story hall with a staircase "wide enough for an army abreast." There was a gold piano on the landing. The rest of the furniture was heavy carved oak pieces and potted palms. In the center of the hall was a marble statue of a nude woman. "It must have weighed several tons," Mrs. Wilson says. "We could not get rid of it so we draped it as much as possible." The final effect was an unhappy combination of a museum and the lobby of the old Waldorf.

The other rooms on the ground floor were an uncomfortable formal French drawing room, a Pompeian dining room, and a "library," whose only book was the New York telephone directory. However, the bedrooms were airy and pleasant. In her diary Mrs. Wilson wrote, "House awful but comfortable."

The next entry is: "September 2, 1916. Saturday. Notification Day. Woke to find it raining. Men on lawn arranging 8,000 chairs. All breakfasted downstairs. People began to come at eleven. Wore my blue dress for lunch. About 300 people for standing lunch. Afterward the sun came out beautifully. Put on my white narcissus dress. Crowd estimated at 25,000. Wonderful speech of Acceptance . . ."

The scene was, in fact, a fine example of a lost piece of Americana—the ceremony of notifying the candidate of something he had known for months. Rollicking shirt-sleeved crowds trampling lawns and flowerbeds in a clambake mood, eating hot dogs and drinking beer while political bigwigs sweating in frock coats and top hats poured forth political oratory that hardly anyone could hear. Wilson's speech was an exception. His clear high voice and precise English commanded attention. After describing the accomplishments of the Democratic Party in implementing the ideals of the New Freedom domestically, he expressed almost for the first time his great aspiration that America should assume the leadership of the world in forming an association of nations to maintain peace:

"If the healing and helpful arts of life are indeed to be revived when peace comes, a new atmosphere of justice and friendship must be generated by means the world has never tried before. The nations of the world must unite in joint guaranties that whatever is done to disturb the whole world's life must first be tested in the court of the whole world's opinion. . . .

"These are the new foundations the world must build for itself, and we must play our part in the reconstruction generously and without too much thought of our separate interests. . . .

"[We] look forward to the days in which America shall strive to stir the world without irritating it . . . when the nations . . . shall look upon our great people . . . as upon a people who, though keen to succeed, seeks always to be at once generous and just, and to whom humanity is dearer than profit or selfish power.

"Upon this record and in the faith of this purpose we go to the country."

At eleven o'clock that night the Wilsons boarded the special train for Kentucky to dedicate a shrine at Lincoln's birthplace. Two days later they were back in Washington for the wind-up of the Congressional session.

On September 8, after signing the final bills at the Capitol, they left in the private car for Atlantic City and the President's long-delayed vacation, which turned out to be no vacation at all. In her diary Mrs. Wilson notes:

"Drove to Hotel Traymore. . . . Had elaborate suite with awful furniture. Dinner was a sacred rite with everything served in frozen eagles or rabbits, and fish cooked before us.

"Went to suffrage meeting afterward. The only speech of my Precious One that I ever failed to enjoy, but I hated the subject so it was acute agony. I had orchids from the suffragettes. . . ."

One of the apparent inconsistancies of Edith Wilson's character was her violent opposition to woman's suffrage. That a woman as intelligent as she, who played so confident a role in great events, should favor disenfranchisement by sex seems extraordinary. It can be explained partly by her upbringing in the South where women traditionally deferred to men and gained their purposes by subtly managing them. What really made her frothing mad was the "unladylike" conduct of the suffragettes. Her anger appears again and again in her diary. In January, 1917, when the suffragettes began picketing the White House with big banners and transparencies, she referred to them as "disgusting creatures," but nevertheless wrote, "I sent Ike Hoover out to invite them in to get warm. They indignantly refused."

By July, with the country at war, Edith was really irritated by these women. She was delighted when they were arrested and sentenced to sixty days in the workhouse for disturbing the peace. On July 17 she wrote in her diary:

"Read in the *Star* that Dudley Malone had espoused the pickets' cause. . . . If anyone had told us that Dudley Malone would be such a traitor we would not have believed that, but he came to see Woodrow who said he could do nothing with him. I hope he will resign and we will never see or hear of him again. My Precious One did not come home from the office until six-thirty and was so weary it broke my heart to look at him. He loved Dudley and said he felt like someone had died.

"July 18. Everyone agitated about those detestable suffragettes. . . .

"July 19. Woodrow decided to pardon those devils in the workhouse. . . . Tumulty came over and agreed with me it was a mistake."

The Wilsons finally got back to Shadow Lawn on September 9, but there was no rest for the weary President. He spent the morning in bed with one of his violent sick headaches, received Governor James F. Felder of New Jersey in the afternoon and then got a telegram saying that his sister, Mrs. Howe, had suffered a stroke in New London, Connecticut.

The next day they started for her home by motor. "Robinson lost the way, so had a rough trip." They stayed at the Mohican

Hotel for three days and then "the *Mayflower* was ordered up from New York. . . . Captain Berry called for us at nine-thirty. When we came aboard the *Mayflower* it was like getting home."

Captain Robert Berry of the *Mayflower,* who doubled in aiguillettes as the President's Naval Aide, was one of Edith's favorite people. He was a rare combination of a splendid sailor and good companion who added enormously to the Wilsons' enjoyment of their frequent cruises.

Mrs. Howe got no better and no worse. Her doctor told the President that she might remain unconscious for months, so it was useless for him to stay in New London. On September 14 the Wilsons returned to Shadow Lawn. They had hardly arrived when word came of Mrs. Howe's death. On the seventeenth they left in the private car for her funeral in Columbia, South Carolina, where Woodrow Wilson had spent his teens.

Columbia, baking in the September sun, was as peaceful as a stagnant millpond, but Wilson remembered it very differently. He told Edith how he had first seen it a few years after the Civil War, when his father had come there to teach in the Presbyterian Theological Seminary. From the ruins of the State House to the Congaree River there had stretched a waste of blackened rubble with a few tar-paper shacks standing on the crumbling foundations of the pillared mansions burned by Sherman's army.

But that had not been the worst of it. The capital of South Carolina became a horrible travesty of Democratic government. With Federal troops in occupation, corrupt Yankee politicians had moved in to prey upon the illiterate Negroes suddenly given the vote. They had elected as governor F. J. Moses, Jr., a Negro who was anathema to upright members of his own race, and proceeded to pillage the state treasury.

Wilson said that from his room in the seminary he had watched the dissolute parties in the governor's stately, classic-revival mansion. Drunken whites and Negroes, spilling out among the Corinthian columns of the gallery, had caroused openly with unfortunate Negro girls and white harlots from the gutters of the northern cities. The revulsion he had felt then was one reason for his abiding horror of war and its aftermath, and the root of his determination to avoid it at any price except that of national honor.

Back at Shadow Lawn the real campaigning began at last. In addition there were the exacting duties of the Presidency. A great stack of mail awaited Wilson and he attacked it with Charley Swem. Mrs. Wilson says that she loved to sit and watch them work. "As Mr. Wilson spoke and Swem wrote a panorama of world affairs passed before me."

When the letters were finished she put them in front of her husband for signing, expertly blotting one as she slipped the next in position. Often he looked up at her tenderly saying, "When you are here work seems like play."

Politicians descended on Shadow Lawn. The few great liberal industrialists who were helping to finance the campaign also came, among them Jacob Schiff and Henry Ford. The latter had pockets full of paper-thin watches he collected, which he boyishly piled on the luncheon table for them to admire.

On Saturdays special trainloads of people arrived to hear important speeches. One day Edith drove to Sea Girt with the President, who was to review a National Guard regiment. In a cutaway and a high silk hat the President mounted a cavalry charger and rode along the lines of troops. Edith thought he looked "very stunning," but Wilson felt ridiculous. "It seems queer to ride a horse wearing a high hat and a cutaway," he remarked. "I do it to emphasize the civil authority over the military."

They got back to find the Young Men's Democratic Club of New York, 1,500 strong, marching up the drive behind a booming band. Wilson made his first purely political speech of the campaign to them. Edith noted, "I like the other kind so much better."

Somehow the Wilsons managed to get in a round of golf most days. The Secret Service men usually caddied for them but one day two elderly members of the Spring Lake Club asked to be allowed the honor of carrying their bags. The one who got Edith's was plainly disgruntled. The fact that she was playing in terrible form that day made him no happier. Hoping to appease him, she asked his advice about a close approach shot. "Do you think I can reach the green with a midiron?"

Sourly he answered, "Yes, if you hit it often enough."

On October 3 they boarded the campaign train for Omaha and parts west. From that moment on they had hardly a break in the dusty round of crowds, handshaking, speeches, handshaking, whistle stops, speeches, politicians giving advice, handshaking, handshaking, handshaking. . . .

The final rally of the campaign was traditionally at Madison Square Garden, which was then really on Madison Square. As the Wilsons approached the square it was jammed by a crowd that overflowed the park and blocked the streets and avenues in all directions. The mounted police could not clear a path for them. Finally they went around to the back of the building, climbed up a fire escape and squeezed through a window.

The great raftered auditorium was a moiling mass of 30,000 perspiring, shouting, frantic Democrats. Al Smith, then sheriff of New York, led the tremendous demonstration when Wilson appeared. It lasted for half an hour, with assorted brass bands blaring out everything from "Dixie" to "The Sidewalks of New York."

Wilson finally began his carefully prepared address. Without benefit of loud-speakers nobody heard a word of it. Even the committeemen sitting on the platform caught only a few disconnected sentences. He might as well have been reciting the multiplication table. Noise was all that mattered.

From the Garden the Wilsons went to Cooper Union, where Lincoln's great speech in 1860 had won him the Presidency. Again his words were lost in enthusiasm, as was the impromptu speech the President delivered to 25,000 people massed in the street outside.

At last the campaign was over and Edith wearily rejoiced in the stunning quiet of the *Mayflower,* as the great yacht steamed slowly down New York Harbor toward the Jersey shore.

In spite of the perspiration and shouting it looked as though the Republicans were winning. Hughes was conducting a dignified—and ineffective—campaign, but Teddy Roosevelt was roaming the land roaring invective against the President, and Roosevelt's close friend, Senator Henry Cabot Lodge, was engaging in an adroit smear campaign. Their virulent hatred of Wilson went far beyond normal political acrimony. In the case of Lodge it became almost pathological. He truly regarded Wilson as the personification of evil.

In late October Wilson had become so convinced of possible defeat that he wrote an extraordinary letter to Secretary of State Lansing, pointing out that if Hughes were elected there would be four months during which "I would be known to be the rejected, not the accredited, spokesman of the country. . . . Such a situation would be fraught with the gravest dangers. . . .

"I feel that it would be my duty to relieve the country of the perils of such a situation at once. . . . I would ask your permission to invite Mr. Hughes to become Secretary of State and would then join the Vice-President in resigning and thus open to Mr. Hughes the immediate accession to the Presidency. . . ."

From the first Edith had been intellectually convinced that her husband could not be re-elected. She was sure that the majority of the American people were for him, but she thought that the huge sums of money and the industrial power which the Republicans poured into the campaign would prevail.

On the Sunday before election she lay in bed thinking of these things and wondering about their future as private citizens. Her husband tiptoed into the room and seeing her eyes open, said, "I hoped you'd be awake."

"I was planning what we would do after we leave the White House in March," she answered.

Despite his own forebodings, Wilson smiled broadly at her.

"What a delightful little pessimist you are," he said. "One must never court defeat. If it comes, accept it like a soldier; but don't anticipate it, for that destroys your fighting spirit."

On Monday Ignace Jan Paderewski came at the head of a mission asking the President to set aside a day to help Poland, enslaved by Russia and submerged by the fighting on the Eastern Front. Edith kneeled in the gallery to look down through the balustrade. She was tremendously moved by the old pianist's tragic features crowned by a swirling nimbus of white hair when he talked of her husband as the hope of Poland and of the world.

Very early on election morning, November 7, 1916, the Wilsons started for Princeton, the President's legal residence, to vote. It was a fine sunny day—Republican weather, people called it. When they reached the polling place in a firehouse, they found a crowd of Princeton boys waiting to greet the President. Edith sat in the open car bantering with them while her husband was voting. It was the nearest she ever came to a polling place, because women did not have the franchise in New Jersey then. In 1920 she and the President voted by mail, and after that she became a resident of the District of Columbia and so (until 1961) lost her vote.

They had a pleasant drive home and worked all afternoon. A family party was gathered at Shadow Lawn: Mrs. Bolling and Bertha; Wilson's son-in-law, Frank Sayre, and Margaret Wilson. The Graysons, who had taken a small house nearby, came in. They had an early dinner, a rather tense meal served in that pseudo-Roman dining room.

After dinner it was a relief to go to the cheerful upstairs sitting room. Admiral Grayson, who was so nervous he could not eat, announced that he was going to run over to the Executive Office that had been set up in Asbury Park. Western Union had offered to install a direct news wire to Shadow Lawn, but the President had declined that special favor, so they had no way of hearing about the election. When Grayson left, the President started them playing a game of twenty questions.

That was perhaps the strangest way any presidential candidate ever passed an election night. It seems inconceivable that Wilson should have been content to sit marooned in that great, gloomy house while his fate and the future of all his plans and his hopes for his country and the world were settled, and while every city, town and village in America was seething with excitement. Surely it was not that he did not care. Indeed he cared more deeply, perhaps, than the cigar-chewing politicians in the roaring headquarters of both parties. His anxiety, however, was less for himself than for his vision of a peacefully united world.

That night he was all Covenanter. Having fought his hardest, he waited with almost inhuman self-control based on Presbyterian determinism—God's will be done!

The other members of the party were not so calm. In fact, the game of twenty questions was rather a failure; all their minds strained out beyond the enclosing walls, thirsting for news with an almost physical craving.

For hours there was not a sound from the outside world except the faint roar of the surf and the sea wind swishing past the windows. The stretched-out silence was ominous. When about ten o'clock the telephone jangled down in the vast shadowy hall it was as startling as a fire alarm. Margaret was first on her feet, clattering down the hall, grabbing the instrument. Edith, listening breathlessly, heard her say, "What do you mean? Why, he's not defeated. . . . I don't care what the *New York Times* says, it's not true. . . . I don't care who gives up, I know it isn't true!"

But when she came furiously back into the room her look told them that loyalty rather than conviction had inspired her words.

The call was from a friend in New York to "condole with you on your father's defeat." He said that the light on the *Times* tower was flashing the prearranged red signal for a Republican victory and the New York Democratic Committee had given up. "It's impossible," Margaret said bravely. "They're still at the polls out West."

Edith flew to the telephone and called the office in Asbury Park.

She found "Mr. Tumulty beyond speech in his impenetrable gloom."

She herself was not ready to give up, though she had expected defeat, and had all along been "secretly preparing an armour against it."

The calmest person in the room was the President. Assaying the news, he agreed that his defeat seemed probable, but not definite until the West was heard from. "Well, I won't send a telegram of congratulations to Mr. Hughes tonight," he said. "For things are not certain."

Then very gravely he faced the future. "There is now very little hope that we won't be drawn into the war," he said. "My defeat will be taken by Germany as a repudiation of my policy. Many of our own people will so construe it and try to force the new administration into war."

Then he resolutely pushed such thoughts away. "We were up pretty early," he said. "Let's have a glass of milk and go to bed."

The funereal-faced butler brought up a tray and the President slowly drank his milk. Then he said "Good night," and started out of the room. At the door he paused and twinkled at the somber faces of his friends and relatives. "I'd stay up later," he said, "but you are all so blue."

Edith joined him soon afterward and sat for a while on her husband's bed holding his hand and talking bravely of all the things they could do now that they were free. In a few moments the hand holding hers relaxed. The President was asleep.

She went back to her own room to lie awake grieving over the ruin of her husband's idealistic plans and still hardly believing that they could all come to nothing. At about 4 A.M. indefatigable Margaret bounced into the room full of excitement to say that she had talked to Vance McCormick in New York. He said that good news was coming from the West and there was still hope. "Let's wake up Father and tell him," she said.

Edith got up and tiptoed into her husband's room. He lay

sleeping so quietly that, as she often did, she went close to the bed to assure herself he was still breathing. Then she went back to Margaret and said, "We'll let him sleep."

News was better still later in the morning. Margaret rushed in to her father, who was shaving in the bathroom, and told him, "The *New York Times* has got out an extra saying the election is in doubt with indications of a Democratic victory."

Wilson waved his straight razor at her and said cheerfully, "Tell that to the Marines!"

The President worked as usual the rest of the morning while people kept bringing in bulletins, and he went for a drive in the afternoon. Though Wilson had a 594,000 popular majority, the vote of the Electoral College hinged on a few thousand votes in California, and the count was very slow.

On Thursday morning the result was still in doubt. The Wilsons played golf with Dr. Grayson at Spring Lake. A friend waved to them in the twelfth hole and shouted, "How's your game, Mr. President?"

Wilson called back. "Grayson has me three down, but I don't care! I'm four states up in yesterday's election."

That night they boarded the *Mayflower* at Sandy Hook to go to Williamstown, New York, for the christening of the Sayres' second child. In the sunny morning as they sailed up the Hudson, Brooks brought in a wireless stating that Wilson had carried California by 3,773 votes, assuring his election.

At Rhinecliff, where they changed to the special train, victory crowds had gathered at the dock and the station cheering wildly. The private car, *Mayflower,* was a conservatory of flowers from well-wishers, and at every station there were great jubilant throngs. The Sayre christening was a quiet interlude, but in the evening an exuberant crowd of students, led by President Harry A. Garfield of Williams College, came in a torchlight parade to serenade Woodrow Wilson. It was like the old days at Princeton.

The next night they came home to the White House. The whole staff was assembled on the great pillared portico, laughing, cheering and pressing forward to shake hands or even touch their clothes. Edith noted gladly in her diary: "The White House looked so big and aristocratic. . . ."

Colonel House came for dinner. He made them laugh with his story of Henry Morgenthau's New York victory dinner on Election night that had turned into a wake when all seemed lost. Most of the guests had drowned their sorrows and senses in bourbon and the bitter branch water of defeat, while Vance McCormick aged before their eyes, turning "a greenish yellow."

The next day Edith sat in on a long serious discussion of affairs in Europe between the President and Colonel House. After the elation of victory the huge insoluable problems were pressing down again. She noted in her diary, "The Colonel does not think things are as serious as Woodrow does. . . ."

CHAPTER VI

NOT PEACE . . .

O<small>N NOVEMBER</small> 25, 1916, Mrs. Wilson wrote in her diary: "I helped Woodrow in the study until nearly twelve. He was writing what he says may prove the greatest piece of work of his life, and oh, if it is only so, for it will mean so much."

The international communication on which Woodrow Wilson was writing might in fact, with better luck, have proved to be his greatest contribution to the world. Ray Stannard Baker says, "To no other piece of work of his entire career, perhaps, did he give more concentrated thought, a greater passion of earnestness. . . ." And Mark Sullivan called it "a high adventure in idealism."

To prepare himself he had called Ambassador Page back from London and Ambassador Gerard from Berlin. With the latter he had long conversations about the attitude of the German government. Gerard wrote that "Mrs. Wilson was present . . . and at times asked pertinent questions showing her deep knowledge of foreign affairs. . . ."

The message was Woodrow Wilson's last great effort to end the war in Europe. Since the very beginning he had hoped and planned, when the right time came, to step in as a mediator to bring about a just peace. Now, with the struggle in Europe bogged down in the morass of trenches and the combatants at a dead center of bloody exhaustion, he believed the time was ripe.

The document he was preparing was a note to all the belligerents calling on them to make a just peace and as a first step to state the grounds on which they would negotiate. But it went much further than that. It promised that if such a peace were made the United States would abandon its traditional policy of isolation and join with the nations of the world in an association to assure peace and punish any nation who attacked another.

Now that we are accustomed to seeing America take a leading part in international affairs this does not appear so very daring. But in all our history up to that time George Washington's advice to avoid "entangling alliances" with European powers had been a sacred shibboleth. Wilson's proposal to put America in the very vortex of international politics with a firm commitment to use force to maintain peace was more than daring. It was audacious.

On December 2 he interrupted his work to go with Edith to New York for the ceremonial first lighting of the Statue of Liberty. They stood with Ambassador Gerard on the bridge of the *Mayflower* as she steamed slowly down the familiar harbor. It was a cold and brilliant night with a thin new moon sinking over New Jersey. An airplane, like a wonderful new toy, flew over them leaving a trail of white fire. Then the President gave an order; a rocket zoomed up from the *Mayflower*'s forward deck and instantly the great dark statue was flooded with light and high above them her torch flared out. It seemed to Edith that hopeful night "a symbol of the thing that is to make the world a place where all men have liberty."

But in the darkness of the *Mayflower*'s bridge Ambassador Gerard spoke gravely to them of new difficulties ahead.

Back in Washington Wilson had nearly finished his note when the dramatic effect he had planned was ruined by events beyond his control. On December 12 the imperial German government issued an astounding proposal to make peace. The German note was couched in the language of a conqueror; nevertheless, it stated that Germany's "aims are not to shatter nor anihilate our adversaries," and that "prompted by a desire to avoid further bloodshed," Germany and her allies "propose to enter forthwith into peace negotiations."

Now the President hurriedly finished his note and dispatched it on December 18. That day was the Wilsons' first wedding anniversary. The President tiptoed into Edith's room at dawn to give her his anniversary present, an exquisite black opal and diamond pendant set in platinum. She was as delighted as a child.

They got up and were out at Kirkside by eight playing golf in the snow; "It was terribly cold and my feet nearly froze," wrote Edith. That evening they went to the Belasco Theatre to see Annette Kellerman's new play.

The next day the reaction to Wilson's peace note burst on them. As a less idealistic man might have expected, it made everybody furious. The Germans regarded the note as an attempt to muscle in on their peace efforts. The Allies considered it support of Germany and an attempt to seduce them from victory. The British were especially bitter because they hoped that America would soon come into the war on their side. When he read Wilson's message the King of England wept.

Even in America there were more harsh words than praise. The pro-ally war party, headed by Lodge and Teddy Roosevelt, were furious. The died-in-the-wool pacifists saw a danger of involvement in future wars.

The Wilsons were astounded and disappointed. Edith in particular, who always saw things in black and white, could hardly believe that people could so misinterpret her husband's noble purpose. Wilson himself merely clamped his lantern jaw shut and persevered, believing still that justice and truth must prevail.

Christmas was a brief happy interlude. The day before being Sunday, the Wilsons went to church and then strolled across to the Treasury to hear some children singing carols. That evening they trimmed the tree and the next night had a family Christmas dinner. All three Wilson girls attended; also, Frank Sayre and McAdoo and all the Bollings who were in town, as well as Stockton Axson—twenty-two very jolly people in all. After dinner they played charades with childish abandon. Nell McAdoo in a brilliant blue velvet evening gown with a handkerchief tied around her head and a kitchen knife in her teeth was a spectacular pirate.

After the New Year the feverish dance of the diplomats continued with both the Allies and the Central Powers refusing Wilson's olive branch, though not quite slamming the door. At the same time the formal entertaining began with the usual Cabinet dinner followed by the traditional chaotic mass receptions. Edith found such affairs more foolish than usual in view of the worsening state of the world. Canceling them, however, would have added frightening gravity to the crisis.

One day the Josephus Danielses dropped in to call and insisted that the Wilsons come out on the portico to see the fine new limousine the government had allotted to them. Up to that time Cabinet officers had been provided with victorias drawn by a pair of handsome horses. Mrs. Wilson wrote wistfully, "It was a lovely car, but I hated to see the horses go."

Despite the dubious reception of his peace proposal Wilson clung unreasonably to hope. He decided to appeal to world opinion and chose the Senate as his forum.

On January 22 Edith Wilson sat in the Senate gallery listening to her husband's inspiring words. She knew that many of his listeners were hostile. For example, Senator Lodge, who the year before had ardently advocated "an association of nations to enforce peace," had reversed himself and declared for isolation simply because the President he hated now proposed it. Edith returned Lodge's enmity with double bitterness.

Wilson told the Senate and the world that every discussion of peace must include a concert of powers to prevent future wars. "Every lover of mankind, every sane and thoughtful man must take that for granted. . . ."

Then he went on to say that "there is only one sort of peace that America could join in guaranteeing . . . not organized rivalries but an organized peace. . . . First of all it must be a peace without victory . . . for victory would mean peace forced upon the loser, a victor's terms imposed upon the vanquished. . . . Only a peace between equals can last. . . ." Then he outlined the fundamental basis of peace. Equality between nations great and small, governments that derive their powers from the consent of the governed, "security of life, of worship and of industrial and social development;" freedom of the seas; limitation of armaments. "These are American principles," he said. "They are [also] the principles of mankind and must prevail."

Having spoken with all the clarity of principle and all the power of his passion for peace, he rode back to the White House with his wife confident that the world would listen. Edith wrote in her diary, "He was so splendid that it makes me feel more and more that he must attain all he is striving for for the good of the world."

Just nine days later Wilson got his tragic answer.

On January 31, 1916, Edith Wilson was waiting in the Oval Room for her husband, who was working late in the Executive Offices. When he came at last he looked like a gray corpse.

"What's wrong, Woodrow?" she asked in panic.

Trembling, he handed her a yellow slip of paper. "Read that," he said.

It was an Associated Press dispatch from Berlin: "The German government has announced that unrestricted submarine warfare will begin around the British Isles tomorrow, February 1."

"What does it mean?" she asked.

"It means war," he said in a despairing voice.

When the official German note arrived from the State Department at eight o'clock, it made matters even worse. Not only did the message announce that every vessel entering the "war zone" would be sunk without warning, but it added insult to injury by proposing to allow one American steamer a week, especially marked and guaranteed to be without contraband cargo, to sail to a specified port in England. For some reason this provision roused more anger in America than anything else; Germany actually dared to dictate where and how our ships should sail!

The President sent for Lansing. Edith sat with them as they talked for hours in his study, deciding nothing. Lansing wanted to break diplomatic relations with Germany immediately. Wilson still waited.

Colonel House arrived from New York early the next morning, gray and gloomy. At eight o'clock the President and Mrs. Wilson joined him in the study. They were all depressed, Wilson most of all. He said frankly that he could not get his balance. "I feel as though the world had reversed itself and instead of turning toward the east were revolving westward," he said.

House had no comfort to give him. They all knew that America would go to war, but Wilson refused to face the fact. Grasping for straws, he brought up the extraordinary theory that America must not dissipate her power by entering the war, but remain strong as a bulwark against the yellow race when the Europeans had exhausted themselves by fighting. "If I thought this I would do nothing, accept any insult," he said.

But they all knew that this was not a valid reason. House writes, "We sat listlessly, killing time. The President nervously arranged his books and walked up and down the floor. We had finished the discussion in half an hour and there was nothing more to say. . . ."

Tormented by her husband's agony, Edith Wilson suggested, "We might play golf. Do you think that would make a bad impression, Colonel?"

"I don't think the American people would feel that the President should do anything trivial at a time like this," House said somberly.

In the end they all went down to the basement and played pool. Both men played very badly.

Reluctantly Wilson faced the inexorable logic of the facts. The country was howling for action. That Sunday hundreds of sermons were preached demanding it. "I think our ministers are all crazy," Wilson told his wife.

On February 3, he went to the Capitol, which was packed to the rafters, and told Congress that he was breaking off diplomatic relations with Germany. Ambassador Count Von Bernstorff was handed his passports that afternoon. But Wilson clung to one faint hope. "I refuse to believe that it is the intention of the German authorities to do in fact what they have warned us they feel at liberty to do," he said. "Only actual overt acts on their part can make me believe it even now."

So the matter remained, but not for long. The next unpleasant surprise was that England intercepted a message from German Under Secretary of State Zimmermann to his ambassador in Mexico, offering President Carranza of Mexico an alliance in the event of war and the "reconquest by Mexico of Texas, Arizona and New Mexico." The idea was so ridiculous as to be incredible, but Zimmermann admitted proposing it. Diplomatic bungling beyond belief!

So the day came for Wilson's second inaugural. March 4 was a Sunday. He went with Edith to the President's Room in the Capitol, where he signed the last-minute bills. She was the only woman in the room when exactly at noon Wilson formally took the oath as President of the United States from old Chief Justice Edward D. White. The official ceremony took place on Monday, March 5. It was very different from the sunny, peaceful scene four years before.

Dressed in somber mourning for her sister Annie Lee, who had died a few days before, Edith Wilson rode with her husband to the Capitol in the presidential landau drawn by four horses, an anachronistic relic of an era already past. Her presence was in itself an innovation, the first time a President's wife had ridden with him. Because of the tension and a suspected plot to assassinate the President, a troop of battle-ready cavalry formed a hollow square around their carriage, and soldiers with loaded rifles stood on every roof-top along Pennsylvania Avenue. When the President and Mrs. Wilson came out on the broad steps of the Capitol a company of Marines with loaded rifles formed up behind them, and the wicked muzzle of a machine gun pointed at the crowd from the pediment on his right.

In that solemn, momentous, even ominous atmosphere, Wilson took the oath a second time and then spoke, not of war, but, even now, of peace:

"We are provincials no longer. The tragical events of the [past] thirty months have made us citizens of the world. There can be no turning back. . . .

"And yet we are not the less Americans on that account. The shadows that lie dark upon our path will soon be dispelled and we shall walk with the light all about us if we be but true to ourselves —to ourselves as we have wished to be known in the counsels of the world and in the thought of all those who love liberty and justice and the right exalted."

In the next four weeks the shadows grew blacker, but one ray of false light illumined them. On March 15 Mrs. Wilson wrote in her diary: "Most thrilling news from Russia today regarding an almost bloodless revolution and the overthrow of the government and taking power by the people. Everyone thinks it a wonderful step in the progress of democracy."

The terrible irony of that entry was evident to virtually no one then, and the fact that Edith Wilson was fooled by the false dawn of democracy in Russia under Kerensky is no discredit to her intelligence. At the time everyone really did think it a great step forward. There is little doubt that it weighed in the President's final decision to take America into the war on the side of the Allies. In his mind the overflow of the Czar removed the last stain of autocracy from the coalition against Germany. With the Russian people freed from despotism Wilson felt he could move with a clear conscience to "make the world safe for democracy."

Nor was Germany long in providing the "overt acts" which

Wilson could not believe they would commit. The British liner *Anconia* was torpedoed with the loss of two American lives, and the American ship *Algonquin* was sunk without warning, though all aboard were saved. Then, within twenty-four hours on March 19 and 20, three unarmed American ships were torpedoed and sunk. Fifteen Americans died in them.

The President of the United States called the Congress to meet in special session on April 2, 1917.

The night of March 31, was warm and muggy. Woodrow Wilson carried his battered old typewriter downstairs and out onto the south portico. In the light of an electric lantern hanging between the tall, fluted columns he sat down to write—alone. That fact was symbolic—this was the cross that only he could shoulder. Even his beloved wife could not help tonight.

She sat upstairs in the Oval Room, listening through the open windows to the hesitant click of Wilson's machine, writing history by the hunt-and-peck system. The Secret Service men guarding the parklike grounds heard it, too, and were careful to keep out of sight. They all sensed that the President must feel himself alone.

Only once was he interrupted. After a bit Edith heard the keys striking more slowly as though with infinite weariness. She went downstairs and into the great, shining kitchen where only a cook's helper sat half dozing. He found milk and crackers for her and put them on a silver tray. She took it and went silently out onto the portico. The air was wonderfully alive with all the sweet smells of a southern spring. Without speaking she put the tray on a little table at her husband's side. Never changing the broken rhythm of his typing, he thanked her silently with loving eyes.

The message was finished after church the next day, Sunday, April 1. The President sent for Frank Cobb, editor of the New York *World*, the wisest journalist he knew. When Cobb reached the White House around 1 A.M. he found the President and Mrs. Wilson waiting up for him in the study beside the big cluttered desk holding the oil student lamp on it.

"You look as though you hadn't slept for weeks, Mr. President," Cobb said.

"I haven't," Wilson answered. "Each night when I go to bed I lie awake going over the whole thing again and again. . . . I have tried every way I know to avoid war."

Cobb answered he was sure of that.

They talked for an hour or more. The President went back to his tragic memories of the Civil War and forward to his prophetic vision of the war to come. "To fight you must be brutal and ruthless," he said, "and the spirit of ruthless brutality will enter into the very fiber of our national life. . . .

"I doubt if the Constitution will survive a war," he continued. "A nation can't put its strength into war and keep its head level. It's never yet been done."

"Perhaps America will be different," Cobb offered.

The President shook his head and Edith saw that his eyes in the yellow lamplight were dark with sorrow.

"I'd do anything else in the world rather than head a great military machine," the President said. "I can foresee what will happen to me—the cheers and adulation as we go forward to victory. The derision and attack when men find that victory is only another kind of defeat."

Edith could hardly bear to look at her husband's face, for his agony of spirit was marked by a sort of dissolution of his features. From his spiritual cross he cried out again, "If there's any alternative, for God's sake let's take it!"

Frank Cobb said somberly, "I see no alternative."

Edith Wilson was determined that her husband must have some exercise to relieve the strain. So they got up at dawn, that fateful second of April, and drove out to Kirkside for a round of golf. If people think it's trivial let them make the most of it, she thought fiercely. I know it's important.

The new Congress met at noon, but it was evening before the message came that they were organized and ready to hear the

President. At eight o'clock he and Edith left the White House in a car surrounded by the troop of cavalry from Fort Myer. A misty summer rain was falling and, as they turned into Pennsylvania Avenue, they saw the dome of the Capitol, illuminated that night for the first time, with the Stars and Stripes flying from its staff.

At the entrance under the steps of the Capitol Edith left her husband and was escorted to her seat in the House gallery, directly facing the Speaker's rostrum. The Chamber was crammed with people. Sitting in chairs facing the rostrum were the nine Justices of the Supreme Court. On either side were the Cabinet and, for the first time in history, the members of the Diplomatic Corps in full dress uniforms. In a few moments the ninety-six senators—most of them carrying little American flags—were escorted to their seats. There followed a tremendous hush, which was broken when Speaker of the House Champ Clark announced, "The President of the United States."

As Wilson's slim figure came through the doors, the Supreme Court rose to their feet, followed by the whole great crowd. He walked to the rostrum in a storm of applause. As he stood there quietly waiting for it to die down he looked up to where he knew Edith was sitting and smiled.

Then Wilson began to speak, huskily at first, but quietly too, for he felt that this was no time for rabble-rousing. His purpose was to appeal to the intelligence of his audience and to their noblest instincts, not to their passions.

After calmly describing the arrogant acts of the imperial German government, he said, "There is one choice we cannot make, we are incapable of making: we will not choose the path of submission. . . ."

At that word the tall white-haired Chief Justice of the United States leaped to his feet, his features distorted, tears raining down his cheeks, and gave the wild Rebel Yell. His action was followed by a crash of sound as everyone stood up cheering.

This was not what Wilson had intended, but the emotions of his audience had been stretched too far by the long crisis. From that time forward they cheered almost every sentence.

Still keeping his voice level and as unemotional as he could, the President called for war—a war without hatred against the German people, a war "to vindicate the principles of peace and justice in the life of the world . . . to make the world safe for democracy . . . we are but the champions of the rights of mankind. . . ."

Then came the tremendous peroration in which Wilson sought to transmute the brutality of war into the nobility of a crusade.

". . . The right is more precious than peace and we shall fight for the things we have always carried nearest our hearts—for democracy . . . for the rights and liberties of small nations, for a universal dominion of right by such a concert of free peoples as shall bring peace and safety to all nations and make the world itself at last free. . . . America is privileged to spend her blood and her might for the principles which gave her birth and happiness and the peace which she has treasured.

"God helping her, she can do no other."

The tempest of cheering was now more than war hysteria. The people were pledging themselves to a great and lofty crusade, and Wilson, standing alone facing the storm of emotion that swept and swayed and bent that assemblage like trees in a typhoon, felt himself uplifted and dedicated afresh to the cause he had proclaimed. In that moment of truth even the bitterest of his opponents could be generous. Senator Lodge pressed forward to grasp his hand saying, "Mr. President, you have expressed in the loftiest manner possible the aspirations of the American people."

In her seat in the gallery Edith thought her heart would burst. Of all those people she was the most deeply moved. For that small beloved figure standing alone facing the tornado of sound was her husband, whom she looked down upon with wonder and awe.

As rapidly as possible she made her way to the entrance, where she found him waiting for her. They quickly got into the car and the cavalry escort formed up around them. Of their departure

Josephus Daniels wrote: "If I should live a thousand years, there would abide with me the reverberations of the fateful, ominous sound of the hooves of the cavalry horses as they escorted Mr. and Mrs. Wilson back to the White House."

That sentence in itself proclaims Americans' touching innocence of what they were getting into—the clatter of cavalry meant war to them, such babes in the wood of war were they.

The President and Mrs. Wilson said not a word to each other as they drove back up the broad avenue through the storm of cheers no rain could dampen, but he held her hand so tightly that it hurt. They went straight to the President's study where Tumulty was waiting for them. He has described how the President came in from his great triumph looking unutterably weary and sad. "Tumulty," Wilson said, "think what it meant, the applause of the people in the Capitol and the people lining the avenue as we returned. My message tonight was a message of death to our young men. How strange to applaud that!"

While his wife and his secretary sat silent wishing to comfort him but unable to find words, he spoke of the tragedies inseparable from war.

Then, according to Tumulty, "President Wilson let his head fall down on his big, old desk and sobbed like a child."

CHAPTER VII

WAR

THE SENATE AND HOUSE debated the Declaration of War for three days. There was no doubt it would pass, but a strong residue of idealistic pacifists opposed it and must have their say.

Just as the Wilsons were finishing lunch on Good Friday, April 6, Rudolph Forster of the Executive Offices brought over from the Congress the completed bill for the President's signature. This would bring America into the war officially and irrevocably. Ordinarily quite a ceremony was made of signing important pieces of legislation, but this was too important for fanfare. The Wilsons got up from the table and went into the ushers' room. With them were only Chief Usher Ike Hoover, who stood with his finger on a button to notify the Navy, Mr. Forster at the telephone to notify the press, and Mr. Starling of the Secret Service.

The President sat down at Hoover's desk and carefully read the document which already bore the signatures of Champ Clark, Speaker of the House and Vice-President Thomas R. Marshall. As he finished, Edith handed him a gold fountain pen and said solemnly, "Please use the pen you gave me."

103

The President took it and wrote firmly at the bottom of the page:

Approved 6 April, 1917,
WOODROW WILSON

America was at war.

Like Eve in Milton's *Paradise Lost*—he for God alone, she for God in him—Edith Wilson conceived her patriotic duty first in terms of keeping her husband as well and happy as possible under the tensions of war. Any time that was left over she devoted to war work. She was able to do quite a lot, for she was a person who could never sit completely idle for a moment. When possible she would do two things at a time, such as knitting and reading. But there was never a question of choice when it came to Wilson's welfare. So she practically forced him to play golf early on the very day after his war speech and noted regretfully, "Only getting my Precious for nine holes."

As the pressures of war increased so did her efforts to make the President get the exercise that Admiral Grayson insisted he must have. She had been told that in the Army training camps for young officers their day began at 5:45 A.M. and ended at 9:00 P.M., which many doctors thought too long for efficiency. At the White House the day began at 5:00 A.M. "Before six the President was at his desk and often he was there at midnight . . . people descended upon the White House until their coming and going was like the rise and fall of the tides. . . ."

Admiral Grayson came to her and said, "The President no longer has time enough for golf. He must take up some new form of exercise."

"What do you suggest?" she asked.

"Horseback riding," said Grayson. "And you've got to make him think it's your idea," the doctor added.

Edith, who had not been on a horse for years, said gamely, "I'll try."

Sure enough, she convinced her husband that the one thing in the world she wanted to do was to ride horseback with him. The unsuspecting President said, "I'll get Grayson to go over to Fort Myer and pick out a couple of mounts for us. He knows horses."

Things happened faster than Edith expected. The next afternoon she got a message from the Executive Offices asking if she could be ready to ride with her husband and Admiral Grayson at five. The request caught her flat-footed. She did not own a single piece of riding gear.

What a scurrying around there was! Margaret Wilson had a pair of breeches that would do. Nell McAdoo supplied a reasonably smart riding coat. But what about boots?—their feet were much too big. Quick, telephone Altrude Grayson! Altrude came tearing over with a pair of Peel's best. Edith tried them on. They engulfed her tiny feet like galoshes, but they would do.

So at five o'clock she was ready on the south portico. Army grooms arrived with the horses. The President came out in a makeshift outfit, Grayson in the immaculate perfection of London's finest tailors and bootmakers. Secret Service men unhappily clambered aboard unwilling nags in their regular dark business suits. And off went the whole cavalcade with a merry jingle of accouterments and rather extraordinary horsemanship. "We had lots of fun," says Mrs. Wilson.

After that the rides became a regular thing. "May 1, went for a nine-mile ride around Potomac Drive. . . ."

They were riding again on Potomac Drive on May 5, and were almost home when Edith's horse stumbled. She pulled him up and thought he was steady when he slipped again and she sailed over his head to a landing on the muddy bridle path. "I was not hurt to speak of and got on him again. But I did feel nervous and shaky."

Nevertheless, on days when there was not time for golf, the rides continued. They were so good for Woodrow.

Late in April the Allied Missions began arriving to co-ordinate the war effort. Wilson had not wanted them to come. He still heeded Washington's warning against entangling alliances. He wanted to fight a lone-wolf war in order to keep America free to act as she saw fit.

However, to refuse to receive the Allied Commissioners would have been discourteous. Rather glumly he wrote to Colonel House: "Of course there is nothing for it but to reply . . . that we shall be glad to receive them."

The British were the first to arrive, headed by Foreign Minister Arthur Balfour. On April 23 the Wilsons gave a splendid dinner for them at the White House. The state dining room was festive that night, literally filled with spring flowers, and with the famous gold plate gleaming on the huge U-shaped table. Helen Bones and Edith were the only women present among fifty-eight men.

Of course Arthur Balfour was on the first lady's right. He was very tall and loose-jointed, his long, fine features eroded by care. Balfour's mind had many facets. Statesman, philosopher, politician and author, he was the quintessential English aristocrat. Edith found him charming.

On her left, by way of contrast, was the Vice-President, Thomas R. Marshall, still remembered for his immortal phrase, "What America needs is a good five cent cigar." Mrs. Wilson later noted, "The Vice-President was at his worst saying all the things you hoped he hadn't."

The next day Balfour had tea alone with the first lady and completed his conquest. She took him out on the south portico to look at her attractive garden. While he stood there drinking in the lovely scents and resting his eyes on the bright flowers, he told of the drab war-weary country he had left. As he talked he looked so weighted with care that he aroused her maternal instinct.

After the British it was the turn of the French. Their mission was headed by Marshal Joffre, the hero of the Marne. At the most critical moment of the war, when the German armies were about to engulf Paris, Joffre had had the supreme courage not to know he was beaten. Now those younger, modern generals, Ferdinand Foch and Henri Pétain were commanding the armies of France.

Joffre was really only a figurehead, sent to arouse American sympathy. However, dressed in his horizon-blue uniform, heavy with gold braid and medals for valor, and with his round, ruddy face and splendidly curling white mustachios, he was a fine figure of a man. America greeted him with almost hysterical enthusiasm.

The real head of the French Mission was Foreign Minister René Viviani, a slight, quicksilver man with a brilliant mind which fascinated Wilson, though it did not take him in. The President was always grateful to Viviani for not boring him with repetitions of the same statement as so many people did. Woodrow Wilson was easily bored.

There was, of course, an equally splendid dinner for the French. Edith looked particularly radiant in her "old black charmeuse gown with white lilacs." Since neither of the guests of honor spoke English, she gamely talked to them in her home-taught French, which, though improved by foreign travel, still had traces of her grandmother's eccentric pronunciation. In spite of that it was "a thrilling evening."

However, the cheers and the banquets were not the main purpose of these star-studded missions. Actually the Allies had some rather delicate explaining to do, and their demands were desperately urgent.

At his first private conference with the British the President learned that the Allies had not been altogether frank in their previous prognosis of the way the war was going. Instead of winning, they were losing it, and losing so rapidly that unless American help came fast the whole Western Front might collapse that summer. The situation was desperate. Thus what most Americans had thought of as an adventure in idealism became, in fact, a fight for survival.

This fact slowly percolated through to the American people. It hit the residents of the White House like a thunderbolt. Wilson immediately ordered a squadron of destroyers to join the British fleet's antisubmarine patrol—it was estimated that U-boats would sink 900,000 tons of shipping during that one month. All the merchant marines of the world could not stand that strain long. The President also gave up any idea of playing a lone hand, and arranged for closest co-operation with the Allies. American Army estimates were upped from six hundred thousand men to four million. The war would not be lost, but America would have to win it.

So even, before the rest of the country, the residents of the White House were grimly aware of what was ahead. Doing what she could in addition to her major task as her husband's playmate and most confidential secretary, Edith got out her sewing machine and set up a Red Cross workshop in a guest room. Later, when the trainees began to pour through Washington and, later still, when the long troop trains started moving through the nation's capital on the way to embarkation ports she joined a canteen. It was established in a shack in the middle of the spider's web of railway tracks in the yards behind the Union Station.

Whenever she was sure the President would not need her for a few hours, she put on her Red Cross uniform to go down there. It was a singularly ill-conceived outfit consisting of a blue and white Mother Hubbard type dress and apron and a Salvation Army style hat that made a frump out of the prettiest woman.

One very hot night Edith, with a basket of cigarettes and chewing gum hung around her neck, was moving through crowds of doughboys who were standing alongside the train in the dim lights and steamy, smoky air, making her offerings. Her hair was damp and disheveled, her face shining with perspiration. A tall western boy in the high-collared blouse, spiral puttees and Rough Rider hat, then the unrealistic uniform of the American troops, hailed her. "Beg pardon, Ma'm, but the boys are saying you're the first lady. Is that a fact?"

Edith gave him her best smile and said, "Yes, I'm Mrs. Woodrow Wilson."

The boy studied her for a moment, then burst out, "Well, Ma'm, you sure don't look it!"

Sometimes when the President got through work he came down to join his wife. Then the young soldiers crowded around, and he laughed and joked with them as he used to do with his Princeton students. It was so like those days and yet so terribly unlike, that as they drove home, Edith knew by her husband's rigidity that he was still wondering if he could have done anything more to keep the peace.

Edith took on one job that sounded easy and turned out to be a great chore. It was renaming the eighty-eight ships taken over from Germany, and also naming the ships that were built, literally by the hundreds, steel ships, iron ships, even wooden ships, to carry the means of making war to America's hard-pressed Allies. The big German boats were easy—the *Vaterland,* the biggest ship in the world, was renamed *Leviathan,* and the smallest became the *Minnow.* The ships like the *George Washington,* which the Germans had tactfully named for American Presidents, were not renamed.

Then the trouble began. Every time Edith thought up a good name and checked in *Lloyd's Register* she found it already had been used. Finally she sent to the Library of Congress for an Indian dictionary, and called the ships by Indian names. The Secretary of the Navy wrote her:

DEAR MRS. WILSON:

I am sure your fine Virginia hand was seen in [renaming] many of the ships we took over from Germany . . . when women decide to become cabinet officers the Secretary of the Navy's portfolio should be assigned to you. Indeed, there seems to be fitness in this for in the Navy we always call a ship "she."

Sincerely,
JOSEPHUS DANIELS

Another minor war effort produced both comedy and controversy. The President purchased a small flock of Hampshire sheep to keep the White House lawn trimmed. This was supposed to save manpower, and set an example to the country by utilizing every available source of food. The result was a howl from cranks who feared that the placid animals would damage the nation's shrubbery. Wilson paid no heed.

One morning Edith, coming out on the south portico, found a lamb apparently *in extremis*. She carried the little thing into the kitchen and sent for Admiral Grayson. He arrived on the run.

"Do you think it's dying?" she asked.

"I'm afraid so," he said kneeling down and examining it.

"Do something," she commanded.

"Whiskey," said the Admiral.

A bottle of bourbon was procured and Grayson forced a good stiff drink on his unwilling patient. The result was miraculous. The little creature opened its eyes. Then it got up and shook itself. Finally it actually stood on its hind legs and walked gaily around the kitchen waving its tiny front hoofs.

There were other relaxations as well. After the first heavy days when the President dared not leave Washington even for twenty-four hours, he began to use the yacht *Mayflower* again as a hideaway. He wrote his daughter, Jessie: "Edith and I are on the *Mayflower* today to get away from the madness . . . of Washington . . . not to stop work (that cannot stop nowadays) . . . but to escape *people* and their intolerable excitements and demands. . . .

"We try to take things light-heartedly and with cool minds, but it is not always possible, and I fear I notice little signs of its telling on Edith. . . ."

Actually, Edith was as strong as a horse, and equal to any strain. However, she may not have been above pretending more fatigue than she felt in order to lure her beloved husband away from those demanding people, for an opportunity to think in the solitude his academically conditioned mind needed.

In August they made a cruise down the Chesapeake that was one of the best-kept secrets of the war. To all appearance their departure Friday evining, August 10, was routine. By the following morning the *Mayflower* lay at anchor off Yorktown, Virginia. When Edith came on deck she saw thirty-five ships of the Atlantic Fleet at anchor in a double column of tremendous armored might.

Secretary Daniels came up in the *Sylph;* the *Mayflower* got under way and the two yachts steamed between the columns of great ships that were soon to join the British Grand Fleet in the perilous North Sea.

Though battleships, cruisers and destroyers were grimly ready for war in the zebra stripe and crazy patterns of camouflage, they were dressed in the gaiety of signal flags while their crews in gleaming white uniforms lined their rails and all the bands played "The Star-Spangled Banner" as their ensigns dipped to the *Mayflower*. However, the long black guns were silent—the usual salutes were omitted at the President's request.

After the review the President and Mrs. Wilson went in the *Mayflower*'s launch to join Secretary and Mrs. Daniels aboard Admiral Henry Thomas Mayo's Flagship, *Pennsylvania,* for lunch. She was the newest, most powerful dreadnought in the Navy with her triple rows of 14-inch guns projecting from three turrets. It is noteworthy that the *Pennsylvania* was still flagship of the United States Fleet on an infamous day in Pearl Harbor.

Twenty admirals sat down to lunch with the Wilsons in the great ship's wardroom. Afterward her decks were cleared and almost all the officers of the fleet assembled to hear the President speak. Edith always remembered him that day, standing bareheaded on the quarter-deck, looking so young and vigorous in his blue jacket and white flannels. If the young officers thought they were just going to hear more patriotic platitudes they got quite a shock.

The President began by telling them that his words were confidential and for their ears alone. Then for once he let go and said what he really thought.

Of England's antisubmarine campaign he said, "We have been hunting hornets all over the farm and letting the nest alone. . . . I am willing, and I know you are willing. . . . I am willing to sacrifice half the Navy Great Britain and we together have to crush that nest, because if we crush it the war is won. . . .

"[But] everytime we have suggested anything to the British Admiralty . . . [they replied] that it had never been done that way and I felt like saying, 'Well, nothing was ever done as systematically as *nothing* is being done now. . . .' "

The President told them he was tired of hearing the British talk about prudence and he said, "Please leave out of your vocabulary the word 'prudent.' . . . Do the thing that is audacious to the utmost point of risk and daring . . . and you will win by the audacity of method when you cannot win by circumspection and prudence. . . ."

The young men and the old admirals cheered their hearts out at that fighting speech. Part of its impact was astonishment at hearing the man who had kept us out of war so long talk in the veritable tongue of heroism.

Edith was not surprised. For she knew her man; knew that in spite of his love for peace, when forced to fight he would be as audacious and implacable as his Covenanter ancestors who stood and won with Cromwell against the professional soldiers of King Charles.

The Wilsons had one last cruise on the *Mayflower* before that lovely toy was put away for the winter. They joined her in New York on September 8, and sailed first to New London and then through the new Cape Cod Canal to Gloucester, Massachusetts, where they called on Colonel and Mrs. House. When they returned through the Canal on September 11, all the banks and bridges were crowded with cheering people.

At the Buzzards Bay end of the canal, they were surprised to find three destroyers waiting for them. An officer came aboard to say that a German submarine had been sighted off Nantucket Island and that he was empowered by the Navy Department to order the *Mayflower* back to the safety of the canal.

The Wilsons talked things over with Captain Berry, who "didn't seem very worried," so the President "pulled his rank" and countermanded the Navy Department's orders. They proceeded at full speed (fourteen knots) to New London escorted by the destroyers with gun crews manning the *Mayflower*'s new antisubmarine guns.

There Wilson got a telegram from Jessie begging him to come to
see her on Nantucket. Submarine or no, the President decided to
go—he thought the German vessel was a figment of inflamed imagination. They arrived in the morning and drove across the island
in an old yellow surrey to Jessie's house in Siasconset. There they
spent a lovely, peaceful day on the beach, "where Woodrow built
a wonderful fort for the children."

After dinner they started home in a fog so dense that they could
not see the horses. The old islander at the reins occasionally
dropped the butt of his whip to the ground and then licked it.
"Taking soundings, Captain?" Wilson asked humorously.

"Yes, President," he answered. "I know the taste of every foot
of ground on this island. I can tell where I am, fog or no fog."

They duly reached Nantucket Town and the *Mayflower*. However she was held fogbound at anchor all night. In these sophisti-
cated times the idea of the President of the United States playing
hide and seek with U-boats, driving around in a dense fog in a
surrey, or lying fogbound in an open roadstead while enemy raiders
were at sea would turn every head in the Secret Service white and
give the whole country the jitters. Apparently neither the President
nor his wife were the least bit worried.

One of the strangest unknown episodes of American political
history awaited the Wilsons on their return to Washington. John
Singer Sargent, the most famous portrait painter of his time, had
been commissioned by a vote of the British people to paint President Wilson. He arrived in Washington about the middle of October and the following day came to lunch at the White House. He
was a most uneasy guest, strained and subdued at luncheon, and
afterward fussing meticulously about a place for the sittings. They
chose the Rose Room on the north side of the second floor, and
draped its huge four-poster bed with dark curtains for a background. Sargent ordered a platform to be built to bring the sitter to
"eye level." Then he and Edith toured the whole house looking for
a chair that would "paint well."

They found the *chaise juste* in an upper hall and brought it to the Rose Room. Standing there leaning on it, John Sargent made a strange confession. "You know, Mrs. Wilson," he said, "I have never been so nervous about a portrait in my life."

Edith looked at him in utter amazement, asking, "Why, what do you mean?"

Sargent, leaning heavily on the back of the chair, said nothing.

Edith prodded him with, "That is surprising for the great Sargent."

She can still remember the strange expression on the painter's face as he said gloomily, "Well, I only hope I can do it."

The mystery of John Sargent's un-Sargentlike nerves was explained the next day, when Edith's old friend Henry White came to see her. "Sargent dined with me last night," Mr. White said. "He's very depressed about the portrait. He said he never dreaded doing a portrait so much."

"I felt that," Edith said. "But why?"

"I can tell you why," Mr. White answered. "Sargent is an old friend of Senator Lodge. He dined with him night before last. It appears that when they were alone together after dinner Senator Lodge said, 'Mr. Sargent, I am delighted you are going to paint the President. You have an opportunity of doing a great service to the Republican party and to America.'

" 'How can I do that, Senator?' Sargent asked.

" 'Mr. Sargent, you are famous for bringing out the worst in your sitters, for associating them with some animal that indicates the beastly side of their nature. Now you must show the hidden evil in this man's face.' "

Even in her intensely partisan dislike of Senator Lodge, Edith Wilson had not conceived the virulence of his feeling for her husband. She was shaken, horrified. She was genuinely shocked.

"Go on," she said, controlling herself.

"Last night at my house," White continued, "Sargent explained his confusion after lunching with you and the President. He said, 'Because of what Senator Lodge had said, I studied the President's face with the greatest acuity and tried to probe his soul. I could find no evil in him. . . .' "

The Sargent portrait of Woodrow Wilson was finally completed. Edith Wilson feels that it is not the artist's best work. "There is a certain weakness in it," she says, "as though for once John Sargent had tried to paint a person sweetly."

Perhaps he did. Perhaps he was afraid to paint the strength he saw for fear it might be misinterpreted.

But the terrible enmity of Senator Lodge, which may have altered the whole course of history so tragically, was plain to Edith Wilson from that time on.

CHAPTER VIII

HIGH MOMENT

THE YEAR 1918 was the year of victory. But its beginning was the darkest hour of the war. The Bolshevik revolution had toppled democracy in Russia and replaced it by a bloodier tyranny than that of any czar. Lenin and Trotsky promptly prepared to make a peace of the vanquished with Germany, which would release nearly a million veteran German troops who could be hurled against the western front. The Italian Army had suffered a terrible defeat at Caporetto and the Allies strained their last resources to shore up the Italian front, teetering toward total collapse. The war had become a race to make American power effective in Europe before the Allies completely disintegrated.

In the fall of 1917 Colonel House headed a mission to France. His long gloomy cables came almost every day. Since only he, the President and Mrs. Wilson knew the supersecret code, she spent interminable hours decoding them and encoding Wilson's detailed replies.

In the United States the mobilization of industrial might was going well, but inevitably there were breakdowns and confusion.

A bottleneck was the railroads, strained to the breaking point by huge troop movements piled on top of the great demands of industry. In December 1917 the President decided that he must take over the railroads and co-ordinate them under a single government authority. Just at this time House returned from Europe. The first day he was home, Edith sat in the study with her husband, the Colonel and General Tasker H. Bliss, the Chief of Staff, while they revised American strategy in the light of House's pessimistic information. "Fascinating talk," she commented.

A day or two later Edith was surprised when Colonel House, who was staying at the White House, dropped in on her for tea, saying there was something he wanted to discuss before dining with her and the President that night. Even though she had never quite forgiven the Colonel for trying to interfere with her marriage, Edith made a point of getting along with him because he was of such great help to her husband.

The Colonel was clearly disturbed. In his hand was a rough draft of the President's proposed speech to Congress about taking over the railroads. They sat down before the fire and House spoke eloquently of his complete disagreement with its policy. Mrs. Wilson says, "He brought up some very good reasons for his side."

"We'll have a very interesting discussion after dinner when you take this up with Woodrow," she said.

"Suppose you tell him about it first and let him think it over," House said, and went off to dress for dinner.

When the President came back from his office Edith gave him a point by point description of the Colonel's objections.

"I'm sorry he feels that way," Wilson commented, "but I'll be glad to hear his reasons. That is really where he gives help."

The three of them went to the cluttered study after dinner, and the President said, "Edith tells me you don't agree with me about this railroad message. Of course I'm disappointed, but let's have it! I want your reactions."

Colonel House was walking nervously up and down the room. In a low, embarrassed voice he said, "Yes, I did tell Mrs. Wilson that, but I reread the whole paper before dinner and agree with every word of it."

Edith's jaw quite literally dropped. She was aghast. "You can't mean that, Colonel," she cried. "Why, you said . . ."

House cut her short with an abruptness far from his usual polished manner. "Yes, I know I did," he said sulkily. "But I've changed my mind."

From that time forward Edith Wilson never trusted Colonel House. "I knew then that he was a yes man," she says. "When he was with Woodrow he agreed with everything he said. But behind his back he criticized everything."

Another trial of the darkest winter of the war was the increase in crank letters. Sometimes they were amusing like the one forwarded to her by Secretary of the Interior, Franklin K. Lane. It began:

HONORABLE SIR,

I am a descendant of Pocahontas and the Powhatan Indians. President Wilson married Mrs. Galt whose name was Bolling. She is an Indian, a descendant of Pocahontas and Powhatan. . . .

Now, Secretary of the Interior, I do not know your name, but Judge Bell referred me to you. President Wilson has broken the greatest law in the United States. He has served wine and liquor to Mrs. Wilson and she is an Indian, and the law says no one shall give or treat or bootleg or sell or blind tag liquor to an Indian et cetera—you can read it yourself.

Now, Secretary of the Interior, I wish you to get out a warrant for President Wilson's arrest immediately according to the laws of these United States. I was given you as the proper one to push this to proper prosecution at once. . . .

I am an educated Indian. My cousin, Judge William Price of Mobile Probate Court, he is said to have sat on Bench so long he wore it out. I will have proper attorneys represent my side at the hearing.

Respectfully,

In his covering letter Secretary Lane wrote:

DEAR MRS. WILSON:

Here is a letter that places terrible power in my hands. If at any time you wish this power exercised I shall not hesitate to do my duty.

Yours for the enforcement of law,

FRANKLIN K. LANE

Other letters, however, were not funny. Many people wrote to Mrs. Wilson threatening to assassinate the President. This did not trouble Wilson. "No man who really intends to kill me is going to write a letter about it," he told Edith. "And I firmly believe that as long as a man is useful in the world he will survive."

Taking courage from her husband, Edith says that she was able to put worry out of her mind: "Just as cowardice is contagious, so trust in one we love dissipates fear."

She had need of that courage the day they went to Baltimore for the opening of the Third Liberty Loan Drive. When they reached the elaborate grandstand, gay with red, white and blue bunting and hundreds of flags, Baltimore's Mayor Preston pulled her aside and said in a conspiratorial whisper, "Mrs. Wilson, I want to apologize to you for the absence of my wife. I have received anonymous letters saying this stand will be blown up today, so I would not let her come."

With a twinkle of malicious humor, Edith said, "Certainly, Mr. Mayor, under such circumstances she is most excusable."

The mayor, openly wiping the sweat of embarrassment from his deeply creased brow, said, "I knew you'd understand, but I did not want to tell the President for fear of making him nervous, as we may be blown up at any moment."

Edith assumed that a President's wife was not supposed to get nervous, and she commented, "With no credit to myself, that happened to be the case."

However dark the prospect, Woodrow Wilson kept the end

clearly in sight. He was determined that the idealistic purpose of America should not be drowned in blood and brutality, or lost in the selfish territorial ambitions expressed by the secret treaties the Allies had made with each other. For this reason he had been working for weeks with Colonel House and Edith and an eminent group of advisers known as "The Inquiry." It was a sort of Brain Trust set up for this purpose. The President was formulating a statement of war aims which should be so unequivocal, so merciful and so just that the German people could accept it, and the Allies would be forced to go along with it.

On January 8, 1918, he went before Congress, and outlined his famous Fourteen Points, which he said were "the only possible program [for peace] as we see it." The program was:

1. Open covenants of peace openly arrived at.

2. Absolute freedom of navigation on the seas. (England did not like that.)

3. Removal of economic barriers. (Nobody liked that.)

4. Guaranteed disarmament.

5. Fair adjustment of colonial claims.

6, 7, 8, 9, 10, 11 and 12 dealt with the evacuation of conquered territory and assurance that the territory of Germany and her allies would not be annexed.

13. An independent Poland.

14. This was the most important, to Wilson's mind. It stated: "A general association of nations must be formed under specific covenants for the purpose of affording mutual guarantees of political independence and territorial integrity to great and small states alike."

The message had a stunning effect not only among the Allies but on the Central Powers as well. Colonel House called it "The most important document that he [Wilson] had ever penned." There can be no question that by assuring the Central Powers that they would receive fair treatment, the Fourteen Points shortened the war by many months.

The winter was a cold and gloomy one. Shortages of food and goods began to be felt. Meatless, wheatless and almost heatless days were called for. Edith was careful to see that every restriction and economy was observed in the White House.

Sometimes during long winter evenings the Wilsons escaped the dreary present by planning a glorious future when they would at last be free to enjoy a private life. One of these daydreams was a bicycle tour through Europe. Unfortunately, Edith did not know how to ride a bicycle—when she was a girl the Bollings had been too poor to buy her one.

All fired up with enthusiasm, the President immediately ordered a fine new Columbia bicycle for her. Teaching Edith how to ride it presented a problem—the first lady could not very well practice on the open White House paths where the public could watch her making a fool of herself. The President said, "I have it. You can learn in the basement."

There was room enough in that cavernous place. Stacking some junked furniture and packing boxes out of the way provided a run about sixty feet long. For several nights the President and two Secret Service men tried to teach Edith to ride. It was a fantastic scene. At first two of them pushed her about, struggling to hold her up, for she was no light weight, all of them roaring with laughter.

Then, when she got a little sense of balance, they let her solo. Off she went zigging and zagging, swooping crazily to a crash landing that skinned her shins and knocked paint off her machine. She never learned to ride, but she said, "We had such hilarious good times that it was real recreation to all concerned."

After the bicycle riding failed, Edith managed to find other forms of recreation for her hard-pressed husband. The golf games continued almost daily, and at least once a week they went to the theater or Keith's vaudeville house. Vaudeville refreshed the President more than anything else. He took a boyish delight in the corny jokes and the acrobatic dancing. Once he said, "I love to see people who have nothing on their minds that they can't express with their heels."

In spite of the crank letters, the Wilsons still went walking in downtown Washington, which even in wartime had a small-town atmosphere. And Edith occasionally drove out in her beloved electric. As she turned out of the great gates she was saluted with a flourish by her favorite policeman.

Years before, when she had been the only woman in Washington to drive an electric, he had made himself her special protector and let her break a few traffic laws. After she had been in the White House for some time she got a letter from him saying that he had been transferred "way northeast, where I never see you any more."

Edith took the letter to the President saying, "Can't you do something for this poor fellow? He has been awfully sweet to me for years."

Though he was generally stern about granting presidential favors, Wilson yielded immediately. Laughing, he said, "I think you might write to Major Pullman [chief of police] and tell him that I would feel more secure with such a disinterested guardian at the White House crossing. I thoroughly approve of policemen who let certain pretty ladies break the law."

In the late summer of 1918 it became evident that the war was won. More than two million American soldiers were in France. The final tremendous massed attacks of the German armies had been stopped, and the Allies were now on the offensive. The enemy was retreating everywhere. Partly due to Wilson's idealistic speeches they had lost the will to fight.

On Sunday, October 6, Wilson learned that a note was on its way from the German government asking for an immediate armistice and accepting the Fourteen Points as a basis for peace negotiations. The President handed the cable to Edith saying, "Here is glorious news!"

But he was not foolish enough to be stampeded into peace, however much he longed for it—the Germans were on the run and an immediate armistice without proper safeguards might give them time to reform for a long war. Instead he wrote a note dotting every *i* and crossing every *t* of his terms so there could be no equivocation or confusion. He also sent Colonel House to Europe to represent him in the councils of the Allies. Again the long coded cables were exchanged across the sea.

The note-writing went on for a month, back and forth, with the Germans becoming increasingly frantic for an armistice as the morale of the German people disintegrated and local revolutions broke out in their great industrial cities and ports. It was evident to everyone that the end was very near.

During these weeks Wilson was considering the advisability of attending the Peace Conference himself. Edith heard all the arguments, pro and con, discussed night after night. For one thing, it was unprecedented—no President of the United States had ever gone to Europe. The State Department regarded this as a great con. To Wilson it was a pro—he loved to break precedents. However, he admitted the force of other arguments, such as the disadvantage of being forced to make immediate decisions on the spot instead of coolly thinking them over at the end of a cable.

Outweighing these objections in his mind was his distrust of the Allied leaders—which was completely justified. They were out for all they could get for their countries and devil take the Fourteen Points. Wilson felt a tremendous moral compulsion to be present in their councils to guard the idealistic principles he had formulated, and to represent the peoples who had put their trust in him—even the enemy peoples.

The question was settled when Edith decoded a cable from Colonel House saying that both British Prime Minister Lloyd George and French Premier Clemenceau opposed Wilson's taking part in the Peace Conference on the grounds that a head of state had no place at the table. The fact that they did not want him aroused both Wilson's suspicions and his invincible Presbyterian stubbornness. "We'll go," he told Edith.

Never for a moment did he think of leaving her behind.

Early in November Edith Wilson knew that the end was only a matter of days. All Germany was now in revolt. The Kaiser fled to Holland and a German Republic was proclaimed. The new German government abjectly accepted every condition Wilson had imposed. It was unconditional surrender in everything but its face-saving name.

Around 1:00 P.M. on November 7 came the flash from the United Press that an armistice had been signed. The message was a mistake, but it set off the wildest celebration in American history. At the President's request Lansing cabled House for confirmation. The Colonel replied immediately, "Armistice has not yet been signed. . . ."

A denial was instantly issued, but nothing could halt the hysterical jubilation of the American people. If it were not true in fact, it was true in essence that the war was over.

A huge crowd of people with a brass band stormed the White House in the afternoon. Edith ran to the President's study. "There's a tremendous crowd out in front calling for you," she said. "Please come out and speak to them, Woodrow."

Her husband smiled at her enthusiasm. "I know the news is not true," he said. "All that's really happened is that the German representatives have crossed the lines under a flag of truce to *ask* for an armistice. I can't make myself a party to the celebration of false news of victory."

Edith showed her disappointment, though she knew he was right.

Finally, about four o'clock, she could stand missing the fun no longer. She ordered an open car, picked up her mother and Bertha at the Powhatan Hotel, where they were appropriately living, and drove down Pennsylvania Avenue. The moment the car was recognized it was mobbed. Edith had the fine feeling of joining her fellow Americans in celebrating the victory that was true even if the news itself was false.

On Sunday, November 10, while some woebegone Germans and pompously correct French generals negotiated with each other in a railroad car in the Forest of Compiègne the Wilsons walked across Lafayette Square to church. That afternoon they went for a long drive, not in an automobile, for it was a "gasless Sunday," but in an old victoria and pair that had been dug up in the White House garage. The Secret Service followed in a moth-eaten surrey with a fringe on top. That drive to the soothing *clop-clop* of their rather flea-bitten team was an oasis of tranquillity from the terrific tension.

That evening Mrs. Bolling, Bertha and Randolph Bolling came for family dinner at the White House. Afterward they sat in the Oval Room, too jumpy really to settle down, because of what was happening in the Forest of Compiègne. Mrs. Bolling got up to leave early. At the elevator she said maternally to her son-in-law, "I do wish you would go right to bed; you look so tired."

"I wish I could," the President answered. "But I fear the drawer; it always circumvents me. Wait a moment until I look."

He hurried to his study and unlocked the center drawer of his Princeton desk where documents requiring immediate attention were always placed. He came back looking dejected, holding five long coded cables. "These are your work, Edith," he said, "so there is no rest in sight for either of us."

Randolph Bolling impulsively said, "Let me stay and help you, Edith."

Before she could tell him no, the code was secret, the President said, "Indeed you can help her and I'll be very grateful."

Wilson went to his study and Edith and her brother went to work on Miss Helm's big table in the west hall. At one o'clock in the morning they took the last of the cables in to the President. It was merely a polite message from Clemenceau saying that he hoped to work in harmony with the President at the Peace Conference.

And still the Wilsons could not go to bed; they sat there talking nervously, waiting for news from the Forest. At three o'clock it came. The armistice was signed. The war was over.

Mrs. Wilson says that many people have asked her exactly what she and the President did in that tremendous moment, and her answer is, "We did nothing. We just stood there dumbly, knowing the news was true, but unable to *feel* it."

On the bright morning of November 11, 1918, they felt the full joyous impact of peace. A little after noon the President drove to the Capitol to tell Congress the news officially. His words were in the spirit of Lincoln's merciful Second Inaugural Speech ("With malice toward none"), for he announced his purpose "to set up such a peace as will satisfy the longing of the whole world for disinterested justice."

And he added, "To conquer with arms is to make only a temporary conquest, to conquer the world by earning its esteem is to make permanent conquest. . . ."

Then the Wilsons drove back up Pennsylvania Avenue in the sunshine through the wildly cheering crowds. Edith remembered the cheers that other time eighteen months before on the declaration of war, and thought happily how different they sounded today. They were different also from the cheering of the false armistice three days ago. Then people had been just wildly, hysterically triumphant. But at the sight of Woodrow Wilson the cheers had a different tone and meaning, as though the American people were pledging themselves to follow his leadership in peace as in war, rededicating themselves to his great ideals.

That was, perhaps, the happiest day of Wilson's life, and he savored the joy of it fully. At four-thirty he reviewed the United War Work Parade and in the evening after dinner he and Edith drove out in the open car to watch the lighting of the bonfires and the victory celebration. The moment the Wilsons were recognized the crowds stormed the car, swamping the Secret Service men, climbing up on the mudguards and reaching out to touch the President and his wife.

They were finally rescued from adulation by soldiers in the crowd, who, locking arms, formed a ring around the car to protect it as it moved slowly back to the White House.

Even then the President was not ready to call it quits. He was like a small boy who cannot bear to see a great day end. One of the most engaging of his characteristics was his juvenile delight in moments like this. In the hall of the White House he said to Edith, "I feel like going to a party. Ambassador Cellere is having one in honor of the King of Italy's birthday. Let's go and surprise them."

"I'd love it," said Edith, always ready for a frolic.

So they dashed upstairs and changed into full fig, and drove to the Italian Embassy. The first Ambassador Cellere knew of it was when a bug-eyed aide dashed up to say the President of the United States was coming in the front door. The Ambassador and his wife broke out of the receiving line and galloped down the marble staircase to greet the Wilsons breathlessly in the hall.

This unexpected arrival lifted the party to heights of gaiety. The President toasted the King of Italy amid thunderous cheers. And Edith herself was radiantly happy at seeing her husband so merry.

They stayed about an hour and got back to the White House after midnight. They were still too excited to sleep so Edith lit the fire in her bedroom. They sat together on the big sofa in front of it and talked most of the night away. Then the President read aloud a chapter of the Bible. After that they went at last to sleep.

CHAPTER IX

TRIUMPH IN PARIS

IN THAT TRIUMPHANT TIME there was one reverse which ulti-
mately robbed the world of the fruits of victory. Many people,
including Mrs. Wilson, attributed it to a mistake made by the President.

The biennial Congressional elections took place on November 5,
1918. It was evident to the Democratic National Committee that
their party might easily lose control of the House and Senate. The
Senate was particularly important because if the Republicans won
there they could appoint a majority of the Foreign Relations Committee which would pass on the Peace Treaty. And because of his
seniority Senator Lodge would become its chairman. Wilson realized that the senator would automatically oppose anything he
wanted.

One evening in the latter part of October, before the armistice
was signed, Edith Wilson came into the study to find her husband
pecking away slowly, almost hesitantly, on his battered typewriter.
He pulled the sheet from the machine and handed it to her. "Tell
me what you think of that," he said.

She read the note with increasing disquiet. It was an appeal by the President to the American people to elect a Democratic Congress in order to show their confidence in his leadership and to make his task easier. Edith, by this time no mean politician, recognized the danger. The war had been conducted on a nonpartisan basis with the full support of the Republicans in and out of Congress. This message seemed to imply that making peace would be a partisan business, because the Republicans could not be trusted.

She put the paper down and said, "Please don't release this, Woodrow. You know you don't feel this way; it doesn't represent your own views."

"You're right, it doesn't," the President said seriously. "But I promised Vance [McCormick] and Burleson that I would do it and I feel I must."

Earnestly, almost passionately, she pleaded. "I beg you not to. It is not like you and I feel it will have a very bad effect."

The President's jaw set stubbornly as he said, "I promised."

The result was actually even worse than Edith had foreseen. The Republicans were infuriated beyond measure. Those who had supported the President most loyally were the most deeply hurt by his apparent ingratitude. Theodore Roosevelt and Henry Cabot Lodge seized the opportunity to rage in speech and print that the President had implied that Republicans were less patriotic than Democrats —something Wilson had been most careful not to do. However, the point was made and there seems little question that many an independent Republican who might have voted for the Democrats changed his mind and resentfully voted the straight Republican ticket.

The Democrats lost control of the House by a sizable majority. The real fatality was that they lost the Senate by one vote. Ironically, John (Honey) Fitzgerald, grandfather of President Kennedy, lost the senatorial race in Massachusetts to Senator Lodge by only 30,000 votes. On so small a turn hung the chance of lasting peace.

When he heard the result President Wilson said, "We are all sick at heart."

Mrs. Wilson says, "That message was the greatest mistake Woodrow ever made."

Perhaps an even worse mistake was Woodrow Wilson's failure to appoint a single well-known Republican to the Peace Commission.

Despite this sinister portent, Wilson was high of heart as he prepared to leave for the Peace Conference. The tremendous enthusiasm of the American people convinced him that with their backing he could, if necessary, defy the Senate.

That was a time of flurry and great excitement for Edith. She had only two or three weeks to make all her arrangements and buy clothes suitable for everything possible from tramping through battlefields to a ball at Buckingham Palace. Until the news that the President was going to Paris was given out, her shopping had to be done secretly, which of course made it even more fun.

According to the Philadelphia *Record* of November 27, 1918, the court gowns for Mrs. Wilson and Margaret, who was in France singing for the troops, were made at Kurzman's in New York. "A large corps of girls and women have been at work making frequent journeys from New York to Washington for fittings and consultations. Mrs. Wilson was not purchasing her order without knowing exactly what every piece would be like."

At midnight on December 3, 1918, the presidential party left Washington in the private car *Mayflower*. Because they were to be the guests of the French government Wilson held his personal entourage to an absolute minimum to save them expense. This group included Admiral Grayson and Miss Benham, the President's secretary, Gilbert Close—Tumulty was left to cope with things in Washington—Charles Swem and Ike Hoover.

In addition Brooks and Susan went along to take care of the President and Edith. The Secret Service men were the famous "Mr. Starling of the White House," looking the perfect flatfoot of fiction with his square, seamed, big-nosed face, derby hat and clumsy booted feet; the comparatively inconspicuous Joseph J. Murphy and a dapper little fellow with a hat cocked jauntily on his curly hair, and a foxy face, improbably named John Q. Sly.

Very early the next morning the train jolted onto a pier at Hoboken alongside the former German liner *George Washington*. The Wilson party went up to the bridge, and preceded by the battleship *New Mexico,* the *George Washington* sailed down New York Harbor amid bellowing foghorns and shrill whistles with airplanes cavorting all over the sky and the forts firing salutes.

Edith thought their suites aboard the liner were like a pleasant summer cottage. The President's included a large sitting room with a round table, a chintz-covered sofa and comfortable wicker chairs; a dining room capable of seating eight; a double and a single bedroom and two luxurious bathrooms. There was also a foyer and an office for the Chief Executive. The suite had been newly decorated and furnished by John Wanamaker's. In the President's office stood a superb Empire desk at which he worked during all the four voyages he made on the ship. Edith's suite was smaller but no less comfortable.

The Belmont Hotel had sent their best chef to cook for the President. Edith found the food "marvelous" but it was too elaborate for Wilson's taste or digestion. Everything came with a French sauce, and he finally said crossly, "I don't see any sense in wrapping food up in pajamas."

The body of the American mission, who were *not* paid for by the French, was very large. The other commissioners were Secretary of State Lansing, slim and elegant and ineffectual; General Bliss, square and solid, his bald head glistening like his cavalry boots. The lone Republican was Edith's friend, former Ambassador Henry White, strolling around the deck in a fur-lined, double-breasted overcoat with a sealskin collar and a derby hat above his wise old face with its drooping walrus mustache. Colonel House, of course, was already in Paris.

In addition there were dozens of experts on all possible subjects whom Wilson had brought along to advise him on the intricate problems he would have to face. William Allen White described Wilson and his experts as "This Yankee knight errant followed by a desperate crew of college professors in horn-rimmed glasses, carrying text books, encyclopedias, maps, charts, graphs, statistics and all sorts of literary crowbars with which to pry up the boundaries of Europe and move them about in the interests of justice . . . and the Fourteen Points."

Other passengers included Ambassadors Jusserand and Cellere with their wives and our new Ambassador to England, John W. Davis, and his wife, he a slight dapper gentleman, she stern and somewhat terrifying in a Russian cossack's fur hat. Of course there were crowds of reporters.

They had a calm and pleasant voyage. Edith was happy to see her husband, who had been completely exhausted, look stronger and happier every day as the sea worked its usual cure. Wilson paid very little attention to his fellow commissioners but he and Edith spent a great deal of time being briefed by the experts. To them he said one day, "Show me the right and I will fight for it!"

They cheered him and, as White puts it, "The world seemed whizzing into its next millennium."

For relaxation the Wilsons went to the movies nearly every night. There was a theater for the Peace Commission and another called "The Old Salt" for the crew. The Wilsons always went to "The Old Salt."

In fact the crew saw more of them than did their fellow commissioners. One Sunday evening they joined the men in a hymn singing. Edith laughed happily hearing her husband's voice soaring loud and clear in the thundering choruses. She knew it reminded him of Princeton days, which had become a nostalgic sort of never-never land for him. And when, as they started to leave, a fine quartet sang "Old Nassau," she saw that Woodrow's eyes were full of tears.

Best of all were their precious moments alone together in their own suite. Edith Benham wrote in her diary, "The more I am with the Wilsons the more I am struck by their unrivaled home life. I have never dreamed such sweetness and love could be. . . . It is very beautiful to see his face light up and brighten at the very sight of her and to see her turn to him for everything, though she is a woman of a lot of spirit. . . ."

On the morning of Friday, December 13—Wilson's lucky thirteen, he and Edith were on the *George Washington*'s bridge at dawn. At twenty-five minutes past seven the great American battleships of the European squadron came over the horizon, dark gray against the lighter gray of sea and sky, lattice masts swaying as they plowed through the waves. The *Texas, Arkansas, New York, Florida, Nevada, Wyoming, Utah, Oklahoma* and the doomed *Arizona* passed the *George Washington* in a thunder of saluting guns and took station in a double column on either side. Then came the four-stack destroyers, their high, sharp bows knifing the sea, and behind them cruisers with an odd silhouette flying the tricolor of France. It was tremendously thrilling to Edith and she knew by her husband's shining eyes that he was as excited as she.

Thus escorted, the *George Washington* entered the great debarkation port of Brest with flags flying, guns firing, airplanes wheeling overhead and the cheering of the people, like thunder across the water. It was only the beginning.

The President of France had sent his royal blue train with *R.F.* —for "République Française"—on every door. The Wilsons had the presidential car, but there was a snafu in billeting the other passengers. The conductor's list read in part: "Room A, Car 3: Secretary of State Lansing and Miss Benham. Room B: Honorable Henry White, Mrs. Lansing. . . ." The proprieties were restored amid gales of laughter, and they were off for Paris.

At ten o'clock of a soft, misty morning the train pulled slowly into Paris. President and Madame Poincaré and the whole French Cabinet were there to greet them with a regiment of crack troops and a band. There were brief speeches, "The Star-Spangled Banner," the "Marseillaise." Then they got into open victorias drawn by high-stepping horses. The two Presidents rode in the first carriage. The second was rather crowded. Mrs. Wilson and Madame Poincaré sat on the back seat with Margaret Wilson and Madame

Jusserand facing them on the jump seats. The mounted Garde Républicaine, splendid in brilliant uniforms and gilt Roman helmets with long horsehair tails, formed up around them with drawn sabers, and they started off at a smart trot, the cavalry cantering alongside, hoofs striking sparks from the pavement.

In the misty sunshine they drove to the Arc de Triomphe where the mounted guards parted and the Presidents' carriage drove alone through the sacred center arch, the first to pass that way since the Franco-Prussian War. The Champs Élysées' dropping away before them, was lined by horizon-blue troops holding back immense crowds of people that extended as far as the eye could see in all directions. All the rooftops were black with humanity and the horse chestnuts bowed like apple trees at harvest time under the weight of people perched there. It seemed to Edith to be raining lilacs and violets and roses; they fell singly and in bunches on her carriage until she was literally buried beneath them. She felt as though not Paris alone, but all France had turned out to cheer the man on whom they pinned their hopes of permanent peace. It is truly said that there had been nothing like that ovation in the whole history of France's ebullient capital, nor was its like seen again. Miss Benham wrote, "They looked upon the President as almost divine. . . ."

In the Place de la Concorde the Wilsons passed the ugly, camouflage-spotted ranks of captured German cannon. Down the Rue Royale past the classic Church of the Madeleine they drove to the beautiful palace that Prince Murat and the French government had lent them for their stay. Its magnificent interior was a scene of confusion as they rushed up to their suites to change for the state luncheon of the Élysée. Trunks were being manhandled through the halls; nobody knew where anything was; a dozen footmen in scarlet livery and white stockings rushed dazedly around. The language barrier was all but impregnable. Nobody on the French staff spoke English, and in the President's party only Miss Benham spoke reliable French.

Somehow the Wilsons got changed in twenty minutes and

mounted their victoria again. With the Garde Républicaine still galloping alongside they drove to the Élysée, the classic palace of French Presidents—and emperors. They passed through the Gate of Kings to the ruffle of drums. The little President of France, looking like a bearded cherub in a frock coat that almost touched his spats, and Madame Poincaré, received them on the portico and took them to the *grand salon* where all the great of the French world were gathered.

After a few minutes of stiff conversation—nobody understood what anybody else was saying anyway—President Poincaré seized Edith's arm in a viselike grip and started for the dining room. He was so short that she felt like a "liner in tow of a tug." The dining room was so filled with tables and servants that she did not see how they would reach their seats of honor at the far end, but Poincaré charged on, and, as Edith says, "mowing down waiters as we went, we arrived breathless and panting."

Once safely at anchor, she enjoyed herself. The table was exquisitely furnished with delicate china and glass and many flowers; and she was thrilled by the sight of the almost mythical heroes of the war—Foch and Pétain and Joffre and "our own Pershing."

There seemed no end to formality. The Wilsons were no sooner back at the Murat Palace, than the Poincarés paid their official call, which the Wilsons returned an hour later. That was quite enough of the Poincarés for one day.

The fact is that ever since she had met him in Spain long ago, Edith had thought Poincaré dull and pompous. She was even less enchanted with the first lady of France—"she was very stuffy."

There was not much rest the next day, Sunday. The Wilsons went to the Presbyterian Church on the Rue de Berry in the morning and, playing no favorites, the Episcopal Cathedral in the afternoon. In between the President and Admiral Grayson drove out and bought a wreath, which Wilson insisted on carrying himself to the grave of Lafayette. On his personal visiting card he wrote, "In memory of the great Lafayette from a fellow servant of liberty." The wreath and the card were later copied in bronze.

Meanwhile the confusion at Murat Palace was gradually sub-
siding. For the first twenty-four hours Miss Benham had to act as
switchboard girl in addition to everything else. Then bilingual telephone operators took over.

Ike Hoover installed himself in the palace antechamber in a
magnificent brocaded armchair with an inlaid Empire table to
write on. A portrait of aristocratic Prince Murat looked down on
him scornfully. He was equally scornful of the peculiar inability
of the French to speak English. This produced problems because
the President's drivers were American service men. So before the
Wilsons went anywhere, Hoover looked up the route on a large-
scale map of Paris. Mrs. Wilson remembers his saying to their
driver, "Now don't forget, you cross one Champs and two roos."

Most of the President's time was taken up by official callers. All
the great men of Europe came in a never-ending stream. When
Marshall Foch was expected Edith and Miss Benham hid behind
a door to watch the greatest soldier in the world. Afterward the
President told them, "I like him. Just as I expected, he is simple,
direct and fine."

When Georges Clemenceau, the octogenarian Premier of France
came, Edith helped receive him. Nicknamed "The Tiger," he was
an extraordinary character, squat and powerful, with his fierce old
face and long white mustachios. He always wore a black skull cap
and, like Robespierre, gray cotton gloves because of his eczema.
Clemenceau was almost the exact antithesis of the President. An
agnostic materialist, he thought Wilsonian ideals were moonshine
and sought safety for his beloved France in military alliances and
the destruction of Germany's ability to fight. He is reported to have
said, "The good God gave us the Ten Commandments and we
broke them. Now comes Wilson with his Fourteen Points—we
shall see."

Despite their fierce clashes Wilson respected the Frenchman's
integrity and the Premier in turn admired him. As for Mrs. Wilson
she says simply, "I liked the old man. You could count on his
word."

Her feeling for British Prime Minister David Lloyd George was just the opposite. She says, "Lloyd George was a slippery character, but very nice socially. Mrs. Lloyd George was with him part of the time—a very uninteresting woman."

Another caller was King Victor Emanuel III of Italy. When he came in the door Edith thought him rather funny, he was so tiny, completely overshadowed by his "queer, double-decker cap." But he won her heart by his forthright, no-nonsense manner. As the little king looked around at the brocaded, gilt and crystal splendor of Prince Murat's *grand salon* he said, "My God, I couldn't live in a place like this!"

All these visits gave the President a chance to know his colleagues—or antagonists—of the Peace Conference. He relied greatly on his wife's sharp human appraisals. Edith was less likely to be taken in by a smooth talker than he; he always expected the best of people, but she was inclined to see their weaknesses. However, Wilson was already becoming impatient to get to work.

In his innocence of the ways of international congresses Wilson had mentally allotted six weeks for the business of remaking the world. In his defense it should be said that the European statesmen were almost completely unaware of what a time-consuming process it would be. There had been no such meeting of world statesmen since the Congress of Vienna more than a hundred years before—which, incidentally, lasted fifteen months. But try as he would, the President could not get his colleagues down to business. Lloyd George had called a General Election in England, with the idea of keeping his party in for five more years by cashing in on victory. He said the Conference could not possibly begin until the election was over. Statesmen from other countries were equally dilatory. To keep the American President quiet the British and Italians suggested that he visit their countries.

On their second Sunday in Paris, Wilson decided that instead of going to church they should visit some of the wounded. Edith Wilson agreed with a sinking heart for she still had a phobia of hospitals. They went first to the American Hospital at Neuilly. As they entered its spotless corridors the smell of antiseptics struck her with such terror and nausea that she wondered if she could go on. She did because she had to.

Together the President and Mrs. Wilson went through the long wards. He, as always, was at his best with young men, joking with them, or compassionate, making them feel that he was something between a friend and a father.

Edith, summoning all her courage, managed to be her warm, gay, beautiful best. The boys loved her.

When she thought the worst was over, they came to the door of a ward where the accompanying doctors paused to give them warning. "This is the facial ward," one of them said. "We put them all up here together so they won't get morbid and self-conscious, so they will sort of help each other."

As the door opened Edith steadied herself on the portal, wondering if she would faint. "There they were," she wrote, "some with their entire noses blown away, some totally blind, others with chins and half their faces gone. . . . I felt so ashamed that I should grow faint from merely looking at these boys who endured without a murmur. . . . Well, I revived and shook myself free from horror and stayed on and told them how proud I was just to touch their hands. . . ."

The Wilsons got home at four o'clock, having spent five hours at Neuilly. They felt too sick to eat lunch. But the President indomitably said that, lest they be accused of favoritism, they must also go to a French hospital. So in the darkness at five o'clock they started for Val de Grace, the biggest French military hospital. Incredibly awful, the hospital consisted of a group of old buildings in the ancient city. Between them ran littered alleyways and noxious open sewers. Instead of the asepsis of Neuilly the whole place smelled of dirt that had been accumulating for half a thousand years. Even the sheets on the patients' beds were gray.

Not that Edith could see them very well. With typical French parsimony the cold, dank wards were lighted by a few twenty-watt bulbs that she says "made it just possible to pick our way through."

To add to the horror a crazy old woman—"She's harmless," they said—clung to Edith's sleeve gibbering at her incomprehensibly.

After visiting the wards they ended up at a Christmas celebration for convalescents. A small room with whitewashed walls was packed with walking wounded in horizon blue. A thin one-legged boy was playing an upright piano. As they came in he struck up the "Marseillaise," and a big man with eyeless sockets in his face began to sing. He had one of the most magnificent voices Edith had ever heard. As the triumphant chords of the great French battle song rang out, she and her husband stood holding hands and weeping.

Since he could accomplish nothing in Paris, President Wilson decided to spend Christmas with the troops. At midnight Christmas Eve he and Edith left for Pershing's headquarters at Chaumont in President Poincaré's special train accompanied by Ambassador and Madame Jusserand, Miss Benham, Admiral Grayson and General Harts, military aide at the White House before the war. The magnificent train was a whited sepulcher, so cold that they could not sleep at all. Jusserand was *"désesperé"* at the inadequacies of his country's transportation.

The next morning at seven o'clock they started out in a windless, heavy snow with General Pershing in his Cadillac to visit the troops. The big car stopped at dozens of farms where the men were billeted mostly in barns, each with a great manure pile beside it steaming in the raw air. Sometimes their cots were placed in rows on the muddy floors beside the stalls for the cattle, at others Edith climbed a rickety ladder to a loft. Luckier men were bedded down in farmhouse cellars. Green boughs and bits of red paper made rather pathetic Christmas decorations which the French children, who were great friends with their doughboy guests, thought wonderful. The Americans were all cold, uncomfortable but very cheerful because they were going home.

Once the Wilsons and Pershing stopped at a cantonment where

field equipment was neatly stacked for inspection. General Pershing picked up a folding tent pole to show them how ingenious it was. Then he threw it carelessly on the ground. "Are these boys likely to be inspected again when we are gone?" Wilson asked.

"Very likely, Mr. President."

Edith saw a devil dancing in her husband's eyes. "One other thing, General," he said. "I am the Commander-in-Chief of the Army, empowered to give you orders. Am I not?"

Bewildered, Pershing said, "Certainly, sir."

"Then, General," said the President, "you will replace that tent pole as you found it."

With a pickle-sour smile the General bent to obey while Wilson winked over his shoulder at the grinning doughboys.

The Army being the Army, there had to be a review, snow or no snow. Edith stood with her husband on an open platform in the middle of a big, muddy field while crack units of the Seventy-seventh New York Division slogged by. In that transition army there were all sorts of anachronisms—infantry, of course, marching by at eyes right with bayoneted rifles sloped evenly as roofs; long modern cannon drawn by teams of six or eight fractious mules; horse artillery at the trot, followed by tanks lumbering along at their best speed of four miles per hour; and finally, like ghosts from Balaklava, a regiment of cavalry dashing past in rulered lines at the gallop.

Then the Wilsons had a traditional Christmas dinner with the troops in a shed as long as a carbarn. Their French aide, General Léorat, was pretty dubious about the pumpkin pie, but, encouraged by Edith, he downed a small piece. Despite the Frenchman's doubts, it was very good pie.

By the time they got to Pershing's headquarters chateau at Chaumont, the Wilsons were frozen as stiff as turkeys in cold storage. Roaring fires and hot tea revived them enough to get back to their train.

On the day after Christmas they left for England to visit the king.

CHAPTER X

BUCKINGHAM PALACE
AND THE QUIRINALE

IN MIDCHANNEL, with the stately formality of a minuet the escorting French destroyers wheeled away and six British destroyers, bowing to the waves, took their places on either side of His Majesty's Ship *Brighton*. The President and Mrs. Wilson, standing on her bridge, saw the white cliffs of Dover come up out of the Channel haze. After brief formalities at the port of Dover they boarded the royal train. On the way to London Edith had a long talk with the king's uncle, the tall old Duke of Connaught, who had come to meet them. He had read of the tremendous reception the French had given her husband and warned her not to expect such enthusiasm in London. "British reserve, you know."

Other people had been advising and admonishing her about the English visit, in particular Mr. Henry White. "I was very fond of Mr. White," Mrs. Wilson says. "A courtly gentleman. However, being trained in diplomacy he was always afraid I wouldn't do the right thing. 'Be very careful with the Queen,' he said. 'She is very stiff, but very nice. You must be careful.' "

Actually Mrs. Wilson found that the king and queen were more nervous about the visit than she was. The Wilsons were the first nonroyal heads of state ever to stay at Buckingham Palace, and the inevitable precedent-breaking meant so much more to royalty, who lived by protocol, than it did to her.

Under the great grimy glass vault of Charing Cross Station King George V and Queen Mary were waiting on the red-carpeted platform with their daughter, Princess Mary, and nobles and notables of the realm. The neatly bearded king was small and nervous. Queen Mary, much handsomer than her pictures, with the corseted wasp waist and pouter pigeon bust of a disappearing age, dominated him. If it had not been *lèse majesté* you might have said she wore the pants. The princess was a shy pretty girl with long golden hair and the lovely strawberries-and-cream complexion that is the compensation for England's atrocious climate.

On this day the climate did not live up to its reputation. The setting sun was shining brilliantly and all England was out in the streets and on the rooftops to see the President pass by. He rode with the king in a high open landau, with the royal arms blazoned on the doors, drawn by four superb horses with an outrider and postilion and four bewigged footmen in crimson liveries. Mrs. Wilson rode in a similar equipage with the queen. Princess Mary sat on the jump seat facing them.

To Edith's surprise the crowds were as wildly enthusiastic as in Paris; evidently the sight of her husband broke down that British reserve. As they drove down the stately avenue toward Buckingham Palace Edith saw an old lady standing on the portico of Marlborough House with only a shawl over her shoulders, waving an American flag. "Good gracious, it's Grandmama!" exclaimed Princess Mary. The Dowager Queen Alexandria was blowing kisses at the President.

The courtyard of the palace was filled with American soldiers invited by the thoughtful king. Those in the front ranks were in wheel chairs or on crutches. After the President had greeted them the royal party went into the palace, where the waltz of protocol began again. The ladies and gentlemen of the king's household were presented. Then the king and queen escorted the Wilsons through the long, freezing cold corridors of the palace to their suite.

First came a big square drawing room with long windows overlooking the grounds. Edith gratefully noted a glowing grate of coals. The President's room had an alcove curtained off with red velvet. The king proudly pulled back the curtains, disclosing a bathtub and an *electric heater*. Edith's enormous, elaborately furnished room had no heat in it at all, but there was a coal grate in her cozy dressing room.

After viewing the rooms the Wilsons made the traditional appearance on the famous balcony of Buckingham Palace. Edith saw the vast cheering crowd extending back down the Mall as far as her eyes could reach. In answer to the cheers the king and queen waved small American flags and President Wilson waved a Union Jack.

Then Sir Charles Cust, the President's British aide, asked them how soon they could be ready to pay their formal calls. "In twenty minutes," answered Edith, who was becoming as adept as an actress at quick changes.

She was ready on the dot in a black crepe de chine gown with a Russian blouse effect and a broadtail skirt and collar. A big black beaver hat with three soft gray ostrich feathers on the side completed her ultrasmart costume.

They went first to Marlborough House where old Queen Alexandria received them with two of her daughters—the Princess Royal and the Queen of Denmark. They were dressed in black with elbow-length brown gloves. Because Queen Alexandria introduced them so casually—"This is Victoria and this is Maud"—Edith was slightly baffled as to just who they were. She talked to "Victoria" and "Maud" while Wilson struggled with the Dowager Queen, who was almost totally deaf.

After a few minutes the Princess Royal said shyly, "Would it be asking too much if I asked you to sign my book, Mrs. Wilson?"

On hearing that Mrs. Wilson would be happy to do so, Queen Maud of Denmark said, "Oh, I so wanted the same thing, but my book hasn't arrived yet, so I must miss this great opportunity."

Smiling enchantingly and inwardly bursting with laughter at the idea of a queen being unhappy at not getting her autograph, Edith wrote her dashing signature, "Edith Bolling Wilson," in the princess' book. The royal eyes nearly popped, and Victoria said, "Oh, you sign *three* names."

Edith was not sure whether or not she had lost caste, since royalty signs only one name, but seeing that Maud appeared even more disconsolate she decided it was all right.

After the required fifteen minutes had passed—"no more but no less," Sir Charles had told them—the Wilsons drove around London dropping cards on other relatives of the Royal Family. That night the king and queen were to dine "informally" in their guests' suite. When Edith asked if she should wear gloves she was told, "Her Majesty will not wear gloves, but she and Princess Mary will carry a new pair with the string still keeping them together, held with the fingers up in their left hands." When they arrived, Edith says, all she could think of was the children's game, "Simon says thumbs up."

Besides the king and queen and the princess, the Duke of York, who later became George VI, his younger brother Prince Henry, and the Duke of Connaught made up the little dinner party. Edith thought it would be, in the English phrase, "a sticky wicket," but it turned out to be a merry evening. The President told a funny story on himself that started them laughing, and the king responded by describing how he was reviewing American troops at the front when he heard one doughboy say, "Who's that bug?"

"The King of England, you dope," said his companion.

The first one shrugged his shoulder skeptically and said, "Where's his crown?"

After an excellent meal the gentlemen remained at the table while the queen took Mrs. Wilson on a personally conducted tour of her own suite. Edith thought it in beautiful taste; she admired equally the exotic Chinese salon in crystal and jade with red lacquer furniture covered with Chinese embroidery, and the queen's work room, whose tall windows looked out on the garden. Its big, leather-covered writing table, easy chairs and overflowing bookcases reflected Queen Mary's real personality. "The only thing lacking," Mrs. Wilson says, "was warmth. I had to clench my jaws to keep my teeth from chattering."

The next day, while the President lunched at 10 Downing Street with the Prime Minister, Edith went to luncheon at Lady Reading's, where she sat next to the famous Margot Asquith, to whom she took an instantaneous dislike. Apparently the lady was at her most Margotish, shoving "her pinched, small face" close to Edith and saying awful things in a loud clear voice: "The lady on my right is the Countess of ————, the biggest liar in London. The next one is an American, but she was ashamed to admit it until Wilson made America fashionable. Now she blows about it disgustingly. Then there is Mrs. Lloyd George; she doesn't count, of course."

Edith in embarrassment tried to stop her by asking if she was going to the state dinner at the palace that night. It was an unfortunate gambit. "I'm not invited," snapped Lady Asquith. "I sent word to the king that I didn't want his food, but I did want to meet President Wilson because he really has brains. I have never met an American with brains."

The state dinner was as magnificently formal as only the English can be. Edith, deliberately democratic in a superbly cut black princess gown with no jewels, walked with her husband through the long corridors of the palace. Walking backward in front of them were two elderly gentleman ushers who made a low bow every third step. They even went up a long flight of stairs backward and bowing.

The Wilsons joined the Royal Family in a small drawing room.

In the blaze of their jewels, especially those of the queen, "who was stunning in a white gown with the blue Order of the Garter across her low bodice, a coronet of diamonds and other magnificent jewels," Edith knew how right she had been not to compete with her own small diamonds.

Because the President of the United States never wears a uniform the king had decided that he and the other gentlemen would wear white tie and tails. During the war no one in court circles had worn evening dress, so overriding the perfume of many flowers, Edith noted a strong smell of moth balls.

From the drawing room they went into a long gallery where the ninety-six other guests were standing in two long lines, the men on one side, the women on the other. The king took the President down the ladies' side, presenting them to him, and the queen took Edith down the other, where all the leaders of the empire stood. She had a Cinderella feeling as she met these world-famous men. Balfour and Lloyd George she already knew, but there was Field Marshal Lord Haig, very neat and military with his white clipped mustache; Admiral Lord Jellico, who commanded the Grand Fleet at Jutland, looking slighter and younger than she had imagined; dashing Admiral Beatty; Lord Curzon of Kedleston, a heavy dark impressive man ablaze with orders of decorations; and Winston Churchill, blond and unimpressive, of whom Mrs. Wilson later said, "Woodrow did not like him. He thought him able, but did not admire him. Of course he must have changed a great deal since then."

After the presentations double doors were flung back, and the king, taking Mrs. Wilson's arm led the way in to dinner. She almost gasped as the full magnificence of that vast room burst upon her. It was ablaze with crimson and gold—crimson walls and two golden thrones covered by a crimson canopy; beefeaters of the Tower Guard in their sixteenth-century red uniforms, standing with halberds stiffly erect; great golden candelabra lighting the table whose massive gold service made the White House's best look like a country cousin. Even the flowers were in key, poinsettia and scarlet anemones.

During the meal the king told Mrs. Wilson that he was going to propose a toast to the President. "It always makes me terribly nervous when I have to speak," he confided.

She wondered if that could be true, since the speech was all typed out, but as he rose to make his graceful tribute she saw that his hands were shaking. Wilson replied without notes in easy, felicitous phrases.

After dinner the women retired to another great drawing room where another quadrille of etiquette was performed. Everybody, including the queen, remained standing while ladies-in-waiting brought different guests up for a few words with Her Majesty. When the gentlemen joined them the same ceremony was repeated with the king. The entire company was kept on its feet for nearly three hours until the palace clocks struck midnight. One of the ladies-in-waiting fainted and was carried out, and Lady Reading whispered to Miss Benham, "No other queen has been able to stand as long as this one."

After the Wilsons had retired to their rooms there was an alarm in the palace. Guards outside their door heard a ticking noise that might be a bomb. Finally they got up courage to knock and warn him. Wilson laughed out loud and said, "Come, I'll show you." He was writing his speech for the Guild Hall next day on his noisy old typewriter.

There was one more day of pageantry and pomp, including the presentation of the Freedom of the City of London at the Guild Hall and luncheon. This was held at the Mansion House and was presided over by the magnificently robed Lord Mayor. At midnight the Wilsons boarded the king's train for Carlisle, where Woodrow's mother had been born.

One may imagine the sigh of relief of both hosts and guests as that train puffed out of the station. The visit had gone off "as

smooth as silk," as the English would say. There had been no
untoward incidents, no real gaffes or contretemps. The high personages involved had all liked and respected one another. They
had even enjoyed each other's company when they got a chance to
do so informally.

Of course the British press had some satirical comments. They
noted that "What astonished the English most was that in his toast
at the state dinner the President addressed the King as 'Sir,' " (instead of "Your Majesty"), and that Mrs. Wilson "Did not curtsey
to the Queen on any occasion." Of course she did not. For Edith
was quite aware that she represented a great nation that would not
bend its knee to any king—or queen.

The papers also had fun with the President's dress. On one occasion he appeared with his left trouser leg accidentally turned up.
The press of England, and France, too, speculated as to whether
this would set a new fashion.

The President caused further consternation by sometimes wearing a shaggy fur coat with his high silk hat. It looked like raccoon
but was actually wombat. "I never liked that coat," says Mrs.
Wilson. However, it made him a fashion plate in America, where
all the college boys began wearing toppers with their coonskin
coats. The British simply shuddered.

But all the gibes were in the spirit of fun. In reality the British
people opened their hearts to Woodrow Wilson. They greeted him
with the same fervor the French had shown. For whatever the
diplomats and statesmen might think, and in their secret hearts
most of them agreed with Clemenceau that his ideas were too
utopian to be safe, the people of all nations instinctively knew that
those same ideas were the only hope of safety for the world.

But there was more than the hope of safety in the hearts of those
people cheering in the London streets. The American President
had lifted them, as he had lifted his own countrymen, above selfish
considerations of security or personal gain to a real, if ephemeral,
concern for all mankind, and they idolized him for it. For this

reason the Wilsons' three days in London were the all-time high of Anglo-American friendship.

Naturally it was raining in Carlisle, but that dampened no spirits. The whole population of the little city turned out. After an early-morning reception at the Crown and Mitre the Wilsons went to the Presbyterian Church where the President's grandfather, Thomas Woodrow, had been the parson. When the time came for the sermon the minister introduced Wilson to the congregation and surprised them by saying that instead of preaching he was going to ask the President to address them.

As he rose, Edith wondered a little nervously what her husband would find to say on such short notice. She had too little faith.

Speaking very gravely, Wilson said, "It is with unaffected reluctance that I project myself into this solemn service. I remember my grandfather very well . . . and I am confident that he would not approve of it. . . .

"The memories that have come to me today of the mother who was born here are very affecting. . . . Perhaps it is appropriate that in a place of worship I should acknowledge my indebtedness to her and to her remarkable father, because, after all, what the world is now seeking to do is to return to the paths of duty. . . . I believe that as this war has drawn nations temporarily together in a combination of physical force we shall now be drawn together in a combination of moral force that will be irresistible. . . .

"Like rivulets gathering into the river and the river into the seas, there come from communities like this streams to fertilize the consciences of men, and it is the conscience of the world that we are trying to place on the throne that others would usurp."

All the time her husband was speaking Edith was thinking of his mother, who had sat in these same pews when she was a little girl, and of how proud she would have been of her son could she have heard and seen him here now.

Back in Paris, the Wilsons started the New Year right by playing a round of golf at St. Cloud on January 1, 1919. The President was wearing a pleated Norfolk jacket and those baggy short pants known as "plus fours." Edith had on stout tweeds with the long cumbersome skirt that modesty still demanded. However, it did not cramp her style for again she, "beat W and Grayson."

Then they started off in another royal train for Rome. It was the most magnificent of all with the servants in royal livery and superb silver and glass and china bearing the arms of the House of Savoy. Their host on the train, representing King Victor Emmanuel, was Duke Dante della Rovere, "a tall lugubrious individual wearing a long-tailed frock coat and looking like an undertaker." In strict observance of protocol he insisted on sitting next to Mrs. Wilson at every meal, which she found "exceedingly fatiguing."

Rome gave Woodrow Wilson the greatest ovation he ever received. The strong golden sunshine was like a benediction after gray northern skies, and the people were idolatrous. All along the route of the procession the medieval cobblestones were covered with golden sand brought from Mediterranean beaches, signifying that the Italians desired to honor the President greatly. The tall windows of the houses and Renaissance palaces were all wide open and from them hung rare old brocades and tapestries and red velvets with armorial bearings. American and Italian flags were everywhere, and the people of Rome were cheering their hearts out, while from rooftops and balconies fell such a tropical deluge of violets and golden mimosa as made the rose-rain of Paris seem a mere drizzle.

Of course the little king and his tall, dark, Montenegrin queen had met the Wilsons at the station, and now they showed them to their suite at the Quirinale Palace. Miss Benham described it as "a wilderness of rooms," and Edith as "gorgeous." It was much more formal than Buckingham Palace. The Wilsons' favorite room was the smallest—a smoking room paneled in Japanese lacquer. All the rooms were well lighted and *heated*.

Their majesties were not living at the Quirinale just then, but

at the comparatively modest Villa Savoia outside the walls of
Rome. In fact, all of the palace except the wing that had been
hastily refurbished for the presidential party (including Margaret
Wilson, Miss Benham and Admiral Grayson) was a hospital
through which the king and queen escorted the Wilsons before
taking temporary leave.

There was just time to change before going to lunch at the Villa
Savoia. As they drove up to that sunny country house set in a
garden of lawns and cypress trees, the king ran down the steps
bareheaded and beat the footman to the car door. When they
entered Edith saw the queen, "dressed in filmy gray that brought
out her dark beauty," standing with four of her children, a boy
and three little girls, in the solarium at the end of the hall. The
children were dressed in velvet and lace. Nearby was a disdainful
Russian wolfhound. In the strong sunshine the group looked like
a painting by Romney.

It was a delightful luncheon, really informal. Everyone talked
English except the queen, who spoke in French. Afterward the
king showed them over the house. His room was so bare that Edith
was astonished—no rug on the stone floor, shelves crowded with
war relics around three sides, a flat-top desk, two straight chairs
and an army cot. The king said, "I'm used to it, so I don't mind
when I join the Army in the field."

By contrast the state dinner at the Quirinale that night was as
formal as in England. In fact it was so magnificent that Edith
teased the king a little by reminding him that he had said he could
not live in a place like the Murat Palace.

"But I don't live here," he answered smiling. "It doesn't belong
to me any more than the White House belongs to you."

On Edith's other side sat the old Duke of Genoa who was stone
deaf and beyond him Margaret struggled valiantly to make conversation. "I was so interested to meet Signor Marconi tonight,"
she said.

"Eh? What?" said the duke.

Just as one of those unexpected silences struck the table Margaret repeated her remark at the top of her voice. All eyes, including those of the inventor of the wireless, were riveted on her, while in an equally loud voice the Duke replied, "Yes, there are more tunnels in it than any other in the world."

The next day Wilson went to call on Pope Benedict XV. This was rather a daring thing for a Presbyterian President to do because of anti-Catholicism at home. It did, in fact, set off a wave of grumbling in rural America. Wilson, however, considered paying such a visit the only courteous thing to do. The President and the Pope got along very well. Indeed, thin, dark Benedict XV, with his aquiline face and rimless spectacles, rather resembled a Presbyterian elder—outwardly at least.

However, when Wilson rejoined Edith at the Quirinale he was in a white-hot rage. There had been an enormous crowd in St. Peters Square when he arrived, and he planned to address it after his audience. He came out of the Vatican to find that the police had dispersed everyone. The official excuse was that the crowd was so large it might get out of hand.

"I know why they did it," Wilson said furiously. "They were afraid that I would talk to them about the League and the Fourteen Points, and by winning their support make it difficult for Orlando and Sonnino to oppose me at the Conference. The people were so friendly there was no danger. That is a plain lie."

On the final day the Wilsons gave a luncheon for the king and queen at the American Embassy, then in charge of Ambassador Thomas Nelson Page. The Ambassador told the President, "It is the custom here to offer the toast to the king after the asparagus."

Wilson waited and waited through interminable courses until the dessert appeared. Then he got to his feet and said, "When I was a boy I learned that when in Rome one should do as the Romans do, so I was waiting for the proper moment to propose the health of their Majesties. However, I shall do so now, as I cannot believe that even in Rome they serve asparagus after the dessert."

At this point Mrs. Page said, "Oh dear, there wasn't any asparagus on the market."

The whole table roared with laughter.

From Rome the Wilsons went to Milan, where more functions had been arranged, among them a gala performance of *Aïda* at La Scala Opera House. They were told about it only a short time before the performance. "We can't go," Wilson said firmly. "It is Sunday night."

Edith was greatly disappointed, but she knew her husband's religious principles too well to argue. The Italians were frantic. Duke Della Rovere arrived looking more funereal than ever. "Every seat in the house is taken, Signor President," he said. "We cannot disappoint so many people. Will you attend if it is a sacred concert?"

Wilson agreed that his conscience would allow that.

When they entered the most famous opera house in the world it was indeed a brilliant sight. The whole bejeweled, bemedaled audience stood cheering and calling for a speech. Wilson gave a short, graceful address, and then the curtain rose revealing the vast spaces of La Scala's stage in the semblance of ancient Egypt. "The Star Spangled Banner" and the Italian national anthem were sung by the full chorus wearing the headdresses and skimpy clothes of Rameses' court. Then two religious chorals were sung. After that "sacred concert" they went right ahead with *Aïda*.

Knowing he had been tricked and that there was nothing he could do about it, the President relaxed and enjoyed the performance. Edith was delighted.

After Milan their final stop was in Turin, where the President was given an honorary degree at the university. With his instinct for charming college boys Wilson stepped forward to make his address wearing the blue cap of a student. Edith, watching fondly as the boys cheered wildly, noted, "How young and virile he looked as he stood there."

CHAPTER XI

THE ROOM OF THE CLOCK

IT WAS A RELIEF for the Wilsons to be back in Paris—not only physically but financially as well. The state visits had been a tremendous drain on their energy and their purse—the tips at Buckingham Palace alone were $800. There were also the gifts to their royal hosts which had to be on a royal scale. With his almost exaggerated delicacy in financial matters the President insisted on paying these semiofficial charges himself.

It was nearly a month since the Wilsons had arrived in Paris and the Conference had still not met. At luncheon alone with Edith and Miss Benham the President said that he believed the other commissions were deliberately holding back, knowing that he planned to go home for the bill-signing when Congress adjourned in March. "But I'll fool them," he said, "for I am going to come back here. When they hear that it will be a bombshell."

Even so, Wilson knew that time was running against him. The people of the world were for him; their supposedly democratic governments were against him. And the controlled French press was already hammering away at his ideals. The important journal

Figaro wrote, "Here and there one hears of people who still dream of a Wilsonian peace. . . ." Ray Stannard Baker called it "The slump in idealism."

Pushing hard, the President brought about the first meeting of the Council of Ten on January 12, 1919. It consisted of the heads of mission and foreign ministers of the five great powers—America, Britain, France, Italy and Japan. The first plenary session of the twenty-seven nations represented—no enemy countries were invited—was held on January 18.

When the conferences began Edith had a great deal more time on her hands. She used it mainly to visit French and American hospitals, rehabilitation centers like the Petit Palais and The Light House; factories, canteens and so forth. One extraordinary charitable institution that she inspected was the poverty-stricken dwelling of an English clergyman in Montmartre. It contained a long attic dormitory where he gave shelter to twenty-two poor girls trying to be virtuous, who were hostesses and dancers in the all-night cabarets that crowded the squares and alleys of "The Hill."

An entirely different kind of visit came about because the Duchess de ——— remarked to the Serbian Minister, M. Vesnitch, that she was tired of hearing about the Wilsons, who were only "ordinary Americans."

"You are mistaken," said M. Vesnitch suavely. "Mrs. Wilson is a royal American princess descended from King Powhatan."

The duchess took the bait. "This is most important," she said. "Naturally I shall call on her and give a dinner in their honor."

Vesnitch came running to Edith with his little joke and urged her to receive the duchess. She in turn told her husband, adding, "I think I'll send her a picture postcard of the Powhatan Hotel and say it's my ancestral palace, now used as a hotel for war workers."

Laughing, the President said, "Please wait until I finish my job here before you go playing jokes on French ladies."

The duchess called and then wrote asking Mrs. Wilson to set a night for dinner. She replied that the President was so busy they could not dine out. A little later the duchess met her at a reception and to Edith's almost uncontrollable amusement curtsied as to royalty. Then she said determinedly, "Mrs. Wilson, I know you visit hospitals."

"Yes, I do," Edith answered.

"Voilà, my house is a hospital, so you will come now?"

"I shall be delighted," Edith said.

On the appointed day and hour she and Miss Benham drove through tall wrought-iron gates into the parklike grounds that surrounded the De ———'s turreted chateau in Paris. As the car drew up, massive doors were flung back and the seven-year-old duke, who was dressed in black velvet and lace, came down the broad steps and, kneeling, presented Mrs. Wilson with a bouquet of pink apple blossoms. Behind him was a cardinal ceremonially robed in red, and the duchess and the ladies of her staff in white with the long nunlike veils of French nurses.

After the usual round of the improvised wards the party adjourned to the great dining room for an elaborate tea. To Edith's amazement, she and the duchess were the only ones seated; the rest of the company remained standing in the presence of royalty!

Occasionally Edith and Miss Benham went on a shopping spree at the great couturiers; Edith did most of the shopping. She was always welcome, not only because of her position, but also because the dictators of fashion knew that her beauty and superb figure would display their creations to the best advantage. M. Worth remained her favorite.

Wherever she went, Edith was always home by the time the President came wearily back from the sessions of the Conference. Often he would throw himself into one of the great embroidered chairs in the salon and, looking at the lackeys standing around in their magnificent liveries, say to her or to Miss Benham, "Will you please indicate to these gentlemen that I would like a cup of tea." His own French was not quite equal to this. The deliberations of the Council of Ten were carried on in English, which luckily almost all the heads of mission spoke.

On the wonderful evenings when he could be alone with his wife, Wilson let off steam by telling her exactly what he thought of his fellow delegates. He found French Foreign Minister Pichon, who was Chairman of the Council of Ten, particularly irritating. Pichon was a bald-headed doctrinaire type, with nose glasses on a broad black ribbon. "He never seems to get the order of proceeding right and his summaries are always wrong," Wilson said.

But if Wilson was annoyed by Pichon, he was infuriated by André Tardieu, afterward Premier of France, who had spent a good deal of time in Washington. The Frenchman had a small black mustache floating on a fat face whose expression resembled a boiled owl. It was not his lack of manly beauty that distressed the President, but his pretention of being an intimate friend who knew exactly what Wilson thought about everything. "We got along all right until Tardieu learned to speak English," the President said.

On one of those evenings Edith told her husband that Henry White, who frequently used her to convey his views to the President, thought that Wilson ought not to leave the Conference at all. It would be an anticlimax if he left and then came back, and White thought it would be better if he remained until the major questions were settled. Edith, who thought there was a great deal of sense in this view, was an excellent advocate.

Her husband said, "I agree about the anticlimax, but I want to go back and get the feeling of the American people. I don't trust the accuracy of our newspapers; they are all owned by the mon-eyed interests."

Miss Benham, who was the only other person present, said, "Don't you feel as though you are getting from some mystic source the consciousness of the new ideals of America and making them articulate?"

Very humbly the President answered, "Yes. I feel so filled with the American spirit that when these ideals come to me I am able to express them so my countrymen will approve."

An early source of trouble was the matter of publicity. Wilson's fine phrase, "Open covenants openly arrived at," backfired, as ringing phrases often do. The American reporters took it to mean that every argument between the Commissioners should be aired in public. "I never meant that," Wilson said. "It's utterly impossible. What I meant was that all conclusions and agreements should be made public."

The French delegation was for complete secrecy in the old tradition of diplomacy, at the same time leaking news favorable to their position to their favorite newspapers. This made the American journalists wild. Wilson fought hard for as much publicity as possible, and Lloyd George as usual oscillated between supporting him and backing Clemenceau. As Mrs. Wilson says, "Lloyd George was a weathervane swinging with every changing wind of opinion from across the Channel."

The situation got so bad, and the news sent back to America so unfavorable to Wilson, that Tumulty cabled in fright that something must be done. The President then appointed Ray Stannard Baker as his press representative to brief the reporters. Baker was an unusual type of journalist. Not only did he possess absolute integrity and have complete devotion to Wilson's ideals, but he was a man of the world welcome in the houses of the great English statesmen, and those of other countries as well. He called a meeting of the irate reporters and said to them, "I cannot tell you everything that goes on, but this I promise you; I will tell you all I can, and I will tell you nothing that is not true."

After that Baker came to Murat Palace every night at seven o'clock to be briefed. Sometimes he had to wait an hour or more for the President as the meetings of the Council dragged on and on. Mrs. Wilson made it a point always to be there and had many enlightening discussions with Baker.

When the President arrived he would tell his press representative everything that had happened during the day. They would then discuss how much they could honorably reveal. In this way Baker was protected in his promise never to falsify. And Edith, who was always present, learned everything that went on behind the double doors of the Conference room in the Quai d'Orsay, and could evaluate the problems her husband had to face.

The French put constant pressure on President Wilson to visit the bombed-out towns and villages of northern France in the hope that it would make him more sympathetic to their point of view. For a long while he resisted. He told Edith, "You know the reason I'm not going to the de*vas*tated regions [so he pronounced it] is that I don't want to get mad. They want me to see red, but I think there should be one man at the peace table who has not lost his temper."

However, Clemenceau's insistence wore him down and he finally agreed to go "from sheer weariness." On Saturday he and Edith drove to Rheims. If Clemenceau had ordered the weather it could not have been more nearly perfect for his purpose. It was bitterly cold, with a fine snow sifting down from an iron-gray sky. The gaping holes and shattered rose window in the great cathedral were the melancholy epitome of war's blight on beauty and piety, while the shattered houses across the street spoke plaintively of human suffering. A frail old priest in a rusty black cassock and medieval black velvet hat pointed a trembling red-gloved finger at the irreparable wounds and said tenderly, "My cathedral stood through three other raids without any bad hurts, but the fourth one broke her."

From Rheims they drove to the Chemin des Dames. Some of the bitterest fighting of the war had turned the countryside there into the desolation of a crater-pocked moonscape; and dead trees writhed with broken limbs. After that they went to Soisson, where American troops had fought so well. The little town looked dead with hardly a person on its deserted streets.

A few miles beyond Soisson they were unexpectedly turned back because a munitions dump had exploded. As they entered the town again they were surprised to find the streets swarming with *poilus* in horizon blue who crowded around their car cheering and smiling. One who spoke English said, "We want a Wilson peace, not a Clemenceau peace. Speak to us."

The President said a few words. Then he asked, "Where were you all when we passed through here before?"

The English-speaking *poilu* answered, "Our officers ordered us to stay in our billets. They did not want us to talk with you, or you to us. When you had gone they let us out. But fate stepped in and brought you back to us."

Mrs. Wilson says that the President sat in thunderous silence all the way back to Paris. Bitterly he noted that this incident was like the authorities' dispersal of the crowds who wanted to hear him speak in Rome—"They are afraid to let me talk with the people."

Because "fate stepped in," Wilson's trip to the devastated regions had the reverse effect from that intended by Clemenceau.

The meetings of the Council of Ten had worked so badly that Wilson, Clemenceau, Lloyd George and Orlando of Italy decided to meet together alone and try to iron things out. "The Big Four," as the newspapers called them, met every afternoon except Sunday. In addition, Wilson had become chairman of the special Commission set up to hammer out the Covenant of the League of Nations. It met at night in the Hotel Crillon. All morning he received reports from his experts and fellow commissioners, and those callers whom he could not in courtesy put off. Thus he was under constant stress all day and half the night. Admiral Grayson's regimen of exercise went by the board. There was not time now to think of health.

Edith was distressed to see her "beloved" growing thinner and older from fatigue. She says that it is literally true that his hair turned from gray to white during the Conference. His saving grace was sleep. Often he came home so harassed that she was sure he would lie awake all night. But when she tiptoed into his room to see if he was all right, she invariably found him sleeping as quietly as a kitten. "Woodrow was not a worrier," she says. "He could almost always put care from his mind and go to sleep."

Not all Wilson's difficulties were caused by the machinations of European politicians. There were jealousies and disaffection in his own delegation as well. Secretary of State Lansing was secretly out of sympathy with his plan to make the League of Nations an integral part of the Treaty. In addition, Lansing was intensely jealous of Wilson's confidence in Colonel House.

One day Henry White invited Edith to go sight-seeing with him in Paris. He was a wonderful guide, having been Secretary of our Embassy there in his youth; but his purpose was not purely to entertain her. "May I talk to you as a friend?" he asked when they were alone.

"Of course," she said.

"Dear lady," he began in his courtly manner, "I want to tell you of a few of the jealousies and sore spots in the Commission. In the first place, Lansing is terribly sore because the meetings of the Commission are held in Colonel House's suite in the Hotel Crillon instead of his. Since he is Secretary of State I think he is right. He is being ignored."

"The President will be grateful to you for telling me this," Edith said. "It is such a small thing I'm sure it never entered his mind."

"It is a small thing," White agreed. "But Lansing is a small man."

The next Sunday, when they went for their weekly drive in the country—"It was raining but we bundled up and went in an open car"—Edith told her husband what Mr. White had said.

"I'm sorry about this," he said seriously. "It never occurred to me, and I'm sure it never did to House. I'll see that it's changed. White is right about it."

Another incident concerned House himself. The Colonel's son-in-law, Gordon Auchincloss, was acting as his aide. One day as the President walked silently down a thick-carpeted corridor in the Hotel Crillon he passed the open door of Room 315, in which he

heard Auchincloss saying gaily to House, "What shall we make
the President say today?"

Wilson kept on, but he saw red. When asked what the President
had said about Auchincloss when he got home that evening, Mrs.
Wilson said, "Even now I shudder when I think of it."

However, Wilson was not so small as to be permanently piqued
by a facetious remark. He continued to give House his confidence.
But the process of erosion which eventually dissolved their friendship may have begun that day.

In the early stages of the Conference Woodrow Wilson battled
to have the Covenant of the League of Nations made an integral
part of the Treaty. He had chosen that name for the instrument,
rather than "constitution" or "charter," because of the Biblical
connotations of the word "Covenant." In fact, the League had
become a matter of almost religious significance to him, for he saw
it not only as an instrument of peace, but also of justice. It would
right the wrongs of humanity in the years to come without recourse
to war. And he felt that it was his sacred duty to bring it into being.

The other members of the Big Four were for making the Treaty
first and talking about the League afterward. Clemenceau thought
the League utopian nonsense; Lloyd George feared it would cramp
the British empire; and Orlando did not give a damn. Wilson was
convinced that if the League were not made part of the Treaty it
would never come into existence. He believed that to fail in this
fight would be to betray the trust of his fellow countrymen and the
people of all the nations who had listened to his speeches and put
their faith in him.

The odds in the Big Four were three to one against him, but for
him were the peoples of all their nations and his Presbyterian zeal
to fight for the right. The peoples and the Presbyterian won.

On February 14, 1919, President Wilson was to present the
draft of the Covenant of the League to a plenary session of the
Peace Conference for acceptance as part of the Treaty. Knowing
how hard he had fought for it and having been his comfort and

counselor throughout the battle, Edith was desperately anxious to be present at the climactic moment. However, the rule was rigid —no unauthorized person could attend a Plenary Session; especially no women.

But neither rules nor princes nor prime ministers awed Edith when she had made up her mind. First she conspired with Admiral Grayson, who was also very anxious to be present. "I'll beard the Tiger in his lair and ask him to arrange for us to see it if you give me permission," he said. "I'm sure that gallant old Frenchman will not refuse you."

Before agreeing Edith went to her husband and told him of her heart's desire and her plan to achieve it. "You can't ask for it," she said, "but Grayson can. Will it embarrass you if M. Clemenceau refuses us?"

The President thought a minute with a fondly quizzical look in his eyes. He would have refused anyone else point blank, but his stern principles became flabby when he looked at her lovely, pleading face.

"In the circumstances," he said at last, "it is more a command than a request, for he could not very well refuse you."

"Then I shall certainly make it," his wife said.

Laughing the President said, "Willful woman, your sins be on your own head if the Tiger shows his claws."

"Oh, he can't, you know," Edith said impishly. "They're always done up in gray cotton gloves."

When Grayson presented his request to the formidable Premier of France the old man's eyes twinkled. "It is impossible," he said. "Almost impossible," he amended. "For so lovely a lady nothing is quite impossible. Let me think. There is a little antechamber off the Room of the Clock, shut off by heavy curtains. You and Mrs. Wilson could hide there. But you must arrive before anyone else, and stay until all are gone."

As Grayson delightedly expressed his thanks the Tiger got a worried crease between his bushy white eyebrows. "For God's sake don't let anyone see her," he said, "for if you do, the other wives will tear me apart."

Mrs. Wilson and Admiral Grayson arrived at the great grimy Foreign Office on the Quai d'Orsay far ahead of the appointed hour for the meeting. An official led them rapidly through long corridors to the famous Room of the Clock, so called because of the great ornate timepiece on one wall. He smuggled them through the huge chamber, containing over a hundred chairs and desks for the delegates; it was empty now and waiting like a schoolroom before the bell rings. They entered the alcove at the far end and pulled the heavy red brocade curtains tight shut. It contained two straight chairs on which the two eavesdroppers sat "hot but happy."

They heard the Conference filling up, as the delegates arrived. The preliminary business took almost an hour, during which they nearly suffocated in their airless hideout. Then Woodrow Wilson stood up to speak, and discomfort was forgotten. Since all eyes were riveted on the President, Edith dared pull the curtains a little apart. Standing under the elaborate clock at the other end of the hall he faced her directly.

First President Wilson read to the delegates the draft of the Covenant which the representatives of the fourteen nations on The League of Nations Commission had unanimously agreed upon. Then he began to speak, explaining its provisions and telling of the high purposes which he hoped it would accomplish. "Throughout this instrument," he said, "we are depending primarily and chiefly upon one great force and that is the moral force of public opinion . . . of the world. . . . Armed force is in the background. . . . But that is the last resort, because this is intended as a constitution of peace, not as a league of war. . . ."

Then the President outlined other objectives of the League besides securing world peace: amelioration of the conditions of labor everywhere; guardianship of undeveloped people; prevention of annexation of territories for exploitation; exposure of intrigue and "designs that are sinister" among nations.

And he told the delegates that "This is at the same time a practical document and a humane document. There is a pulse of sympathy in it. There is a compulsion of conscience throughout it. It is practical, and yet it is intended to purify, to rectify, to elevate. . . ."

And finally he said: "Many terrible things have come out of this war, gentlemen, but some very beautiful things have come out of it. Wrong has been defeated, and the rest of the world has been more conscious than it ever was before of the majesty of right. People who were suspicious of one another can now live as friends and comrades in a single family, and desire to do so. The miasma of distrust, of intrigue, is cleared away. Men are looking eye to eye and saying, 'We are brothers and have a common purpose. We did not realize it before, but now we do realize it, and this is our covenant of fraternity and friendship.' "

As the President finished speaking, the leaders of the nations sat silent for a moment, then burst into a tornado of applause. The vote to accept the draft of the Covenant as a basis for discussion and inclusion in the Treaty was unanimous.

Edith, who had been peering through the curtain with tear-dimmed eyes, later wrote: "It was a great moment in history, and as he stood there, slender, calm, and powerful in argument, I seemed to see the people of all depressed countries—men, women and little children—crowding round and waiting for his words. . . ."

Admiral Grayson and Mrs. Wilson obediently waited in their cubbyhole until the last delegate had left the room. Then they scurried out to mingle with the crowd outside the building. Edith saw the familiar Cadillac with the blue presidential flag flying from its mudguard and knew that Woodrow was waiting for her. She got in beside him and, as the car drove off, he doffed his silk hat and leaned his head back against the seat.

"Are you so tired?" she asked maternally.

"Yes, I suppose I am," he said. "But how little one man means when such vital things are at stake."

Then enthusiasm overcame fatigue. "This is our first real step

forward," he said. "For once established the League can arbitrate
and correct mistakes which are inevitable in the Treaty. The re-
sentments and injustices caused by war are still too poignant, and
the wounds too fresh. They must have time to heal. Then the mistakes can be brought to the League for readjustment. It will act as
a clearing house where every nation can come, the small as well as
the great."

Then turning to his wife with a radiantly happy smile he said,
"It will be sweet to go home, even for a few days, feeling that I
have kept the faith with the people, particularly with these boys,
God bless them."

The following day the President and Mrs. Wilson sailed in the
George Washington for home.

CHAPTER XII

SWEET TO BE HOME?

Aboard the *George Washington* the President's wonderful re-cuperative powers again restored him. In a few days he was in fine fettle. Not so poor Herbert Hoover, whose great humanitarian work for the starving people of Europe had made him a world figure. He came down with pneumonia and had to be left on the ship when they all landed. All through the Conference Wilson relied heavily on Hoover for advice about food supplies for the people of Central Europe and consulted him on financial matters as well. Hoover's rather cold manner repelled Mrs. Wilson, who "did not care for him too much then," though she respected his ability. She was very glad when he recovered in time to join the Commission in Paris.

On this same trip home the Wilsons saw a good deal of Assistant Secretary of the Navy and Mrs. Franklin D. Roosevelt, who were aboard. It was the first opportunity Edith really had to know F.D.R. The Roosevelts seemed to her simply "very delightful companions," which, at the time, was all they were.

The President as usual, consorted as much as possible with the

wounded men the *George Washington* was bringing home, and
with the members of the crew. On one gala evening the latter gave
an impromptu show which the Wilsons attended. Exiting up the
aisle after one roaring chorus an exuberant sailor chucked the
President under the chin as he passed.

Edith shuddered as she saw Wilson's hair-trigger temper flash in
his eyes. She knew that he demanded the utmost respect for his
office and that he also hated to be touched familiarly. However,
Wilson quickly recovered and turning to the horrified captain said,
"I don't want that boy punished. He meant no harm."

On the ship the Wilsons received news that an assassin had
leaped out of a Paris crowd and shot the French Premier. "How
well he shoots," Clemenceau said as he fell forward in his automobile.

Luckily the fellow had not shot that well. Clemenceau was only
wounded. Despite their differences Wilson felt that his loss would
have been a calamity. Edith, thinking of his kindness and his
honesty, was deeply thankful that Clemenceau had lived to fight
again.

Coming into Boston Harbor in fog and darkness on the morning
of February 24, 1919, Captain McCauley got lost and very nearly
piled up the President's ship and her escorting destroyer on
Thatcher's Island. Bellowing fog horns and running feet woke
Edith but did not upset her. It turned out to be only a near miss.

Governor Calvin Coolidge of Massachusetts met the Wilsons at
the dock and drove with them at the head of what became a triumphant procession through the city. It was a day of crisp, brilliant clarity. Half the people of Boston seemed to be in the streets
to welcome their President home. Their greeting was not, perhaps,
as idolatrous as those he had received in Europe but it was defi-
nitely heart-warming.

The Republican governor looked a bit pickle-faced—but then
he always did. Certainly his introduction of the President to the
great roaring throng in Mechanics Hall expressed the sentiments

of his commonwealth and the vast majority of his countrymen when he said, "We welcome him as . . . a great statesman, as one to whom we have entrusted our destinies, and one whom we shall support in the future in the working out of those destinies as Massachusetts has supported him in the past."

Wilson replied with one of his rousing orations. He told how the commissions of every nation that came to Paris brought their problems first to the representatives of the United States. "Why?" he asked. "Because—and I think I am stating the most wonderful fact in history—because there is no nation in Europe that suspects the motives of the United States. Was there ever so wonderful a thing seen before? Was there ever so moving a thing? Was there ever any fact that so bound the nation that had won that esteem forever to deserve it?"

Then he spoke of the inspiration that American ideals had brought to Europe and how our soldiers there were loved by the people. And he said, "I do not mean any disrespect to any other great people when I say that America is the hope of the world. And if she does not justify that hope the results are unthinkable."

Finally he said, "Probing deep in my heart . . . I feel that I am interpreting the thought of America. And in loving America I find that I have joined the great majority of my fellowmen throughout the world."

If the crowd's greeting to the President had been enthusiastic, their farewell was an ovation. On the presidential special to Washington Wilson could say happily to his wife that having renewed his strength by contact with the American people he was sure that he was on the right track and that they were behind him.

Things were very different in Washington.

At first it was truly "sweet to be home." Edith found that the staff of the White House had planned a surprise for her by giving it a thorough housecleaning from basement to attic. According to the Raleigh *Observer*, "The rugs have been beaten, the stonework honed, the walls scraped and the hardwood floors planed and polished." Gleaming outside and in, and filled with flowers, it was indeed home after the cluttered splendor of Murat Palace.

Of course the women of Washington were anxious to see Mrs. Wilson's new Paris clothes, for she was an acknowledged fashion setter. The Washington *Star* reported:

"They gasped over the cut of her clothes and those who had bought lengthy hobble skirts and extreme coats must be disappointed in them when they see Mrs. Wilson's long, narrow skirt, and conservative but faultlessly tailored coat. The entire suit is of dark maroon cloth with which she wears a small black hat when out walking.

"She has been occupied since her return with visiting with her family and superintending the opening of the many mysterious packages . . . [which contain] souvenirs consisting of rare paintings, books, statues, cigarette cases and other beautiful things brought over in boxes weighing hundreds of pounds and worth hundreds of pounds of sterling." These were, of course, the gifts, royal and otherwise, which had been showered upon the Wilsons.

The first thing the President did on his return to Washington was to invite the members of the Senate and House Foreign Relations Committees to dinner at the White House to discuss the draft of the Covenant. As usual Mrs. Wilson was the only woman present.

Henry Cabot Lodge, Chairman of the Senate Committee, was the ranking guest. As a result, in Mrs. Wilson's own words, "I went out to the dining room with that stinking Senator Lodge and sat next to him at dinner. He pretended to me that he approved of everything Woodrow had done."

In fact the Senator from Massachusetts was at his most charming. With his curly beard and lively smile-wrinkled eyes he looked like an amiable raccoon. Edith was lulled into confidence.

The President's after-dinner discussion with the committees was also very friendly. He gave his wife a word-by-word description of it when they had left. According to him Senator Lodge and his colleagues were fearful that the Covenant might constrain the

Monroe Doctrine. He assured them that he would have the Conference accept an amendment preserving it. Other minor changes
were proposed by the senators, to all of which the President agreed.
There were no arguments.

As the meeting was concluding the President addressed himself
directly to Lodge, saying, "Of course you understand, Senator,
that I shall have to go back to Paris and resubmit this to the Conference, for while it is not essentially changed, it is not what they
accepted the day I left, and I have some pretty stubborn men to
deal with. But I am going to do my best. If this new draft is
accepted as it stands, do you think it will go through the Senate?"

Lodge answered, "If the Foreign Relations Committee approves
it, I have no doubt it will be ratified."

"Very well," Wilson said. "I consider that, armed with your
approval, I can go back and work feeling that you and your associates are behind me."

Lodge bowed his head.

Naturally Wilson was very happy that night believing that the
senators who must ratify the treaty were with him. Neither he nor
Mrs. Wilson perceived the slight catch in Lodge's remarks: "If
the Foreign Relations Committee approves it." Actually the Senator had no intention of letting that happen. In fact, two days later
in a Senate speech Lodge violently attacked the Covenant of the
League of Nations.

Furthermore, on the eve of President Wilson's return to Europe,
as he was about to make a farewell speech at a public meeting in
New York City's Metropolitan Opera House, he was presented
with a round robin signed by Lodge and thirty-six other senators
—four more than the third of the membership necessary to defeat
ratification of a treaty—stating that they would not vote to approve
the Covenant in its present form.

In his anger and sense of betrayal that night Woodrow Wilson
said a thing perhaps better left unsaid: "And when that Treaty
comes back gentlemen on this side will find the Covenant not only
in it, but so many threads of the Treaty tied to the Covenant that

you cannot dissect the Covenant from the Treaty without destroying the whole vital structure. The structure of peace will not be vital without the League of Nations, and no man is going to bring back a cadaver with him. . . ." It was a public challenge flung in the face of the Senate.

Nearly half a century has not lessened Mrs. Wilson's bitterness about Senator Lodge. With her eyes flashing their ancient fires she said recently, "Oh, he was a snake in the grass! Or rather, not in the grass. He was a snake in the open!"

On the return voyage to Europe President Wilson was not disheartened by the unexpected opposition the Covenant had received in America. If some Republican senators were against it, others approved it and he knew the American people were for it.

Foremost among the pro-Republicans was former President Taft. Indeed, Taft's support and admiration had been a great strength to Wilson for years. In 1918, Colonel House sent Wilson a letter from H. H. Childers, of Washington's National Press Club, in which the reporter described how, at a private party, former President Taft had said that there was "something providential in the fact that Woodrow Wilson occupied the presidential chair at this time."

Taft added, "The manner in which he has grasped the tremendous problems of the war, and the execution of the plans that emanated from his wonderful brain, is such that there is not another living man in this or any other country who could accomplish as much. . . ."

Childers added that what Mr. Taft said was not for publication.

Across the face of the letter House wrote with humorous affection, "Pretty good for your fat friend! E.M.H."

And again at the Metropolitan Opera House, Taft, presiding at the great meeting which filled it to overflowing, had spoken strongly for the Covenant. In addition, such great Republican leaders as former Secretary of State Elihu Root and Wilson's old opponent,

Charles Evans Hughes, were for it. Finally, the President was confident that in the last resort the people themselves would follow him
if he went to them.

Wilson was, in fact, far more worried by the reports reaching
him from Paris. The situation there was worse indeed than he
imagined.

The American Commission had been left under somewhat ambiguous leadership. Lansing as Secretary of State was now its
titular head, but Wilson had told the Council of Ten that he had
asked Colonel House to take his place while he was away. Mrs.
Wilson had begged her husband not to do this. "He never dis-
agrees with you," she said, "and I think it's impossible for two
people always to think alike. While I like Colonel House, he seems
to me absolutely colorless and a 'yes, yes' man."

Wilson answered, "I don't think that's altogether true. You forget that it's my constitutional duty to formulate policies and take
the responsibility. House thinks straight and can get the real views
of men in a way that's impossible for me, because so few people
are natural and frank with the President. House brings me something I cannot get any other way."

"That's true," Edith said, "but he is still wishy-washy. Remember that time when he changed his mind about your railroad speech.
I distrust the judgment of people who change sides abruptly, as he
did."

However, Wilson convinced her that House was the only instrument at hand. After all they both knew that Lansing agreed with
Clemenceau that the League was a fantasy. House, on the other
hand, had always been for it. So he was given temporary authority
to speak for America.

Not only that, but Wilson was so sure that their minds were in
tune that he did not leave very specific instructions with the
Colonel.

As soon as Wilson left for America Clemenceau and Winston
Churchill, who had temporarily taken Lloyd George's place, went

to work on House. The old Frenchman once said, "House is an ear, not a mouth." Now he proceeded to twist the ear.

Before he left, the President had agreed to the making of a preliminary treaty embodying *only* military terms. Using this loophole, Clemenceau insisted that the "whole of the preliminary peace terms be pressed forward with as little delay as possible in order to take advantage of the present situation in Germany."

In effect this was going back to the idea of making peace first and talking about the League afterward. Lansing thoroughly agreed with this. Poor House was completely outmaneuvered. This amiable gentleman, who hated an argument and wanted to be loved by everybody, had neither the stamina nor the inclination for a first-class fight.

As the anchor chains of the *George Washington* rumbled down in the harbor of Brest a tender came alongside carrying the usual officials and, to everyone's surprise, Colonel House. The President, feeling that something dire was afoot, said, "Edith, will you receive the officials while I talk to House?"

The greeters were all familiar to her, Ambassador Jusserand, of whom she was very fond, French Minister of Marine Leygues with his fatigued walrus mustache, and the ancient white-bearded Admiral of the Port. She listened to the speeches, which seemed unending, and replied in broken French, all the while wondering what was going on in the President's office.

It was too late to go ashore that night, so when the officials left she went to her cabin and sat waiting and wondering. It seemed as though everyone else on the great ship had gone to bed. And after days at sea with the constant rumble of the engines and the creaking of beams, the utter stillness was oppressive.

It was after midnight when Edith heard the door of the President's room open and the Colonel's voice saying goodnight in the passageway. As the hall door clicked shut she quickly opened the connecting door into her husband's room. He was standing uncertainly in the middle of the floor. His appearance stopped her heart. His face was haggard and his long jaw was rigid with the strain of self-control. In three hours he seemed to have aged ten years.

Without speaking he held out his hand and she ran to clasp it crying, "What is the matter, Woodrow? What has happened?"

Making an enormous effort to speak calmly, her husband said between clenched teeth, "House has given away everything I had won before we left Paris. He has compromised on every side. The League is out of the Treaty. I'll have to start all over again, and this time it will be harder because they'll think that my own delegation is against me."

All Edith could say was, "Oh Woodrow!"

Wilson continued, "House says that with a hostile press in America and Senate speeches against the League as part of the Treaty, he thought it wise to yield on some points lest the Conference withdraw its approval altogether. So he has yielded until there is nothing left."

Knowing that the great majority of American newspapers had endorsed the League, Edith was thunderstruck. She stood there holding her husband's hand, so boiling mad that she dared not speak for fear she would say something that no lady should say.

Her husband recovered before she did. She could almost feel his courage mounting; his eyes lighted with the spirit of battle.

"Well," he said, and threw his head back, "thank God I can still fight. And I'll win it all back or never look these boys I sent over here to fight in the face again. They lost battles—but won the war, God bless them. So don't you worry too much."

After that they sat talking until it was almost dawn. Mrs. Wilson says that night was the crisis of Woodrow Wilson's life, the beginning of his long illness and the wreckage of his great plans for his fellowmen.

Certainly it was the beginning of his estrangement from Colonel House. Their relationship grew ever more distant and once the Treaty was signed they never saw each other again. And yet, a long time later, after Wilson had been stricken and after the Treaty had been killed by the Senate, when a Cabinet member made a belittling remark about House, the President rebuked him by saying, "I have a great affection for Colonel House."

CHAPTER XIII

VERSAILLES

W HEN THE WILSONS REACHED PARIS they found a new residence waiting for them. The Conference was lasting much
longer than expected and they could not keep Prince Murat out on
the street indefinitely.

Their new home was smaller and simpler than Murat Palace,
though still amply large. It faced on a square which the French
courteously renamed La Place des États-Unis. From the center of
the square a statue of Lafayette gave them a friendly greeting.

However, one room of the house was more fanciful than anything the Murats had dreamed up. It was Mrs. Wilson's bathroom,
an enormous room with a sunken green tub like a small pool. On
the walls were painted four life-size apple trees in full bloom. A
few petals were painted on the edge of the tub as though they had
just fallen there. Where the four trees met in the ceiling a chan-
delier hung from a painted bough with glass birds perching on it and
jeweled butterflies hanging from silver wires over it. A musicians'
gallery on the wall opposite the tub completed the picture.

When she saw the room, Edith ran to fetch her husband. The

177

President surveyed the *bijouterie* with a twinkle and said, "Like the King of Italy, I don't think I could live in this place."

Wilson found that French opinion had, indeed, written off the League of Nations. Ray Stannard Baker records that the first well informed man he met on his return to Paris said, "Well, your League is dead."

The President wasted no time, but immediately gave it drastic artificial respiration. On the day after his return, March 15, 1919, he called Baker on the secret American telephone line connecting with the Hotel Crillon and told him to make this official announcement:

"The President said today, that the decision made by the Peace Conference at its Plenary Session on January 25, 1919, to the effect that the establishment of a League of Nations should be made an integral part of the Treaty of Peace, is of final force and that there is no basis whatever for the reports that a change in this decision is contemplated."

What a row that blast raised! It blew everything done while Wilson was away right out the window. British and French newspapers roared with rage; PYRRHIC VICTORY and HOLDUP! they called it. Even men of good will who saw their hopes for a quick peace fade were disconsolate. But the other three-quarters of the Big Four knew a stone wall when they saw one. There was no further mention of dropping the League.

However, even though this gesture was effective, it proved costly. Wilson found his colleagues' attitude hardened by frustration. Now there was one fight after another.

The Big Four held daily meetings in Wilson's study. The gaily decorated house on the Place des États-Unis became a combined business office and council chamber. Great maps were hung on the walls of the President's study and the corridor connecting his room with Mrs. Wilson's. The gilt and crystal ballroom was filled with desks and noisy clacking typewriters. Crowds of secretaries and experts pouring through or waiting to be summoned turned the front hall and salon into a small replica of the waiting room at Grand Central Station.

In addition to attending the afternoon meetings of the Big Four, Wilson was working every night trying to force the Senate-proposed amendments to the Covenant through the League of Nations Commission. Knowing he had to have those amendments to appease the senators, the other commissioners fought them in order to win concessions to their territorial ambitions. The wrangling often lasted until after midnight.

One of those nights Edith said to her husband, "Oh, if only Colonel House had stood firm while you were away! I think he's a perfect jellyfish."

Smiling tolerantly the President answered, "Well, God made jellyfish, so don't be too hard on House. It takes a pretty stiff spinal column to stand up against these people here."

In helpless anguish Edith watched her husband growing thin and gray and old under the strain. His spirit drove his flesh beyond endurance. The inevitable happened. He caught influenza and in his weakened state the germs had an easy conquest.

While he was in bed, the other members of the Big Four pushed hard for their special interests. The President sent word that unless they were afraid of the disease, he would like them to meet in his bedroom.

Mrs. Wilson says they came every day and solemnly took their place around a table in his room. The door was closed. While the long hours passed she and Admiral Grayson sat outside that closed door "fuming" because they knew that the President was bankrupting his last reserve of strength.

The flu germs redeployed and counterattacked. The President collapsed with a high fever and pains in his chest. Then Admiral Grayson ordered, "No more work!"

While the President was completely *hors de combat,* Clemenceau, Lloyd George and Orlando had things pretty much their own way. The news of what they were now demanding—enormous, unpayable reparations from Germany, territorial grabs—was so serious that Edith was afraid to tell her husband about them lest he collapse again. But patriotism and loyalty to him demanded it. So with her courage in her hands and fear in her heart she sat down beside his bed and briefed him on what was taking place.

She had done him less than justice. Instead of weakening, his fighting spirit rose. "I can never sign a treaty with such conditions in it," he said strongly. "If all the rest of the delegates have determined on it, I will not be a party to it. If I have lost my fight, which I certainly would not if I had been on my feet, I will retire in good order. We will go home. Please call Grayson for me."

The little Admiral hurried in, his face sharp with worry. In the tone of the Commander-in-Chief, Wilson said, "Grayson, I want you to send word to Captain McCauley that I want the *George Washington* brought over for my return trip as soon as you think it safe for me to travel."

That news hit the other commissioners like a shell from Big Bertha. Despite the ebbing tide of idealism in the world Woodrow Wilson's prestige was still so high that in the eyes of the world a treaty without his signature would be no treaty at all. His absence would expose it as a great betrayal.

The High Commissioners came rushing to the door—first Clemenceau, looking like a worried walrus; then Lloyd George, smoothly diplomatic, and, finally, spaniel-eyed Orlando, almost in tears. All of them were met by Admiral Grayson's statement, "The President is too ill to receive anyone."

Of course they did not believe him—they knew all about diplomatic illnesses—and this upset them more than ever. They all wrote letters begging Wilson to stay, and expressing their admiration and confidence in his integrity and leadership. These sentiments were not merely diplomatic forms. It was what they truly felt.

There have been many speculations as to whether Wilson ever really intended to leave Paris. Mrs. Wilson says that he unquestionably did. But equally certainly he did not want to. When he saw that the fight was not yet lost, he canceled the *George Washington.*

And as soon as he was able to stagger out of bed, the meetings began again.

There were still some sharp conflicts. Prime Minister Orlando wanted Fiume and most of the Dalmation coast for Italy. Since the inhabitants were Yugoslavs, Wilson would not stand for that. When he told Orlando of his irrevocable decision the poor man burst into tears right there in the conference room, and left Paris. Mrs. Wilson says, "Orlando was a very sweet person. I liked him. Woodrow felt very sorry for him when he had to refuse Fiume to Italy. Orlando was a very gentle man."

So the Big Four temporarily became the Big Three, but the sparring went on unceasingly. Because of the necessity of getting the senators' amendments approved, Wilson gave in on many things which neither his judgment nor his conscience approved of. However, he believed that when the League began to function it would remedy these injustices.

At one point things got so tense that Lord Balfour sent his secretary to ask the President if that day they could meet in Lloyd George's apartment as, "It is neutral territory, and they would rather go there than come here."

The President said, "Certainly!" And then in humorous despair, "What children!"

Meanwhile there were other petty annoyances, among them Queen Marie of Rumania. The blond, blue-eyed queen was considered to be the most beautiful royal lady in the world, an opinion in which she enthusiastically concurred. Her charm was quite lost on the Wilsons, both of whom disliked her heartily. However, they could not be rude to the wife of Czar Ferdinand of Rumania, so when she graciously invited herself to luncheon they braced themselves for the inevitable.

The day before, a Saturday, Queen Marie telephoned to announce that she was bringing nine people with her—her sister, the Infanta Eulalia, her two daughters, a lady-in-waiting and five gentlemen. The Wilsons had already invited Miss Benham, Ad-

miral Grayson, General Harts and two young aides for the young
princesses. According to Miss Benham, the latter turned out to be
"fat and dull—little lumps." Even their mother much preferred
her third daughter, whom she described to Edith as "dark and
passionate, my love child." Paris gossips gleefully said Czar Ferdinand was not her father.

The presidential group gathered in their salon promptly at one
o'clock. It was a lovely spring day with the scent of lilacs in the
park drifting through the open windows. They chatted gaily until
the clock struck the next quarter. The President began to fidget—
he was very prompt and Edith never kept him waiting one minute.
By twenty past one he was furious. Miss Benham said, "As the
minutes flew by I could see all the provinces of Rumania disappearing as the President fumed."

Finally at one-thirty Wilson said abruptly, "This is extremely
rude. We have waited long enough. Let's go in to lunch."

Caught between a dilatory queen and an impatient President,
Mrs. Wilson was frantic. She says, "Just then I heard the motors
throbbing and motorcycles sputtering. My goodness, I was glad!"

Even so she had to fairly drag the President to the front door to
greet his royal guest. The queen, looking radiant, was softly allur-
ing as she took the President's hands in both of hers and begged
him to forgive her. Not without satisfaction Edith observed that
her husband was impervious to blond blandishment.

Miss Benham and the French Chief of Protocol had done the
seating, but Queen Marie upset it with a royal gesture, saying,
"But this is all wrong! My sister, the Infanta, not the Princess,
must be on the President's left."

Throughout luncheon she worked on the President for "my poor
country." She told tales of pillage and rape in such plain language
that the President looked more and more the Presbyterian elder,
and Edith was "quite startled." Miss Benham says, "Poor, shy
Admiral Grayson fairly curled up with embarrassment."

What a relief when they finally left! Bernard Baruch, dropping
by to take Admiral Grayson to the races at Longchamps, found

the President in a holiday mood. "Let's all go for a drive," he said.

Grayson muttered unhappily, "I have a stiff neck. A drive might make it worse."

"Then you'll come, won't you, Bernie?" Wilson asked.

Poor Baruch was trapped.

A few days later Mrs. Wilson, referring to something else, said to Grayson, "I heard about you the other day."

The little Admiral turned as pink as a shrimp and said, "How did you find out I went to the races Sunday?"

This was the first Edith had heard of his treachery but she said smugly, "I have spies everywhere."

In spite of premiers, foreign ministers and difficult royal beauties, the Treaty was finally whipped into shape. Four months of unremitting work had produced a big white volume of 214 pages and 440 articles which, as Baker says, "was packed and crammed with meaning for the whole of humanity." It was far harsher than Wilson thought right, but it was the fairest Treaty he could obtain. Indeed, he had fought so strenuously for the rights of small nations, and even for those of the enemy peoples who had trusted his word, that he was sometimes referred to as "The Commissioner for the World."

He was also called "pro-German" by the extreme jingo press of France and England.

On April 30 the German delegates arrived to receive the Treaty and hear their country's fate. The next day was May 1, traditional occasion of leftist rioting in Europe. The French authorities regarded May Day as especially dangerous that year because of the Bolshevik turmoil in Russia and the presence of the Germans at Versailles.

When Mrs. Wilson as usual drove with the President to the Quai d'Orsay that morning she saw heavily armed troops stationed in the Place de la Concorde, and the glittering sabers of a cavalry regiment guarding the bridge across the Seine. Her husband advised her to stay home the rest of the day. But she says, "It was much too nice a day to waste so Miss Benham and I drove to the Bois in the afternoon and walked home."

The President was understandably upset when he heard about this. It was sheer luck that Edith did not find herself involved in a first-class riot, of which there were several that day.

The Treaty was presented to the Germans on May 7, 1919, in the incongruously frivolous Trianon Palace at Versailles. Edith desperately wanted to see the ceremony, but for once she cajoled her husband in vain. There was hardly room in the little straw-berry-ice-cream palace for all the delegates, let alone their wives.

So she had to hear at second hand from her husband and Mr. White of the tense, solemn ceremony and the brief, harsh words with which Clemenceau presented "The Book," as he called it, to the sullen Germans. Many of those present considered the attitude of thin old Count Brockdorff-Rantzau, the head of the German delegation, unfittingly arrogant. But kindly Mr. White told Edith that the ancient German aristocrat's knees were shaking until he could hardly stand, so perhaps there was an excuse for him.

The Germans were horrified when they read the document, and, indeed, as news of its terms leaked out, so was liberal opinion in many nations. The Paris edition of the Chicago *Tribune* said: "GERMANS STUNNED BY TREATY TERMS. 'Let the Allies occupy the whole country, we'll never sign,' they say." *La Presse* of Paris headlined: "THE DEFEAT OF WILSON: A Bismarckian Peace." In spite of Wilson's best efforts it was, in fact, an imposed, a victor's peace.

Then for seven weeks the Allied statesmen jittered, wondering if the Germans would sign; and, if they did not, what should be done. Implacable Foch, backed by Clemenceau, was ready to begin the war again and march on Berlin.

During these weeks of waiting, the Big Four—Orlando had soon returned—continued to hold frequent meetings to consider German objections to the Treaty and the changing situation of the world; for example, Bavaria had gone Bolshevik and defied the government of the new German Republic. As all Germany tottered on the brink of revolution it looked like a race between peace and chaos.

However, much to Edith's delight, her husband now had far more free time to spend with her. He did not though recover rapidly from the strain of the Conference. Frequently he was laid low by the violent neuralgic headaches which had plagued him in the past. Following Grayson's long-neglected prescription of exercise, Edith made Wilson take long walks with her and even got him out on the links once or twice. Never once did she make an engagement of her own when there was the faintest chance he might be free.

Miss Benham wrote in her diary: "Probably no one will realize fully . . . how much Mrs. Wilson has done to make it [the President's work] possible. She is the most wonderful wife in the world to a man who needs love and care more than any I have ever seen. Without it I don't believe he could live. . . ."

On May 30, Memorial Day, Edith drove with her husband to the big, sad American military cemetery at Suresnes. It was new and bare and brown, an ugly gash in the green countryside. While Edith listened from the car to which she was confined by an infected foot, the President made perhaps the most moving speech of his whole life.

"These men who lie here are of a unique breed," he said. "Never before have men crossed the seas to a foreign land to fight for a cause which they did not pretend was peculiarly their own, which they knew was the cause of humanity and mankind. And when they came they found fit comrades for their courage and their devotion. . . . Joining hands with these, the men of America gave the greatest of all gifts, the gift of life and the gift of spirit. . . .

"So it is our duty to take and maintain the safeguards which will see to it that the mothers of America and the mothers of France and England and Italy and Belgium and all the other suffering nations shall never be called upon for this sacrifice again. This can be done. It must be done. It will be done . . . [through] the great instrument which we have just erected in the League of Nations. The League of Nations is the covenant of governments that these men shall not have died in vain. . . .

"If I may speak a personal word, I beg you to realize the compulsion I, myself, feel that I am under. By the Constitution of our great country I was the commander in chief of these men. . . . I sent these lads over here to die. Shall I—can I—ever speak a word of counsel that is inconsistent with the assurances I gave them when they came over? It is inconceivable. . . . So I say: 'Here stand I, consecrated in spirit to the men who were once my comrades and who are now gone, and who have left me under eternal bonds of fidelity.' "

Looking out of her car, Edith saw that the motorcycle soldiers of her escort were weeping. As she was.

One day the Paris papers carried the headline: "King of Belgium Comes Unexpectedly to Paris by Air."

The story opened: "For the first time in history a king has arrived in Paris by air. Yesterday morning the King of the Belgians glided down to Le Bourget Airport in a biplane which brought him from Brussels. . . ."

The tall blond hero-king had come to call on the Wilsons and invite them to visit his country. Much as they loathed the thought of another royal razzle-dazzle, they felt they could not refuse his courteous invitation.

The Belgian visit proved to be the most strenuous of all. Since the Belgians wanted it that way, the President took an unusually large entourage, which in addition to Grayson and Miss Benham included Margaret Wilson, Bernard Baruch, Vance McCormick, Ambassador Davis and Herbert Hoover, who because of his great relief work was a hero to the Belgian people. They arrived in the French President's train—Belgian royalty was too poor to own one —at Nieuport near the French border, at 7:30 A.M. King Albert and Queen Elizabeth were there to meet them. The long-nosed Queen of the Belgians wore a frumpy white cotton dress and white cotton stockings. The King was in uniform and Woodrow Wilson, always unconventional about dress, wore a cutaway and a tweed golf cap. As usual Edith was smartly turned out in a large-brimmed summer hat, dark silk dress and matching parasol. Miss Benham looked as though she was about to take off in a winged Valkyrie helmet of feathers.

After greetings aboard the train the party started out in thirty automobiles to see all the devastation they could find. Miss Benham says, "They led us a pitiless chase."

Over the war-torn, dusty roads of Belgium they raced at fearful speed. King and President in the first car were not so badly off, but the rest of the company were smothered and covered by layers of dust. The queen said, "Mrs. Wilson, I have terrible hay fever, so I hope you won't mind if I keep all the windows shut."

Mrs. Wilson noted, "I certainly did mind, but what could I say?"

It appeared that the queen was particularly susceptible to roses. "I do hope they don't give me any today," she said.

At the very first village two great bunches of roses were thrust into the car. The queen immediately dissolved in tears. "Quick, throw them out!" said Edith.

Between sneezes the queen gasped, "No! It would hurt their feelings. Wait until we get out of town."

When they stopped at the next village Margaret Wilson, looking like a gray plaster image of herself from dust, begged a ride in the closed car. There was plenty of room for three in the back but the queen made Margaret sit on the tiny jump seat. As the car leaped off again Margaret landed on the floor at their feet. When they stopped to right her, more roses were thrust into the car.

On they raced at sixty miles an hour, through the ravaged countryside and ruined villages, at each of which they stopped to sign "The Golden Book." "These people are crazy about signatures," said Miss Benham.

They had lunch in a big tent in the Forest of Houthoulst, which before the war had been a lovely woods and now looked like the Dismal Swamp with nothing but the naked shards of once fine trees standing around shell craters.

In the afternoon they passed through "the awful desolation around Ypres" and came to Zeebrugge on the North Sea, which Edith found the most interesting place of all. Here the Germans had built a great U-boat base. The British, in perhaps the most daring enterprise of the war, had sailed against the mole a ship loaded with explosives and blown her up, completely blocking the port. British Captain Carpenter, who had commanded the raid and lived to tell the tale, was there to show them around. He looked so young and carefree that Edith found it hard to believe that he had once stood on this long concrete pier in a deluge of steel and fired coolly directing his men as they blew the huge water gates off the locks that were the U-boats' lair.

The motorcade had started at 8 A.M.; it was seven o'clock at night before they boarded the train again for Brussels. In eleven hours the women had not had a moment's privacy. They heard that the queen had trained herself to go all day without the need to retire. Lacking such royal discipline, the American women were very unhappy.

Dinner was served on the train and they arrived at Brussels in a rose-pink sunset to be greeted by a idolatrous crowd that almost equaled Rome's. There was an informal reception at the palace, a balcony appearance for the cheering crowd and bed for a few brief hours.

The next day was a typical round of official sight-seeing and ceremonial meals. At the American Embassy lunch given by Ambassador and Mrs. Brand Whitlock they all had their pictures taken in the lovely summery garden. King Albert was so tall that he dwarfed even the Wilsons, while Admiral Grayson looked like a small boy in uniform. Only Bernard Baruch, thin and elegant, in his shiny high silk hat, topped King Albert.

On the last day they visited Cardinal Mercier, who had so bravely defied the Germans throughout their four years of occupation. The Cardinal towered over them all in his red robes, with the great jeweled cross on his breast. His worn, ascetic face and gentle smile seemed truly saintly. He gave them tea in the great

salon of the Archepiscopal Palace. It was splendid with heavy
gilt furniture and crimson brocade and mirrored walls. But the
mirrors were all shattered and the sky was blue through a bomb
hole in the vaulted roof.

Then the Cardinal drove with them to Louvaine near the German border to see the famous ancient library which the Germans
had destroyed. Only its unroofed walls were standing and the
final touch of poignancy to Edith was that the rubble on its floors
was covered by heaps of flowers to soften its desolation. Just as
she had feared the President saw red.

Then they drove back to Brussels—such a tiny country—and
the state banquet at the palace. So finally, with enormous relief
they boarded their train back to the house on the Place des États-
Unis that was almost like coming home.

In Paris the best possible news awaited them. The Germans
had agreed to sign!

Never was there a more beautiful day than June 28, 1919; and
hardly ever in history a more hopeful one. Everyone knew the
peace was not perfect, but it was *peace*. The President said, "The
real peace of the peoples ought to follow, complete, and amend
the peace of the statesmen." That day almost everyone believed
that was the way it would be.

Early in the morning the President gave his wife a corsage of
her favorite orchids, and what touched her even more, a lovely
beaded bag of gray and blue which he secretly had made to match
her gown. With it was a single red rosebud, of which he said,
"This is the nearest I can get to making it our American red, white
and blue."

She carried the bag and the rose that one day and kept them
always.

A little after noon they started for Versailles in the President's
car with his big blue and gold flag flying from the fender. The
streets of Paris were jammed with people waving flags of all the

Allies and the long white country roads were bordered by horizon-
blue lines of *poilus*.

The great square of the palace was guarded by French cavalry
with colorful pennants flying from the tips of their lances, and on
the broad marble staircase stood the Garde Républicaine in glittering cuirasses and horse-tailed helmets. The French knew how
to stage this sort of thing. Perhaps they knew too well.

Mrs. Wilson wrote that the ceremony was held in the Hall of
Mirrors "where curiously enough the German Empire had been
proclaimed in 1871." There was nothing curious about it. Of
course the French had staged it there to make the Germans eat a
little more dirt, just as the Germans in their turn staged the surrender of France, in 1940, in the same railroad car in the same
part of the forest where the Armistice was signed in 1918. "What
children!"

At the entrance to that long, long gallery, the President left Mrs.
Wilson to join his delegation, and she was escorted to a seat in the
front row of spectators facing the end of the hall where the dais
had been placed for the signing.

After what seemed a long time the double doors were thrown
back and Clemenceau, the old Tiger, looking both fierce and gay,
led the French delegation to their seats and took his place as President of the Conference in the center of a long table covered by a
tawny golden cloth.

Then came Woodrow Wilson leading the Americans. Mrs. Wilson writes, "I felt a curious tightening of my throat as I looked at
his dear figure, grown more slender in those months, but alert and
alive." The President took his place on Clemenceau's right and
Lloyd George marched briskly in to his place on the Tiger's left.
The other delegations followed.

Then there was a long wait while secretaries ran back and forth,
delegates asked each other for autographs and there was a rather
disorderly let-down of solemnity. It ended as the trumpets blew
to announce the German delegates, and with a single motion all
the men of the Garde Républicaine sheathed their shining sabers.

In a terrible, venomous silence the two miserable men who were the only representatives the new German Republic could find to perform the humiliating final act of the tragedy of the German empire walked in, accompanied by an officer of each of the Allied armies, who seemed more like jailors than a guard of honor. The Germans wore rusty black clothes, celluloid collars, black bow ties and spectacles. They trembled a little with the emotion they desperately sought to hide.

One of them was tall and angular, with light hair and pale blue eyes; the other short with an overlarge head covered by dark hair in a stiff pompadour. As they marched stiffly down the enormous length of the room that whole great company remained seated in utter, hostile silence.

When the Germans had taken their lonely places, Clemenceau rose to speak. He was all Tiger now, his voice a harsh growl. He fairly spat out a few brief sentences, then pointed like an avenging god at the big White Book of the Treaty lying open on the table with the gaily covered ribbons of the delegates already in place— Wilson had sealed it with his ring of California gold.

Clothed now in the dignity of despair, the Germans mounted the steps and in the appointed place signed their names:

Hermann Müller
Johannes Bell

Then President Wilson who, with rare unanimity *all* the delegates had chosen to be the first to sign, rose and walked swiftly to the table where the Book lay open with a fresh page turned. He write "Woodrow" firmly and then shaken by emotion, added with difficulty, "Wilson." Colonel House, Secretary Lansing, General Bliss and Mr. White wrote their names beneath his.

As the President walked past Edith on his way back to his seat he gave her one of his most radiant smiles. Mr. White, hobbling on his cane at the tail of the procession, stopped and made her his Court of St. James bow.

The last of the representatives of fifty-one nations present

signed the Book of the Treaty at 3:40 P.M. As he laid down his
pen, artillery in the park crashed out the beginning of the 101-gun
salute. It was taken up by the great seige guns of the outer forts
and echoed by antiaircraft batteries along the road to Paris until
the joyful sound reached the capital, where pandemonium broke
loose.

Everything that could make a noise howled and bellowed and
changed and boomed. The bells of half a thousand churches tolled.
Sirens screamed and taxis tooted. Truck drivers gaily made their
engines backfire and Parisians without artificial sound-makers just
yelled. From the roof of the Invalides the Prussian cannon captured by Napoleon belched smoke and flame for the first time since
the Battle of Jena in 1806.

In the Hall of Mirrors Clemenceau rose and abruptly declared
the Conference of Versailles adjourned *sine die.*

President Wilson hurried through the mob scene to join his wife.
But no sooner had he greeted her than the photographers were
upon them begging him to come out on the terrace with Clemenceau and Lloyd George so they could get a proper picture. Smiling, he agreed, and Edith said, "I'll wait for you here."

She went to one of the long windows that looked down on the
lovely vista of flowers and green lawns, the long mirror lake and
all the famous fountains playing for the first time since the war.
Behind a cordon of police was a seething mass of people cheering
and waving flags of all the Allies.

Then she saw the famous Three come out of the palace in the
formality of shiny silk hats and frock coats. But there was nothing
formal about their manner. Lloyd George's curly white hair flowing under his hat made a nimbus around his smiling face. Clemenceau, no Tiger now, looked like an amiable Skye terrier between
his taller companions. Woodrow Wilson's face had the joyous ex-
pectancy of a schoolboy at the beginning of the summer vacation.

Linking arms like youthful comrades, they strolled across the broad terrace, with the little fighter biplanes of France swooping overhead and the fountains glittering in the golden sunshine.

It was too much for the crowd. Shouting *"Vive Wilson! Vive Clemenceau! Vive Lloyd George!"* they gave a mighty, spontaneous heave that cracked and submerged the cordon of police like a broken dam. Edith's heart almost stopped as she saw the mass surge toward the Three. She thought they might be trampled to death by that stampede of people who wished them only well.

But there was no danger for them in France that day. Laughing and cheering, the first people to reach them joined hands and made a circle around the laughing statesmen. Those behind halted and braced themselves to hold back those farther in the rear. In this little magic circle of loving, laughing people that moved with them they strolled on with the old Tiger waving his cane in sheer exuberance.

The President had decided to leave Paris that very night and sail from Brest the next day. Admiral Grayson had asked, "Aren't you too good a Presbyterian to sail on a Sunday?"

The President grinned at him, and said, "Don't you mean that the Grand Prix is to be run at Longchamps on Sunday and you want to see it? I'm not as green as I look."

So they hurried back to the Place des États-Unis to dress for the last state dinner, the Victory Dinner at the Élysée—the only really jolly party they went to there. Then they rushed home again to change for traveling; and back to the station, where the French President's train waited to take them on their last trip in Europe. All the leaders of the nations were there to see them off. Despite his great age and the terrific day he had put in, the Tiger was among them. He and the President shook hands with real emotion.

Edith knew that there was genuine affection between these two antagonists—the affection of mutual respect. Wilson loved Clemenceau for his integrity and fighting spirit. He felt far more secure in the old Tiger's open hostility than in Lloyd George's ambivalent support.

As for Clemenceau, he watched the long blue state train of France sliding away with an unexpected mistiness in his eyes. Almost to himself the Tiger said, "There goes a very great man."

Alone in their familiar stateroom after that day of high emotion, the Wilsons stood at the open window as the train clicked over the switch points and the jumbled tenements of Paris gave way to the fragrant fields and woods of the lovely land of France. Taking Edith's hand in his he summed it all up with the words, "Well, little girl, it is finished. And as no one seems satisfied, it makes me hope that we have made a just peace. But it is all in the lap of the gods."

CHAPTER XIV

APPEAL TO CAESAR

PRESIDENT WILSON'S ARRIVAL in New York on July 8, 1919, was almost a repeat performance of Boston in February. As the *George Washington* steamed up the harbor, preceded by the battleship *Oklahoma* and the Navy dirigible *C-4*, Edith stood beside her husband on the bridge enjoying it hugely, while guns boomed from the old forts and the whistles on all the ships from tugs to liners were tied down, and fireboats almost rivaled the fountains of Versailles. It was a maritime preview of the tremendous welcome awaiting them on land.

The *George Washington* docked at Hoboken. Gaily the President remarked, "This is the first time Hoboken ever looked beautiful to me."

He and Edith were in high spirits at getting home. The President was rested by the sea voyage, which Admiral Grayson had prolonged two days by having the ship slowed up. Each time Wilson had a few days of enforced quiet he made one of his amazing comebacks. Nevertheless, Mrs. Wilson sadly observed that each time he achieved a little lower level of vitality. The graph of his strength had its peaks and valleys, but on average it was a descending line.

From Hoboken the presidential party, which had been joined by Vice-President Marshall and young Governor Al Smith of New York, crossed to Manhattan on a ferryboat. In an open touring car under a blazing July sun they drove through crowds almost as delirious as those on Armistice Day to Carnegie Hall, where the President spoke of his joy at being home and ended by saying:

"I have come back with my heart full of enthusiasm for throwing everything I can, by way of influence or action, in with you to see that the peace is preserved. . . ."

Right after that they were on their way to Washington in their familiar private car, *Mayflower,* which looked finer to them than all the royal trains of Europe.

The White House limousine with Robinson at the wheel was waiting for them at the station and the people of Washington were waiting in the streets that summer night to welcome them as wildly as the people of New York. Then they were home at the White House, which was, in fact, the only home they had known together. Mrs. Wilson wrote, "How good to be surrounded once more by the single dignity of the White House, spick and span with cool linen on the chairs and flowers everywhere."

And the President said to her exuberantly, "After what I have seen today I believe that eighty per cent of the American people are behind me and the League."

So they were that night.

Almost at the same time a very curious scene was taking place in the office of Senator Lodge of Massachusetts. It was described to this writer by the late William Phillips, former Ambassador to Rome and Under Secretary of State.

The senator sat behind his broad, bare desk with his whiskers bristling and his eyes glaring at Phillips. "The League of Nations must be killed!" he said fiercely.

"But Senator," the other protested, "how does it happen that you

who have favored international co-operation for so long, and even
wrote a book about it, are so determined that America shall not
join the other nations of the world in the very thing you have proposed?"

The senator's face turned turkey red, his eyes glittered with a
fanatic light and his fist crashed down on the desk. "Don't you
realize," he roared, "that if Wilson gets his League, the Republican
party will be done for fifty years?"

Ignoble as that reason was for destroying the great design of
world co-operation, it was probably not even the truth. In fact, if
any other Democrat had proposed the League, Lodge might have
gone along, even though with partisan misgivings. But his personal
hatred of Wilson had so warped his mind that he truly believed
anything proposed by the President was evil.

"How are you going to defeat the League when it's plain as a
pikestaff that a vast majority of Americans believe in it?" the visitor asked.

With a sly twinkle that would have been almost ingratiating had
it not been so malicious, the senator said, "We shall make reservation after reservation, amend and amend, until there is nothing
left."

Edith Wilson's greatest joy in getting home was the fond and
foolish dream that she and her husband could resume the happy
and comparatively tranquil routine of the first year of their marriage before the war, and then the peace, had thrown them into
the vortex. The dream lasted about twenty-four hours.

Two days after their return she rode with her husband to the
Capitol to hear him present the Treaty of Versailles to the Senate.
Always before when she had heard him speak she had felt the
warmth of the audience rising toward him. This time she sensed
the tension and hostility as she took her place in the balcony of
the Chamber.

Though more than half the senators present favored the League
in some form, the others were strongly against it. Among the most

adamant were the "Irreconcilables," including Senators Hiram Johnson, William E. Borah, James A. Reed and Robert LaFollette. Their opposition did not stem from hatred of Wilson, but from a genuine belief that America should not get involved in the tangled affairs of Europe. Having saved the world, our country should return to the splendid isolation in which she had grown great. The Irreconcilables were honest and conscientious men who did not realize that the land they loved could never again renounce her responsibility for world leadership. Senator Lodge, who knew better, used them adroitly for his purpose.

So as Wilson explained the Treaty to the Senate point by point, and described the difficulties and complexities of its making, these men sat in hostile silence. Their integrity made them no less implacable.

Even as he left the Chamber amid cheers from the galleries and from pro-Treaty senators, Wilson realized that he had a hard fight on his hands. He decided that if he could not win them en masse he would try to reason with the senators individually.

Mrs. Wilson describes how all during the suffocatingly hot months of July and August the senators came for conferences with the President. Many of them were on his side. Chief among those favoring ratification was Senator Gilbert M. Hitchcock of Nebraska, Democratic minority leader of the Senate. The President supplied these senators with arguments for their speeches explaining why, if the Senate made vital reservations to the Treaty, all the other nations who had signed would have the right to do the same. This would produce chaos.

Other senators who were troubled but unprejudiced came to talk with the President. One of these was kindly Warren G. Harding of the Foreign Relations Committee. Harding was responsive but irresolute.

The Irreconcilables also came. Bridling his temper, a feat which became more difficult every day, Wilson patiently explained and clarified point after point in the long document. Oddly enough the senators did not question him closely about the obvious injustice of terms which land-hungry European statesmen had wrested from him. It was the Covenant of the League of Nations to which they objected, and especially to Article X which read:

The members of the League undertake to respect and preserve against external aggression the territorial integrity of all members of the League. In case of such aggression, or in case of any threat or danger of such aggression, the Council shall advise upon the means by which this obligation shall be fulfilled.

They feared that this article might compel the United States to enter another European war and regarded it with horror. Wilson, on the other hand, considered it "The heart of the Covenant," and the best guaranty of the peace of the world.

Mrs. Wilson writes, "Day after day, week after week these conferences continued, but nothing seemed to result except increasing fatigue for the President. He had, of course, many other problems to work out. . . . There were constant addresses to the Congress, one on the high cost of living [we call it inflation now], another urging co-operation of railway employees . . . still another urging increased domestic production and economy.

"Anyone who knows the heat of Washington in July and August can picture the way energy is sapped. . . . The increasing demands on my husband's brain and body exacted a toll which pyramided, while I looked on with an anxious heart. . . ."

Edith had another cause for anxiety. Early in August the President decided that since he was getting nowhere with the senators he must carry his cause to the people—"The appeal to Caesar," he called it, for to him the people were the final court of appeal. Baker writes, "He believed, all but mystically, in the people."

Wilson also knew that although he had the power to inspire the people and lead them, and to make them revere him, he lacked the element of personal popularity. Once he said sadly, "I want the people to love me. But they never will."

Both Admiral Grayson and Mrs. Wilson were terrified by the President's proposed trip. They pictured in their minds what the strain of a nationwide whistle-stop campaign in the heat of summer would do to a man already so exhausted. With arguments reinforced by medical logic and love they dissuaded him—temporarily.

Meanwhile the debates in the Senate grew more shrill, the level of oratory more partisan. The night of decision was August 19, 1919.

That evening the President invited all the members of the Foreign Relations Committee to dinner at the White House. As usual Edith was present at the dinner and tried to make herself agreeable to Senator Lodge. After dinner the men adjourned to the East Room for the conference. Before entering that room a member of the senators insisted that everything said there should *not* be regarded as private or confidential. This suited Wilson to a T. He asked Charles Swem to make a record of all that was said.

While Edith sat upstairs, waiting anxiously, the conference lasted for over three hours. It opened with a short statement by the President and afterward became a free-for-all of question and debate, the angry clash of conflicting opinion at close quarters. Josephus Daniels writes, "The President was never quite so much the master of any gathering in the logic and brilliancy of advocacy of a cause."

But brilliance is of no avail against the blind, and logic is shattered against a closed mind. When the President came at last to his wife in her sitting room he was grim and exhausted. "It's no use," he said. "They are determined to wreck the Covenant. I must go to the people. Only they can prevail."

Admiral Grayson and Edith made one final effort to reason with him. They went into the President's study one morning and the Admiral described the hardships and danger of a month's "swing around the country," such as the President proposed—the heat and dirt of the train, the unceasing strain of delivering one or two major speeches every day, the endless banquets, luncheons and receptions, and the thousands and tens of thousands of hands to be shaken. "As your physician I cannot answer for your health," the devoted doctor told him. "It may kill you."

Edith could only reinforce the Admiral's words by an appealing look.

Wilson got up, and walking to the window, stood looking out at the Washington Monument for several moments. Then he turned to them and said, "Yes, all that is true; but I feel it is my duty. If the Treaty is not ratified by the Senate the war will have been fought in vain, and the world thrown into chaos. I promised our soldiers, when I asked them to take up arms, that it was a war to end wars, and if I do not do all in my power to put the Treaty into effect I will be a slacker and never able to look those boys in the eye.

"I cannot put my personal safety and my health in the balance against my duty. I must go!"

Edith wrote, "To this neither Doctor Grayson nor I could find an answer."

Before they left Mrs. Wilson gave what turned out to be her final party at the White House. It was a lawn party for the wounded men from the Naval and Walter Reed Hospitals. Perhaps, it was the most successful one she ever gave. Every President since has followed her lead.

Meanwhile Tumulty was carefully planning the itinerary of the trip, charting the course of the train in long diagonal swoops through the Midwest and far West, where opposition to the President was strongest, avoiding the East and South, where the League was popular. Tumulty also had the task of co-ordinating arrangements for the speeches, parades, banquets, receptions and hotel space with advance agents and pro-League citizens in each locality with whom he prepared detailed schedules called "maneuver sheets."

It was a complex business. Everyone wanted as much of the President's time as possible and he had so little time. To keep him on schedule and still avoid slighting any important local politicians or organizations was an extremely delicate feat of politico-social tightrope-walking. Tumulty managed it with great dexterity.

Routing the train was an equally complicated operation which White House aide Edward Smithers worked out with executives of the railroads involved. But paying for it was no problem. The custom was that the President would purchase a drawing room at the regular fare and the railroads would provide a private car attached to a special train. On this trip the roads lost no money because over a hundred reporters accompanied the President, and their fares brought in a substantial sum. The private car was the usual *Mayflower*.

Admiral Grayson ordered Tumulty to arrange for a week's layover at the Grand Canyon to give the President a breathing spell. When he heard of this Wilson vetoed it, saying, "We must do nothing to give the public the impression that this is a holiday. It is too vitally serious for the country."

Had Grayson's schedule been followed the course of world history might, perhaps, have been changed.

Tumulty was, in fact, the only person close to the President who favored the trip. He had complete confidence in the President's persuasiveness and he was sure Wilson would create such overwhelming sentiment for the League that the Senate would be forced to accept it. For so great a cause he was willing to gamble on the President's health. As was Woodrow Wilson.

As the President's long train pulled slowly out of the tangled railway yards of Washington, there was a very gay party in his private car. Wilson was in high good humor. With decision taken and action impending, his doubts and anxieties slipped from his shoulders. Edith, who could be gay at the slightest excuse, or none at all, if she thought it would help Woodrow, was bubbling with merriment. Tumulty was at his Irish best, keeping them all roaring with dialect stories, while Admiral Grayson encouraged him, and contributed his own share to the fun.

Loath to break up the party, they sat talking for hours while the train went through the Baltimore tunnel and swung westward, swaying and puffing through the Alleghenies toward the heartland of America.

It was a night of good omen, September 3, 1919—the fifth anniversary of the night Edith Bolling Galt had promised to marry Woodrow Wilson.

CHAPTER XV

THE LONG TRAIN

THE NEXT MORNING as the train rumbled through the big flat cornfields of Ohio, the President held a press conference in a Pullman car. Some reaction had set in after the gaiety of the night before, and Mrs. Wilson noticed that he appeared a little edgy. However, this was not surprising, for she knew that press conferences usually made her husband nervous. "They ask me such foolish questions," he said.

The opening meeting of "the swing" was in Columbus, Ohio, at noon that day. It was a prototype of all the others—the local committee coming aboard at an earlier stop to be greeted and entertained, jammed into the small saloon compartment of the *Mayflower;* then the arrival at the station, and the motorcade through the roaring crowds in the noonday heat; the hasty fried chicken lunch—Edith thought what a massacre of cockerels their trip caused—and on to the hall in an atmosphere of clamorous confusion.

Quite suddenly all confusion ended as the President began to speak. Edith marveled that those thousands of people, packed sweating in the great, flag-draped hall, could sit so still and be so attentive as her husband's voice, carrying to the rafters without benefit of loud-speakers, brought the clarity and light of reasoned argument to that emotional gathering.

In Columbus, as at all those other stops, the President explained one of the aspects of the Treaty in profound yet simple words that his listeners clearly understood and approved. It was a major policy address, which under modern circumstances would take weeks of preparation by a trained team of writers.

In the afternoon the train coasted over the border of Indiana to a stop at Richmond where Edith stood on the rear platform beside her husband while he made a trenchant impromptu speech to the crowd of farmers and their wives that overflowed the railroad yards and backed up all the side streets. In the evening they went to the Coliseum at Indianapolis for another major address which carefully examined still another aspect of the Treaty.

During the night the train rattled on to St. Louis. There at a huge Statler Hotel luncheon Wilson analyzed the controversial Article X of the Treaty in a highly intellectual address. That evening he spoke to ten thousand people in the St. Louis Coliseum, where he pointed out that the alternative to joining the League was America's standing isolated in a hostile world, armed to the teeth with fear of attack hanging over her. As always, he kept his arguments on a high plane free of politics: "Forget that I am a Democrat. Forget that some of you are Republicans. Forget all about that. . . ." Only the League mattered.

On through the fields of eight-foot corn, green and golden and ready for picking, the train steamed to Kansas City, Missouri, Des Moines, Iowa, Omaha, Nebraska. Then it turned northward through the wheat fields, left bare behind the reapers, to South Dakota. In every city Wilson made at least one major speech—in St. Paul, Minneapolis he made three in a single day—and almost every time the train stopped he talked from the back platform, making a tremendous effort to project his voice so that farmers holding their teams at the far edge of the crowd could hear and understand.

In all those places the newspapers gave him headlines that streamed across the whole front page. And everywhere the crowds grew bigger—in Bismark, North Dakota, there was no place large enough to hold them and the President spoke in an enormous circus tent pitched in a wheat field. Wilson knew he was winning—winning the people over—so he redoubled his efforts.

The opposition was badly frightened. They hastily raised some funds and sent Senators Borah, Reed and Johnson out on the President's trail to try to stem the tide, speaking in the cities where he had spoken, savagely attacking the League. The papers called them "The Bitter Enders" and "The Battalion of Death." The latter description was almost true.

The President's wife and his doctor knew that while he was gaining the public he was exhausting his last reserves of strength. In her memoirs Mrs. Wilson wrote: "Never a moment to relax and rest. And so on across the continent. From one city to the next a small local committee would accompany us, which meant constant entertaining even on the train. . . . I could not remain blind to the physical sacrifice he was making and must wonder if it were not too great. . . . Dr. Grayson's disregarded warnings against attempting the tour haunted my sleep. . . ."

When asked how she, herself, stood the tremendous strain complicated by her deep anxiety, Mrs. Wilson answered simply, "Oh, I did not matter."

On the high plateaus of Montana the President first began to fail. The altitude, compounded by heat and dust, brought on a recurrence of the asthma that had troubled him ever since his illness in Paris. He lost his wonderful recuperative power of sleep. And he began to suffer blinding headaches. Often Edith would come into his compartment to find him in a chair holding his splitting head in both hands. But he would not slacken his pace. Mark Sullivan, who was on the trip, wrote: "In proportion as he was ill . . . he was more meticulous than ever to keep every engagement, to appear at each meal . . . to respond to every call from wayside crowds for additional train-platform speeches. . . . He even planned to extend the trip, carry the fight into the enemy's country—Lodge's New England."

But everything was not grim for the Wilsons. There were little breaks, charming episodes that gave them a chance to laugh together. Edith made the most of these respites, never letting her husband see her tragic fear for him. She was grateful to Tumulty for the laughs he brought them and wrote, "Tumulty was great fun on a trip."

A reporter in Oregon wrote: "The President can truly say that Mrs. Wilson sustains him. As Mr. Wilson, standing in his automobile, bowed right and left waving his brown fedora in answer to the cheering thousands, she constantly held her hand against his back, supporting him against the possibility of a fall."

A touching vignette occurred in Billings, Montana, where two little boys climbed in the back platform of the train. One said, "Here, Woody!" and gave the President a small American flag. The other boy had no flag, so he searched through his pockets until he found a dime which he solemnly presented to his friend, "Woody."

"I like to think of it as the widow's mite," said Woodrow Wilson.

Many years later Mrs. Wilson found the dime carefully wrapped in tissue paper in the change purse her husband always carried.

On September 12, the great train climbed over the Rockies and came down to the coast at Seattle, Washington, where the Wilsons spent two nights in the Hotel Washington. But there was nothing restful about that. On September 13 President Wilson delivered four major speeches at the Stadium in Tacoma, the Armory in Tacoma, the Hippodrome in Seattle and the Arena in Seattle. In between he reviewed the Pacific Fleet.

The review was almost a holiday for the Wilsons, for they both loved ships, especially Navy ships. It was likewise the most dangerous moment of the whole trip for the President.

Their good friends, the Secretary of the Navy and Mrs. Daniels, had come all the way to the Coast to join them on this occasion. They all met at the dock where Admiral Hugh Rodman's barge was supposed to be waiting. By some mischance it was not there, so Daniels' aide commandeered a small launch. As everybody piled aboard, the launch sank lower and lower until the gunwale was only a few inches above the water. In his excitement the young officer in command gave a series of ill-timed orders. The launch started off at full speed, rammed a Navy whaleboat and almost capsized.

The President only laughed. But Mrs. Wilson was furious, not at the danger to herself, but at the danger to Woodrow.

Almost awash, the launch finally reached the famous old battleship *Oregon* which had fought in the Spanish-American War. Safely on her high bridge, they waited for Captain Ivan C. Wettengel to get under way. But he was being remarkably cautious. Mrs. Wilson noted her husband's impatience rising. "Why are we waiting?" he asked.

The Captain answered, "Until the destroyers have taken position."

Wilson looked over the fleet with an expert eye. "They are not moving, Captain, they are hove to," he said in his Commander-in-Chief's voice.

"Aye, aye, sir," said the Captain, saluting.

The *Oregon* got under way and steamed past the great battleships, the cruisers, destroyers, submarines and other craft in the thunder and smoke of saluting guns, while Edith watched her husband standing suddenly young and gay again with the salt wind combing the pain from his head and his eyes shining with a boy's delight in the noise of guns as he took his last salute from the Navy.

That night, after the speech at the Hippodrome, they came back to their suite on the top floor of the hotel. From it they looked down on the magnificent harbor where the fleet lay with strings of lights outlining masts and hulls and the busy searchlights sweeping the stars out of the sky. For a little while they sat together in darkness looking down on the beautiful ships.

After Seattle came two speeches at Portland, Oregon. And then the train made the long run down the West Coast along the bluffs above the Pacific, through the pines and the redwood forest to Oakland. When Mrs. Wilson examined the "maneuver sheets" for Oakland and San Francisco her heart sank. It was a schedule that might have knocked out a prize fighter at the peak of his form.

Wilson was almost spent. This was the fifteenth day and six thousandth mile of the trip. He had made twenty-two major speeches, each of which was entirely new and different, and an uncounted number of rear-platform talks. He had conferred with hundreds of political leaders, who had "to have a word with the President;" and shaken, perhaps, a hundred thousand hands. "How long can he keep it up?" was the question Edith and Grayson asked each other mutely.

Wilson kept to the letter and minute of his schedule in San Francisco and they went on to Los Angeles. They were to be there over Sunday and Edith had counted on a day of rest, for her Presbyterian husband would not speak on the Sabbath. But important visitors who could not be denied stole the morning from them. In their kindness the Wilsons had invited an old friend for lunch.

It was the famous Mrs. Peck (by now Mrs. George Hulbert). Mrs. Wilson says she was glad to receive her to show "my disdain for the scandals." She came, "a sweet, faded-looking woman," weighed down with personal sorrows and oppressed by the importunities of yellow journalists. After lunch they sat in the sitting room of the suite, the Wilsons together on a sofa and Mrs. Hulbert at the apex of the triangle, talking that precious afternoon away as she told all her troubles. Edith saw a restful nap for the President go glimmering, and then her cherished plan for "a nice long ride."

The President was emotionally drained by the lengthy, sad conversation. "Is there nothing we can do for you, Mary?" he asked.

"Nothing for me," she said resignedly. "Perhaps for my son."
And launched into *his* misfortunes.

Charitably Mrs. Wilson wrote, "Poor woman, weighed down by
her own problems, of course she did not understand. Darkness
had fallen when she finally rose to go."

They were at Sacramento the next day, and then the train turned
homeward at last on a long slant north and east that took them to
Reno, Nevada, Ogden, Utah and then to Salt Lake City. It is
probable that the great meeting in the Tabernacle there was the
final straw that broke Wilson's back.

September 23 was a blazing hot night, but apparently everyone
in Salt Lake wanted to hear the President. Fifteen thousand people
were jammed into the great Mormon temple two hours before the
time set, and fifteen thousand more were storming it from the
streets outside. The police could not hold them back and they were
forced to close and bolt all the doors. Slowly a cordon of police
forced a way for the Wilsons' car through the enormous crowd
and battled to hold a lane from it to the door.

Mrs. Wilson wrote: "The fetid air we encountered on entering
the great building was unlike anything I have ever experienced.
Imagine fifteen thousand human beings in hot weather shut up
tight with no ventilation for over two hours! I felt sick and blind.
We were pushed at last to the rostrum and seated on the long
benches where the Apostles sit during the Mormon service. The
seats rose in tiers and of course the higher one went the worse the
heat and the human odors. To this day I cannot conceive how the
President spoke under such conditions. . . ."

Edith borrowed a big handkerchief from a Secret Service man
and, soaking it with lavender salts, sent it to her husband. Then,
almost fainting herself, she waited for him to speak.

And speak he did, one of the longest, most closely reasoned,
brilliantly expressed orations of his life which ended with pure
idealistic fervor couched in almost Biblical language suited to a
place that was called a "tabernacle":

"We want America to be a body of brethren . . ." he said. "Then you may be sure that its leadership will bring the same sort of comradeship and intimacy, of spirit and purity of purpose to the counsels and achievements of mankind."

When the Wilsons got back to the hotel they were both close to prostration. The President was soaking wet, and when he changed it was only a few moments before he was soaked again.

Through the furnacelike plains they pushed on to Cheyenne, and that night the President could not even pretend to Edith that he was not ill. From there they went to Denver, reaching the Brown Palace Hotel at 10:30 P.M. As they sat alone for a moment in the high-ceilinged, overcrowded sitting room of their suite Edith looked at the frighteningly pale, drawn face she loved so desperately and for a moment lost her courage. "Let's stop," she said. "Let's go somewhere and rest. Only for a few days. . . ."

Gathering himself with a tremendous effort, Wilson said, "No! I have caught the imagination of the people. They are eager to hear what the League stands for. I should fail in my duty if I disappointed them."

It was true. The windstorm of his oratory was bringing the dead ashes of American idealism back to flame. The people who had grown selfish after the great selfless effort of the war were awakening again to the high spirit in which it had been fought. He was winning them; winning them to the cause of all mankind.

Then seeing his dear wife trying to summon courage to accept his decision, he added with a smile, "Cheer up! This will soon be over. And when we get back to Washington I promise you I'll take a holiday."

The President spoke at the Denver auditorium at nine-thirty the next morning. Then they got on the train once more, to Pueblo, Colorado, where they reached the fair grounds at three o'clock of a blazing afternoon. In spite of the headache, which never let up now, Wilson joshed the reporters in the press box. "This will have to be a short speech," he said. "I should think you fellows must be getting pretty sick of this."

It was not a short speech, but longer even than the one in the Tabernacle, and this speech was as clear and closely reasoned as any he ever made. And yet it was the most emotional. For near the end he recalled the mothers who had lost sons in the war but still took his hand and asked God's blessing on him. And he spoke of the cemetery at Sursesne and the Americans lying in the long rows of graves who had not died in vain, for "France was free and the world was free because America had come. . . . There seems to me to stand between us and the rejection of this Treaty the serried ranks of those boys in khaki, not only those boys who came home, but those dear ghosts who still deploy upon the fields of France. . . ."

Then the President's eyes flashed and his voice rang out as he proclaimed his imperishable faith in his fellow countrymen. "There is one thing that the American people always rise and extend their hand to and that is the truth of justice and of liberty and of peace.

"We have accepted that truth and we are going to be led by it," he said. "And it is going to lead us, and through us the world, out into such pastures of quietness and peace as the world has never dreamed of before."

When he had done Edith sat weeping in the harsh western sunshine. And all around her, people were weeping too. There were tears on her dear husband's cheeks, so that later men were to say that he broke down at Pueblo, Colorado, and lost command of himself.

That was not true. If he himself had been carried away by emotion, he had carried all those thousands of people with him at a country fair on a summer afternoon. . . .

The great long train stood still in the deserted countryside twenty miles east of Pueblo. In front the twelve-wheeled locomotive panted hoarsely as engines do when they stand with steam up. A quarter of a mile of cars further back was the glittering private car with the President's seal, sitting there in the middle of nowhere. It was one of the strangest sights of the trip.

After the mighty effort of the speech at Pueblo, Woodrow Wilson was totally spent and suffering torture from the headache that had returned with blinding force. Mrs. Wilson and Admiral Grayson, at wit's end, consulted together as to how to revive him. The doctor had used up all his skill and was at at loss. "Perhaps a quiet walk in the fresh air would help you," he said to the President. "Would you like that?"

"Yes, I would find it refreshing," Wilson answered.

Grayson sent for Captain Dave Hardester, conductor of the train, who climbed up over the tender to confer with the engineer. As a result the train was halted on an empty stretch of prairie. Only three people got off it. Somehow word was passed to the hundred-odd reporters and photographers that the President must have a few moments alone, and they loyally remained in the stifling cars. The President and his wife and Admiral Grayson clambered down the railroad embankment and walked along a dusty country road in the gentle slanting sunshine of early evening. Once a farmer in a flivver came rattling along and slammed on the brakes incredulously as he recognized the President. He climbed down to shake his hand, and insisted on giving him a head of cabbage and some apples, "for dinner tonight."

A little farther on they saw a gaunt frame farmhouse with a soldier in uniform sitting in a chair on the porch. "That fellow looks sick to me," Wilson said; and Grayson answered, "Yes, he certainly is."

So the President climbed over a low fence, and walked across a dry, dusty field with Grayson and Edith following. As he shook hands with the young man, the father and mother came out on the porch with flustered gratitude.

Then the Wilsons and Admiral Grayson walked back to the train carrying the cabbage and the apples.

The outing really seemed to do the President good. His head felt better and the three of them had a gay little dinner. Afterward the train stopped at Rocky Ford, Colorado. Tumulty said, "There's a big crowd outside. Do you feel up to shaking a few hands, Governor?"

"Wait until just before we start," Grayson urged, anxious to spare him. For once Wilson obeyed his doctor's orders. Just before pulling out he appeared on the rear platform to grasp the hands of those nearest it. As the train slowly moved off he stood there waving to them. Then he went to his compartment and to bed.

At eleven-thirty that night Edith was getting ready for bed with the help of her maid. They talked in whispers for fear of waking the President, although the train was roaring and rattling down the long slope of the plains toward Wichita, Kansas. There was a sharp knock at the connecting door, and her husband said, "Can you come to me, Edith? I'm terribly sick."

She found him sitting on the edge of his bed with his head pressed against the back of a chair. "I can't sleep because of the pain," he said. "I'm afraid you'd better call Grayson."

Mrs. Wilson later wrote, "That night was the longest and most heartbreaking night of my life. Nothing the doctor could do gave relief. Finally the President got up and dressed. He said he could not stay in that tiny room; he must move about. . . ."

They took pillows into the office room where his old typewriter was set up on a Pullman table and tried to make him comfortable, but he could not keep still. It was five o'clock in the morning when he finally fell asleep, sitting almost straight up on the bench-like seat. Edith nodded Grayson out of the room and sat watching her husband, scarcely daring to breathe, hoping against hope that he would awaken feeling well; knowing that she hoped in vain. . . .

For the President's face was deeply lined and the left side drawn up unnaturally. Edith remembers that "As I sat there watching the dawn slowly break I felt that life would never be the same . . . and from that hour on I would have to wear a mask —not only to the public but to the one I loved best in the world;

for he must never know how ill he was, and I must carry on. . . ."

The President woke at seven and said that he must dress and shave to be ready for his speech at Wichita. Edith knew he could not speak. She helped him to his room and called Grayson and Tumulty. While they were still trying to decide what to do Wilson returned, shaved and dressed, but moving feebly. His speech was indistinct.

Doctor Grayson told him that he must cancel the rest of the tour and go straight back to Washington. With "a flash of his own grim resolution" the President said, "I must go on. I should feel like a deserter. My opponents will accuse me of having cold feet should I stop now."

Grayson said, "I owe it to the country, to you and to your family not to permit you to continue. If you try to speak today you will fall down on the platform before the audience."

Tumulty came in and the President said to him, "My dear boy, this has never happened to me before. I don't know what to do."

"You must give up the trip and get some rest," the secretary said.

Again Wilson said, "Don't you see, if we cancel this trip Senator Lodge and his friends will say that I am a quitter, that the trip was a failure! And the Treaty will be lost!"

With his Irish heart on his sleeve Tumulty grasped both the President's hands saying, "Governor, what difference does it make what they say? Nobody in the world will consider you a quitter. It is your life we must consider."

Still Wilson would not give up, and it was Edith, with her heart breaking, who finally had to tell him that he could not let the people see him as he was that day.

He believed her. Turning sadly to Grayson he said, "I suppose you are right."

Then with tears raining down his cheeks he said, "This is the greatest disappointment of my life!"

By the time the President heeded their pleas the train was slowing down for Wichita; the reception committee was waiting in the outskirts and the auditorium was filled with people. The reporters were already climbing into the automobiles of the motorcade and the committee was impatiently wondering why they were not invited aboard the car. Then Tumulty, stony-faced, came out on the platform and announced that the President was too ill to speak. Tumulty said that he had suffered a digestive upset brought on by exhaustion but the Irishman knew, and the world suspected, that it was far worse than that.

Then the tracks were ordered cleared; a pilot engine was sent out ahead and the train started for Washington at the utmost speed. When it had to make a stop, great crowds gathered, curious, respectful and hushed. Edith ordered the shades of the car pulled down.

So she sat beside her husband with "the structure of our life lying in ruin around us." And she bravely tried to amuse him with small talk, while she did some knitting to make it seem an ordinary occasion. But despite her gallantry the darkened car appeared to her "like a funeral cortege."

At eleven o'clock on the morning of Sunday, September 28, the Presidential train rumbled into the cavern of Union Station. A silent crowd, held back by police, filled the concourse and the plaza outside. The President felt equal to the long walk from the platform to where Margaret Wilson was waiting with the automobiles. Quickly they got in and were driven swiftly to "the blessed shelter of the White House." Mrs. Wilson with typical understatement admits, "I was rather unstrung."

But home was not peace. All that day the President, tormented by unceasing pain, prowled up and down the long corridor between his study and Edith's room. He could settle to nothing. He could neither work nor read. The next day, Monday, was the same.

Great headlines in the papers had followed the course of the train. Because of Grayson's ambiguous bulletins speculation was wild. Trying to damp it down, Mrs. Wilson invited ten of the White House correspondents to tea with her. But the President felt

too ill to appear. The *New York Times* for September 30, announced: "Wilson Sleeping Better. Condition improving. He was
allowed to do a little work."

On Wednesday, October 1, it looked to Edith as though the tide
had turned. She went for a pleasant ride with her husband in the
afternoon and he felt so much better that after dinner they watched
a movie in the upper corridor of the White House. In their room
afterward Wilson read her a chapter from the Bible almost as he
used to do. Then he stood up and wound his watch. And said,
"Good night."

A little later Edith noticed the watch lying on the table and
took it in to him. He seemed upset and said, "That worries me.
It isn't like me to forget my watch."

It was not like him, but Edith said brightly, "Nonsense! Everybody forgets things. I do it all the time."

Ever since that horrible night on the train Edith had only cat-
napped. So half a dozen times this night she stole into her husband's room to make sure he was all right. The last time was at
5:00 A.M. She found him deep in tranquil, silent sleep. Thank-
fully she went back to bed and slept until a little after eight.

In the bright morning light she went again to his room. The
President was sitting on the edge of his great bed trying to reach
the water bottle on the bedside table. In that terrible instant she
saw that his left arm was hanging uselessly at his side. "I have no
feeling in that hand," he said with difficulty. "Will you rub it for
me? But first help me to the bathroom."

With the strength of fear and love, she half carried him to the
bathroom. "I'm going to leave you just long enough to call Grayson," she said.

Edith went into her own room and called; even now she did
not want to be overheard on the White House switchboard. "Dr.
Grayson, come immediately," she said. "The President is very ill."

When Edith got back to the bathroom the President was lying
unconscious. He was not hurt at all, as has been said; he had
simply slid from a sitting position to the floor. She did not lose her

head, but almost instinctively did the right thing. Running to the bed, she grabbed a blanket and a pillow. She wrapped him up carefully where he lay to keep him warm.

While she was slipping the pillow under his head he stirred and asked for a glass of water. She held it out for him and he was able to sip a little. Then she sat beside him on the floor waiting numbly for Grayson.

Mrs. Wilson says, "Except for those few minutes, Woodrow was never unconscious. For the moment he came to, his mind was absolutely clear, thank God! He was always able to speak understandably."

At last there was a knock on the locked door of the room. Edith opened it for the frightened doctor. He knelt beside the President. It took his trained eye but a moment to diagnose the condition. "A cerebral thrombosis, a stroke," he whispered to Edith. "His whole left side is paralyzed."

Even then Edith did not give way, for she, too, had known his true condition. It was like a nightmare that was too awful to be real. All feeling was mercifully blotted out.

Together she and the little Admiral lifted the President's limp body, and laid him gently on Lincoln's bed. . . .

CHAPTER XVI

EDITH WILSON'S STEWARDSHIP

THE NEXT FEW WEEKS represent the most difficult and the most controversial period of Edith Wilson's life. Even now historians argue as to whether she did right or wrong; how much authority she usurped and why. Charles Willis Thompson called it "Mrs. Wilson's Regency," and others spoke of her as "Acting President." In *Liberty Magazine* George Sylvester Viereck wrote: "For six-and-a-half months Edith Bolling Wilson was not only acting President, but secretary of the President and Secretary of State." This is the wildest sort of exaggeration. At most her "regency" lasted six weeks.

The truth is that even to this day Mrs. Wilson does not realize the power that she wielded. She simply acted as she thought she must.

At first, of course, there was no thought of politics, or almost none. Specialists were summoned. Ike Hoover was instructed to get the nurse who had taken care of Ellen Axson Wilson on her deathbed. Drs. Sterling Ruffin, F. X. Dercum and Rear Admiral E. R. Stitt arrived. Later several other specialists came, among them Dr. Charles Mayo. The President's room was turned into a private hospital, with every facility that medicine then afforded. By modern standards it was primitive.

The only political action of this first dire day was Admiral Grayson's bulletin. It was anything but frank:

THE WHITE HOUSE

October 2, 10 P.M.

The President is a very sick man. His condition is less favorable today and he has remained in bed throughout the day. After consultation with Doctor F. X. Dercum of Philadelphia, Doctor Sterling Ruffin and Doctor E. R. Stitt of Baltimore in which all were agreed as to his condition, it was determined that absolute rest is essential for some time.

(signed) CARY T. GRAYSON

Not a word there about what was wrong with the President; and only a hint that he was close to death. Instead of telling the truth as James Hagerty did when President Eisenhower suffered a heart attack, Grayson decided to tell nothing he was not obliged to.

This was a terrible error. Those mysterious bulletins, intended to soothe public opinion, had exactly the reverse effect. Since the unknown is always more frightening than the truth, however grim, the wildest rumors started circulating. According to hearsay, the President was unconscious; he was totally paralyzed; he was a raving madman. In proof of the latter theory people pointed in horror to bars on certain windows of the White House; bars which had actually been put there in Theodore Roosevelt's day to keep his young sons from batting baseballs through the windows.

This failure of communication, with all its unfortunate consequences, must be blamed directly on Admiral Grayson and Edith Wilson. They knew nothing about public relations. Until she married the President, Edith had shunned publicity as a well-bred southern lady should. Though she had learned to live in its glare graciously, she had never trusted the press, except for certain journalists like Baker, whom she knew and liked. Admiral Grayson was a Virginia gentleman with an equal distrust of journalists, and absolutely no sense of public reaction. Their decision for concealment was unfortunate but understandable.

An even graver error may have been keeping the truth from members of the Cabinet and, particularly, from the United States Senate. But having embarked on the course of withholding it, this became a logical necessity. Had the Republican senators, for instance, been informed, the whole policy of "protecting the public" would indubitably have been blown wide open by calculated or accidental leaks. Mrs. Wilson and Admiral Grayson found themselves in a trap. Either everyone must be told the truth, or no one.

When the medical routine had been established and everything possible had been done for her husband, Edith Wilson faced the constitutional crisis. After all, the patient was the President of the United States. He had certain duties that could not be delegated; they could only be postponed temporarily. It was an almost unprecedented situation. Since no one knew the medical truth except the doctors, there was no one else to whom she could turn for advice.

In her *Memoir* Mrs. Wilson tells how two days before the President's collapse in the White House, Sir William Wiseman, a British secret agent, had asked to see the President to give him some important information. She refused to allow him an interview —"I never liked this plausible little man"—and made him tell her instead. Then she conveyed the message to Wilson. She writes, "This was the only instance that I recall having acted as intermediary between my husband and another on an official matter, except when so directed by a physician."

In that last phrase lies the nub of the matter. Everything Edith did was by the advice of the doctors. But doctors are neither politicians nor constitutional experts. Actually, the history of the United States was changed by the advice of a man who even now is almost unknown to historians. It was Dr. F. X. Dercum.

The time of the decision was a day or two after the President's stroke when the immediate danger of his death had receded. Mrs.

Wilson called the doctors to her, asked for the complete truth about her husband's condition and demanded a prognosis. The medical men were all agreed that he had a cerebral thrombosis, a blood clot in his brain, which had paralyzed his entire left side. However, there was no lesion. With luck the clot would dissolve. As Dr. Dercum put it, "He might live five minutes, five months or five years."

They were also agreed that his mind was as clear as ever and that his recovery was highly probable. "But," they said, "we can promise nothing unless the President is protected from every disturbing problem during his convalescence."

"How can that be done?" Edith asked. "Everything that comes to the Executive is a problem. How can I protect him from problems that the President must face?"

It was Dr. Dercum who answered her. First he told her that Pasteur had suffered a stroke almost exactly like that of President Wilson, and yet the great French scientist had done some of his most brilliant work afterwards. Then, according to Mrs. Wilson, Dr. Dercum leaned toward her with almost passionate earnestness and said, "Madam, this is a grave situation, but I think you can solve it. Have everything come to you. Weigh the importance of each matter and see if it is possible to solve it by consultation with the head of the department involved without your husband's advice. In this way you can save him a great deal. And always keep in mind that every time you take him a new anxiety or problem to excite him you are turning a knife in an open wound. His nerves are crying out for rest, and any excitement is torture to him."

"In that case shouldn't he resign and let Mr. Marshall succeed him, so that he can get the complete rest so vital to his life?" Edith asked.

Dr. Dercum knew that this was the inevitable question. He had thought about it almost continuously and had his answer ready. "No," he said, "not if you feel equal to what I have suggested. For Mr. Wilson to resign would have a bad effect on the country and on our patient. He has staked his life and made his promise to the

world to have the Treaty ratified. If he resigns, the greatest in-
centive to his recovery—his very will to live—will be gone. His
mind is clear as crystal and he can still do more with a maimed
body than anyone else. Dr. Grayson tells me that the President
has the utmost confidence in you. That you know his mind . . ."

Though the decision was put up to Edith Wilson, once these
words were spoken she had no choice. In her heart and mind the
welfare of her husband came first—it came even before the best
interests of her country. But when these two were joined together
in the doctor's logical argument there was only a question of her
own courage. And of that she had plenty.

Of course the matter was not settled without more discussion.
Admiral Grayson ardently backed his colleague's point of view.
Both as physician and friend his first duty was to his patient. The
other doctors, too were bound by the Hippocratic oath. Also, in
the thoughts of the least political-minded of them, and especially
in Edith Wilson's, was the picture of that amiable nonentity, the
Vice-President, succeeding Woodrow Wilson. Even to many of
the President's opponents this must have seemed a last resort.

In the final analysis the whole question was academic. Even if
his doctors and his wife had decided differently and earnestly urged
the President to resign, it seems certain that Woodrow Wilson
would have refused. Though he lay half paralyzed in mortal
weakness, his brain was functioning lucidly. He was as determined as ever to pursue his fight for the League and as fearful as
ever that the world would think him "a quitter." It is inconceivable
that he would have quit.

In corroboration: on Sunday, October 5, three days after his
stroke, the President called for his stenographer, Mr. Swem, saying
that he wanted to dictate some important letters. Edith was able
to dissuade him only by telling him it was the Sabbath.

Of course it probably lay within the doctors' power to declare
Wilson incompetent to perform the duties of the Presidency; that
is a constitutional question which has never been decided. But had
they done so with Mrs. Wilson's approval, it would most likely

have killed him. And if he had recovered his wrath would have been terrible.

The test of their decision was not long in coming. On Tuesday, October 7, Secretary of State Lansing, having conferred with the Cabinet, came to Tumulty and tried diplomatically to pave the way for a possible take-over by Vice-President Marshall. He read aloud the section of the Constitution setting forth the conditions under which the Vice-President shall assume the powers of the Presidency ("In case of the . . . inability of the President to discharge the duties of said office . . .").

Though Tumulty had not been taken fully into the confidence of Admiral Grayson and Mrs. Wilson, he was passionately loyal. As Lansing pursued his legalistic argument Tumulty's temper approached the flash point. Finally he interrupted the Secretary of State, saying, "Mr. Lansing, you are mistaken. The Constitution is not a dead letter at the White House. I have read the Constitution and am not in need of any tutoring at your hands in the provisions you have just read. Furthermore, you are shirking the question as to who should certify as to the disability of the President to perform the duties of his office."

Lansing said nervously, "That would be a job for either you or Dr. Grayson."

Fairly roaring, Tumulty replied, "You may be sure that while Woodrow Wilson is lying flat on his back in the White House I will not be a party to an attempt to oust him."

At this point, either fortuitously or purposely, Admiral Grayson came in. He was like a fighting cock pitched into the pit. "If any such attempt were to be made," he said fiercely to Lansing, "I should completely disavow it. I shall testify that the President is completely competent to perform the duties of his office."

This ended the only serious effort to oust Woodrow Wilson from the Presidency.

After her conference with the doctors Mrs. Wilson wrote, "So began my stewardship. . . ."

She used the exact word to define her position as she saw it. Stewardship implies the faithful use of delegated authority; the function of a trustee; or the guardianship of property while the owner is absent. Mrs. Wilson did all these things. In a real sense she was the Steward of the Presidency.

Fortunately, she was better qualified for the task than any other first lady in American history. Not that she was necessarily the most sagacious or the most brilliant, but because she was more completely in the confidence of the President than any woman before her.

Very few husbands and wives have ever been as close as the Wilsons. The President's need for companionship; his complete devotion to his wife; his trust in her judgment; and, paradoxically, his lone-wolf method of conducting the government which required a confidant rather than advisers, had led him to expose to her, and her alone, his most intimate thoughts, and to make her a party to his every decision. Because he depended on her love so much, he made her a full partner in his life.

And Edith Wilson was peculiarly suited to the role. Her love for her husband was both maternal and a little awe-stricken. She never got over her sense of wonder at the brilliance of his mind and the nobility of his character. She too had a good mind, but at the time she married Woodrow Wilson it was virtually a clean slate politically, since she had never interested herself in public affairs. He was able to form it almost in the image of his own.

Mrs. Wilson once said, "No two people ever think exactly alike." And she also said that quite often she disagreed with the President. But she did know exactly how he thought and what he thought about virtually every problem of the nation. She could become his second self. And in exercising her stewardship she was careful to think and act, not as Edith Wilson, but as she knew the President would.

The technique of government which she developed was this: Every paper, letter or document that the members of the Cabinet and the senators sent to the President was given to her. She read them with the greatest care. If they seemed at all important she would send for the official concerned and confer with him directly to see if he himself could not solve the problem. Whenever she felt something must be decided by the President she made a brief digest of the situation and then read it to him with a few words of explanation. "At first I was only able to discuss affairs of state with him for about ten minutes a day," she says.

When asked how she determined what was important enough to bring to his attention, she said, "I just decided."

But she added, "I had talked with him so much that I knew pretty well what he thought of things. If there was a doubt in my mind, I would mention a problem tentatively. Often he said, 'That's not important.' "

When her husband told her what he wanted done she made careful notes of everything he said and sent for the head of the department to come to her sitting room next to the sickroom. There she told him the President's decision, and discussed it with him. In rare cases she would go in to her husband and request further clarification. Edith hardly ever wrote to the Cabinet officers, but always spoke to them personally. She says, "When I did write anything to go outside, I always read it to Woodrow before I sent it." And she says stoutly, "I, myself, never made a single decision regarding the disposition of public affairs. The only decision that was mine was what was important and what was not; and the very important decision of when to present matters to my husband."

However, this sort of censorship by selection requires statesmanship of a high order. And, of course, the way in which problems were presented to the President had a powerful bearing on his reaction to them. It is doubtful if Mrs. Wilson fully realized the enormous influence she thus wielded on the government of the United States. Nevertheless, she was completely aware of her heavy responsibility. She had aid, of course. "During those months Daniels and Baker were most helpful. I saw them often," she says. "And I could always call on the wisdom of Mr. Baruch. I did not see much of Lansing, for I never liked him."

Poor Lansing was thus in an unfortunate position. He had less legal authority over his department than the other members of the Cabinet. The Constitution virtually makes the Secretary of State a messenger boy; it expressly charges the President with the conduct of foreign affairs. Lansing was in fact a messenger boy without even a message.

In the Senate, which was violently agitated by the Treaty fight, Senator Hitchcock became Edith's principal adviser and strength. Even at his sickest Wilson maintained a vivid interest in the maneuvers for ratification. Mrs. Wilson writes, "He asked me a thousand questions and insisted on knowing everything, particularly about the Treaty. He would dictate notes to me to send to Senator Hitchcock. . . . Or he would tell me what senators to send for and what suggestions to make to them. . . . This method of handling interviews was another suggestion of the doctors. . . . [They] said that if I could convey the messages . . . to the President he would escape the nervous drain that audiences with these officials would entail. . . .

"These instructions from the medical men were far from easy to carry out. . . . Upon all sides I was literally besieged by those who 'must' see the President. But I carried out the directions of the doctors—and my heart was in it. Woodrow Wilson was first my beloved husband. . . . After that he was President of the United States."

On other matters Edith sometimes conferred with Tumulty, though Tumulty himself did not see the President for six weeks. As to Grayson she says, "Admiral Grayson took no part that I remember in political decisions, only those which had to do with how much work or strain the President could safely stand."

So Edith Wilson bore the crushing burden almost alone. David Lawrence described the burden in an article printed in November, 1919:

"Picture the heroic determination on the part of a worried

woman to save her husband's life and fight to the bitter end the political calumny that is being avalanched upon the man. . . . It has been renewed with vigor in the last few days. It is not directed at the Cabinet nor at the Secretary to the President, but against an unidentified power in the White House. . . . Between the President and the outside world stands Mrs. Wilson as devoted and faithful companion as ever nursed a sick man. . . . Mr. Tumulty helps to determine priority and relative importance [of the problems] but Mrs. Wilson finally decides. . . . It is doubtful if ever a woman in American history had such a burden. As between the chance to save a life and answer the numerous attacks that are being made upon the President, Mrs. Wilson has chosen the course of stoical silence."

Unbiased observers testify to the success of Mrs. Wilson's stewardship. The sensational reporter for the London *Daily Mail* stated catagorically, "Though Washington tongues are wagging vigorously no suggestion is heard that Mrs. Wilson is not proving a capable 'President.'" And Republican Dolly Gann wrote: "If she did run the country, I say all the more credit to her! I'm glad there was a woman in the White House who knew how to take the reins and use authority when it was pressed upon her."

Mrs. Wilson had no sooner evolved "a workable system for handling the affairs of state," than she was suddenly faced with her gravest decision. On the night of October 13 the President's recovery was interrupted by what Mrs. Wilson calls "a stricture blocking elimination from the bladder." If it continued for even a few hours death would certainly follow.

The regular team of doctors was hastily summoned, reinforced by two specialists, Dr. Hugh Young of Johns Hopkins and Dr. H. A. Fowler of Washington. They worked for some time with local applications, trying unsuccessfully to relieve the President. Then they all retired to another room for one of those secret consultations which can mean life or death. Edith sat by her husband's bedside in dread anticipation.

After what seemed an interminable time Admiral Grayson appeared in the doorway and beckoned to her. She joined him in her dressing room, eagerly searching his face for a ray of hope. Grayson was distraught. He could not speak, and they stood silently side by side looking out of the window at an autumn morning whose beauty mocked them.

Finally Grayson, with an obvious effort at control, said, "Mrs. Wilson, this is the situation. Drs. Young and Fowler, who are specialists in this thing, both say that the President's condition cannot be relieved without an operation. The others agree with them. When they told me I went out and walked around the block trying to pull myself together before talking to you. I feel sure the President cannot stand an operation; it would be the end. Therefore, while I hate to put this responsibility on you, it is you who must decide."

Mrs. Wilson later said, "I felt that another chasm had opened under my feet and that this time I did not know how to bridge it." But she did not hesitate. "Then we will not operate," she said. "You know more than anyone else of the real chances of recovery. Go down and tell them that I feel sure that nature will take care of things. We will wait."

Grayson left her then, but in a moment he was back with Dr. Young, who looked both angry and anxious. "If you understood this situation, Mrs. Wilson, you would see things differently," he said.

He took a pencil and paper and began to draw diagrams that Edith's tear-blinded eyes could hardly follow. Then Dr. Dercum came in, followed by Dr. Ruffin, her personal physician before she met the President. They supported Young's argument, while Admiral Grayson stood pale and silent.

The pressure on Edith Wilson was enormous. These men were the leaders of their profession, far better known in the medical world than Grayson. They were united in their advice, and she stood against them supported only by her faith in the man who had taken care of the President for so many years. Mrs. Wilson was an extraordinarily resolute woman but this was the ultimate test of moral courage. Every instinct of self-preservation must have urged her to give way; for if she were wrong and her beloved husband died, she faced a future of unbearable self-crimination. Edith Wilson believes that some force beyond herself "kept me steady."

In the middle of the argument, the frightened nurse came in to say, "The President is asking for you, Mrs. Wilson."

She flew from them, but as she left the room Dr. Young called after her, "You understand, Mrs. Wilson, the whole body will become poisoned if this condition lasts an hour, or at most two hours longer."

It sounded to Edith like "the tolling of a funeral bell." She swiftly crossed the room to her accustomed chair beside the great carved bed. Her husband gave her a faint welcoming smile and slipped a thin hot hand into hers.

She sat beside the bed watching the nurses come and go, seeing the doctors glumly make examinations every half hour. Each time they took the President's temperature it was a little higher, and although they preserved their professional mask she could sense their reproach. Mostly she was aware of the racing clock. One hour went by and then the two, which Young had set as the outer limit of hope. Her own life seemed suspended in a vacuum. But she remained steadfast.

It was well into the third hour when the tension suddenly relaxed and Wilson's body resumed its normal functions. As suddenly as that the danger vanished. To Edith it seemed something like a miracle.

That was the last crisis of Wilson's illness. Thereafter the graph went gradually upward. Grayson's bulletins certainly made light of what had happened. The one dated October 14 read: "The President did not have a restful night last night. His restlessness was caused by a swelling of the prostate gland, a condition from which he has suffered in the past and which has been intensified more or less by his lying in bed. His general condition, however is good."

There was more justification for the bulletin the following morning: "The President had a good night's rest, enjoyed his breakfast, and, in spite of a slight headache, continued to make improvement. The condition which caused the restlessness Monday night about which Dr. Fowler was consulted gave no trouble during the night."

By October 30, Wilson was well enough to receive visitors. Typically, the first people from "outside" that Mrs. Wilson let him see were a king and queen. She knew that while politicians and officials might prove a drain, royalty would only amuse him.

King Albert and Queen Elizabeth of Belgium had been on the high seas for a state visit when the President was stricken. They were obliged to retire into incognito and tour America unofficially. However, when they reached Washington, the Vice-President and Mrs. Marshall entertained elaborately for them and Mrs. Wilson asked them to tea at the White House. They were accompanied by young Crown Prince Leopold and came bearing a magnificent gift of Belgian china decorated by pictures of all the cities of their realm. They had tea with Mrs. Wilson in the Red Room. After a little, Edith invited the king to come up to the President's room. As yet no American unconnected with the medical profession, not even Tumulty, had set foot there. King Albert and Wilson had a brief pleasant chat.

Then Edith took the Belgians on a tour of the White House. When it was over the queen said, "Please, may I see the President for just a moment? I so want my son to meet him."

Edith was nonplused. But she remembered that her husband always enjoyed the company of attractive women. So they all went up to the sickroom. The President had been changed from the handsome dressing gown in which he had received the king to the old gray wool sweater he always wore in bed. He had not been shaved for nearly a month and had a short white beard. In fact, he was hardly looking his best, but this did not embarrass him at all. He greeted the queen almost with his old gaiety. She in turn was delighted that they had found him studying their china gift through a magnifying glass.

The visit had repercussions for Edith. As she saw her royal guests to the door they were besieged by reporters—after all, the Belgians were the first outsiders to see the President since his illness. "How did the President seem? What did you talk about? What was he wearing?"

To the latter question the queen answered, "He looked very comfortable in a worn wool sweater."

It came out in the papers a *torn* wool sweater. Edith received at least a hundred letters from motherly old ladies reproaching her for not mending the President's sweater.

Wilson's next visitor of record was also royal—the young and glamorous Prince of Wales. Mrs. Wilson says that the prince was much more nervous than the President. He sat beside the bed fidgeting with his necktie.

However, Wilson could always charm young men. He told the prince a story about the visit of his grandfather to the White House when the older man had been Prince of Wales and how, after he had officially gone to bed one night, he had slipped out of the window to go to a private dance. The story amused the prince and he asked delightedly, "Was it this window, sir?"

Obviously it was not, since that particular window was at least fifteen feet from the ground, but the prince was now no longer nervous.

Meanwhile the Senate of the United States was in an uproar and the innuendos in the press against Mrs. Wilson became bolder. The curtain of mystery that had been dropped between the President and the world gave some cause for this, but it did not justify the venom of the attacks. Wilson's opponents were using his illness as a weapon in their fight against the League.

No expression of sympathy was voted in the Senate. Instead there was a series of speeches intended to cast discredit on those who were speaking on behalf of the President as well as to injure

Wilson himself. First came the debate about whether the President's signature on documents was his own, the inference being that it was forged by Mrs. Wilson. She herself states that "Within two weeks of his stroke the President was able to sign public documents."

It is true that, at first, he had to be helped, but he always knew what he was signing and fully intended to do so. Nor was this an unprecedented situation. When President Garfield was shot, a rubber stamp was made of his signature and he used it on public documents.

Then reports were circulated by several senators that Wilson's brain was permanently affected and that the office of President would soon be declared vacant. David Lawrence wrote, "It is Mrs. Wilson who is compelled to bear the whole burden. . . . It is not pleasant for a woman . . . to read the bitter attacks that are being heaped on 'someone in the White House,' but Mrs. Wilson is probably hopeful that the age of chivalry is not past and that the American people will not approve of the campaign to force the President into activity that may cost him his life."

The fact that four royal personages had seen and talked with the President, and reported him sensible and even witty did nothing to mollify the opposing senators. In fact it infuriated them further. Finally the uproar reached such a pitch that Edith realized it was seriously damaging the chance of ratification of the Treaty. Since she knew this was dearer than life to her husband, she arranged for two senators to see him. Ostensibly they wanted to consult the President about new difficulties in our relations with Mexico. But everyone in the country knew that they were really going to see if he was in his right mind. Wilson was furious at what he called "The Smelling Committee."

The chosen emissaries were Senator Hitchcock and Senator Albert Fall, who a few years later achieved the unique distinction of being the only Cabinet member ever to go to jail; he was convicted of receiving a $100,000 bribe from oil magnate Edward L. Doheny in the Teapot Dome scandal.

Mrs. Wilson ushered these gentlemen into the President's room one morning. Wilson had been shaved and was reclining in bed in that gray wool sweater. He greeted his old friend and ally Hitchcock with great warmth. Then Fall approached the bed. In his slightly oily way he said, "Mr. President, we have all been praying for you."

Edith saw a flash of the old fire in her husband's gray eyes. "Which way, Senator?" asked Woodrow Wilson.

They talked for quite a while about the Mexican situation and then took their leave. When the reporters outside the White House asked Fall if he was entirely satisfied with the President's mental condition, the Senator replied, "Yes, sir, entirely so."

Two more comments on that famous meeting are worth recording. Admiral Grayson said that the stimulation seemed to have done the President good. This might indicate that Edith was being overprotective.

President Wilson himself said, "What does that fellow Fall mean by praying for me? Does he want to get me in wrong with the Almighty?"

CHAPTER XVII

DEFEAT WITH HONOR

THERE SHOULD HAVE BEEN NO QUESTION in anybody's mind as to Woodrow Wilson's mental powers after December 3, 1919. On that day he sent the Congress a long, intricate message. There could be no doubt that he wrote it himself, or rather, dictated it to Mrs. Wilson. It was in his own precise style. No one in the White House entourage had either the knowledge or the ability to formulate it; only Woodrow Wilson at his best could have done it. So instead of lasting for six and a half months, as has been claimed, Mrs. Wilson's "regency," if such it can be called, is proved to have lasted less than two months. Actually it was much less than that. On November 11, the first anniversary of the Armistice, Wilson had dictated a moving message to the American people. By November 18 he was well enough to sit in the sun on the south portico of the White House in an Atlantic City boardwalk chair. Edith had rented it for him. Later she bought the chair outright.

From that time forward she says that she went over every communication with the President whether it was important or not.

Her only remaining function of a "regent" was to protect him from too many visitors by acting as a go-between. She continued to do this until April, 1920.

As has been noted, even in the crisis of his illness Wilson continued to direct the fight for the ratification of the Treaty. But without his physical presence it went badly. First, however, came a minor victory.

Senator Lodge had dragooned the Foreign Relations Committee into voting a series of amendments. They were so outrageously drastic that many of his own party joined the Democrats in defeating them. He then proposed a series of much milder "Reservations."

Even though they changed the essence of the Treaty by severely limiting American participation in the League, many friends of the Treaty favored accepting these Reservations in order to assure ratification. Bernard Baruch, who was one of the few people Mrs. Wilson allowed to see the President, urged Wilson to agree to them.

On November 18 Senator Hitchcock came to see Mrs. Wilson. Very gravely he told her that unless the Democrats accepted the Lodge Reservations the Treaty would be beaten, not on its merits, but because the struggle had narrowed down to a personal fight against the President by Lodge. In desperation Edith went to her husband and said, "Woodrow, for my sake won't you accept these Reservations and get this awful thing settled?"

The President turned his head on the pillow and reached out to take her hand. "Little girl, don't you desert me," he said in an agonized voice. "That I cannot stand. Can't you see that I have no moral right to accept any change in a paper I have signed without giving every other signatory, even the Germans, the right to do the same thing? It is not I who will not accept; it is the nation's honor that is at stake."

Then after a moment his eyes lighted with mournful fire as he added, "Better a thousand times to go down fighting than to dip your colors to dishonorable compromise."

Mrs. Wilson says that she "felt like one of his betrayers ever to have doubted. . . ."

She rejoined Senator Hitchcock and told him that for the first time she saw the whole thing clearly as Woodrow Wilson saw it. "Never again," she told the senator, "will I ask my husband to do anything dishonorable."

When Hitchcock had gone she went back to the President's room. He made his decision a matter of record by dictating to her a letter that is preserved in Senator Hitchcock's papers:

THE WHITE HOUSE
Washington, November 18, 1919.

MY DEAR SENATOR:

You were good enough to bring me word that the Democratic senators supporting the Treaty expected to hold a conference before the final vote on the Lodge resolution of ratification. I should hesitate to offer it in any detail, but I assume that the senators desire my judgment on the resolution. . . . On that I cannot hesitate, for in my opinion the resolution in that form does not provide for ratification, but rather nullification of the Treaty. . . .

I sincerely hope that the friends and supporters of the Treaty will vote against the Lodge resolution. I understand that the door will then probably be open for a genuine resolution of ratification.

I trust that all true friends of the Treaty will refuse to support the Lodge resolution.

Cordially and sincerely yours,
WOODROW WILSON

The signature is in lead pencil, but boldly written with a flourish as though the strength of the President's emotion inspired his hand.

With that letter President Wilson signed the death warrant of the Treaty. On the vote the next day the Democrats defeated the resolution ratifying the Treaty with the Lodge Reservations. On the next vote the Republicans defeated the ratification of the Treaty without reservations.

There will always be a question as to whether Wilson was right or wrong. William Allen White points out that he was enclosed in the isolation of his sickroom. His last contact with the world had been the fair at Pueblo and the emotional cheers of the crowd were still ringing in his ears. He did not realize how greatly the American spirit of idealism had deteriorated or how damaging had been his enemies' attacks while he lay helpless. He did not know this was the end. However, even if he had, his sense of honor was so delicate that he might still have remained steadfast.

As to Edith Wilson, she was so deeply in love with her husband and so in awe of his nobility of thought that, as she said, she could argue no more.

Though, in effect, the vote that day was conclusive, the fight for ratification went on for weary months. The President expressed his willingness to accept interpretations which he felt did not fundamentally alter the structure of the Treaty, and on that basis Hitchcock and the faithful Democrats tried again. On March 19, 1920, the Treaty was finally defeated.

Edith Wilson says, "That was a terrible night!"

It was indeed. The President had never really believed that the Treaty would be beaten. When the unthinkable became an unalterable fact he almost broke down. Grayson writes that Wilson said wearily, "I feel like going to bed and staying there."

He went to bed but he could not sleep. All night long Edith and Grayson were in and out of the room. At 3 A.M. the President said, "Doctor, the devil is a busy man."

Later he called again for his wife and his friend. To Grayson he said, "Doctor, please get the Bible there and read from Second Corinthians, Chapter 4, verses 8 and 9."

In a trembling voice Grayson read:

"We are troubled on every side, yet not distressed; we are perplexed, but not in despair;

"Persecuted, but not forsaken; cast down, but not destroyed . . ."

Then Woodrow Wilson said to them, "If I were not a Christian, I think I should go mad. But my faith in God holds me to the belief that He is in some way working out His own plans through human perversities and mistakes."

Nevertheless, the President seemed crushed. Once he said, "It probably would have been better if I had died last fall." That was not just a sick man speaking, but a historian who knew that if Abraham Lincoln had lived to fight for his ideas on reconstruction, the radicals in the Congress might well have destroyed even him.

On April 13, for the first time, Wilson spoke of resigning. According to Grayson's book, *An Intimate Memoir,* the President said to him that morning, "I am seriously thinking what is my duty to my country because of my physical condition. My personal pride must not be allowed to stand in the way of my duty to the country. If I am only half efficient I should turn the office over to the Vice-President. . . . What do you think?"

Grayson and Mrs. Wilson both thought that it would be fatal for the President and for the country. After pointing out how much of the work of his office Wilson was actually doing, the Admiral took his courage in both hands and suggested that the President call a meeting of the Cabinet. Although Wilson had seen most of its members singly, they had not met with him as a body since his illness.

The President agreed eagerly, and called the meeting for 10 A.M. the very next day. The members of the Cabinet who had not yet seen the President were shocked when he limped into the room leaning heavily on a cane. Secretary of Agriculture David F. Houston described the scene:

"The President looked old, worn and haggard—it was enough to make one weep to look at him. One of his arms was useless. In repose his face looked very much as usual. When he tried to speak there was marked evidence of trouble. His jaw tended to drop on one side, or seemed to do so. His voice was very weak.

"I shook hands with him. He greeted me as of old, and put up a brave front, spending several minutes cracking jokes. . . ."

It had been arranged that after an hour Admiral Grayson was

to come in. This would be the signal for adjournment. However, when he appeared, the President shook his head and Grayson backed out. Finally, after an hour and a half, Edith came in with the Admiral and broke up the meeting.

Grayson writes, "[The President] plainly showed that it had done him a lot of good."

After that Wilson held Cabinet meetings regularly. Several changes had been made in it since his illness. The first to go was Secretary of State Lansing. He was, in effect, fired.

This took place in February when the President learned for the first time that Lansing was actually calling meetings of the Cabinet. This had been going on ever since his illness but Wilson had been kept so isolated from affairs that he did not know of it. He was furious. However, his reason for dismissing Lansing was not only this. In addition, he knew that his Secretary of State had been undercutting his policy on the League of Nations ever since Paris. For example, at the time Wilson was campaigning in the West for the League, William Bullitt testified before a Senate Committee that Lansing had said to him that "the League Covenant was thoroughly bad and, in his belief, if the Senate thoroughly understood, it would reject it."

But the thing that brought Wilson to a boil was learning Lansing's maneuver to oust him at the time of his stroke.

On February 7 the President dictated to Mrs. Wilson a letter to his Secretary of State in which he asked, "Is it true as I have been told, that you have frequently called the heads of executive departments of the Government into conference?" And Wilson went on to point out that "under our constitutional law and practice . . . no one but the President has the right to summon the heads of executive departments into conference. . . ."

Lansing replied explaining, not unreasonably, that "Certain members of the Cabinet, of which I was one, felt that in view of the fact that we were denied communication with you, it was wise for us to confer informally together." Nevertheless he tendered his resignation.

Wilson accepted it because he felt that "you accepted my guidance and direction . . . with increasing reluctance . . . [and it will] afford me an opportunity to select someone whose mind would more willingly go along with mine. . . ."

The President added, "I need not tell you with what reluctance I take advantage of your suggestion, or that I do so with the kindest feeling. . . ."

Mrs. Wilson did not approve of this letter at all. In her tigress rage against anyone who threatened her husband's peace of mind, she urged him to make public what she considered Lansing's "accumulation of disloyalty in discharging the great trust he had accepted at the hands of the President."

Perhaps she was right, because the public, not knowing all the circumstances, concluded that the President had dismissed his Secretary of State on rather trivial grounds, and got the false impression that it was the act of a querulous invalid.

Lansing was replaced as Secretary of State by Bainbridge Colby. Of him Mrs. Wilson says with her usual candor, "I liked Colby. He was very delightful socially, but not an able Secretary of State."

The other Cabinet officer who resigned was Secretary of the Interior Franklin K. Lane. There was no acrimony in this resignation, although Mrs. Wilson was relieved to be rid of him. For months, she says, he had been urging the President to lease the oil lands owned by the Navy to private interests for development—"He wrote reams on the subject."

The President refused to alienate public lands. "Thank goodness he did," says Mrs. Wilson, "in view of that awful Teapot Dome scandal under Harding."

Lane's replacement was Judge John Barton Payne. As the newspapers reported, Mrs. Wilson conducted the preliminary conversations with him, and Payne himself did not see the President until the first Cabinet meeting. Before receiving the Judge in the Red Room, Edith got complete instructions from her husband. He told her to inform Judge Payne about his opinion on the oil leases and to instruct the Judge to make an exhaustive study of them for Wilson's information. Payne accepted, and as a result of his report the leases were not signed.

The year 1920 was an election year. The leading contenders for the Democratic nomination were Attorney General A. Mitchell Palmer and William Gibbs McAdoo. Among the minor candidates was James M. Cox. Herbert Hoover, who was uncommitted to any party, was mentioned hopefully, but eventually decided that he was a Republican.

Neither the President nor Mrs. Wilson was particularly enchanted by any of the candidates. At the Democratic Convention in San Francisco, they all made efforts to get the President's backing, but he would not even put in a word for his son-in-law. William Allen White says, "McAdoo . . . could have been nominated . . . if Wilson had said the word." The President's refusal may have been based on his distaste for nepotism; Mac's enemies at the Convention jeeringly called him, "the Crown Prince." On the other hand, Josephus Daniels writes that in 1918 Wilson said to Postmaster General Burleson, "Do you think Mac has got it in his head to run for the Presidency?"

Burleson replied, "I believe he has."

"He's not fit for it," said Woodrow Wilson.

Some of the Democratic leaders at San Francisco wanted to soft-pedal Wilson. But at the first mention of his name in the Convention such a roaring ovation took place that it was evident he was still first in the hearts of the delegates. As Brand Whitlock wrote from Belgium to Ray Stannard Baker, "The grim old schoolmaster there in Washington still has power in the land. . . ."

Wilson remained absolutely neutral throughout the convention. Tumulty thought that he secretly hoped to be nominated himself. Mrs. Wilson says, "That is nonsense. He was much too ill to contemplate campaigning."

In spite of that the question is debatable. It is certainly true that Wilson was too ill to electioneer. But if the Democrats had nominated him by acclamation, which at one point nearly happened, weakness, doctors and Edith combined might not have prevented the old Covenanter from trying.

After one of those interminable wrangles typical of Democratic conventions under the Two-Thirds Rule, it ended with the nomination of a dark horse, James M. Cox, and a brilliant young man, Franklin D. Roosevelt.

When Wilson heard of Cox's nomination he said, "They've picked the weakest one."

Almost the first action of Cox and Roosevelt as nominees was to make a pilgrimage—that is the right word for it—to the White House. When they arrived, the President and Mrs. Wilson were waiting for them on the south portico. It was the first time young Roosevelt had seen the President since the *George Washington*. Edith saw the shock and pity in his sensitive face at the sight of his once vigorous chief. By now she was used to that reaction.

Looking back at the Roosevelt of those days Mrs. Wilson says, "He was socially wonderful—truly he could charm the birds off the trees. I thought him more charming than able then, but I changed my mind later because the rude discipline of polio changed him."

Although the Democratic platform favored America's joining the League of Nations, Cox had hesitated about making it a major issue of the campaign. Now, however, after greetings had been exchanged, he said politely, "Mr. President, I have always admired the fight you made for the League."

Before Edith's eyes Wilson's whole posture changed. His eyes glowed as the light of his fighting spirit shone through and his voice rang with youthful timbre as he said, "Mr. Cox, that fight can still be won!"

The visitors stayed for luncheon and heard Wilson repeat his previous comment that the election should be "a great and solemn referendum on the League of Nations."

As they were driving away Cox said to his young running mate, "Frank, we'll make the fight on the League."

Even as he said it Cox knew in his heart that the fight was lost.

The American people were fed up with idealism. Republican Candidate Warren G. Harding's slogan "Back to normalcy" expressed the feelings of the majority. As most of the political commentators pointed out, Cox was not running for President. Woodrow Wilson was running by deputy. But his deputy lacked the passionate eloquence to reignite the flame of American idealism.

However, Harding had good reason to be thankful for Wilson's idealism. Mrs. Wilson says that she was sitting with her husband on the south portico on another sunny morning when Tumulty came dashing out waving a piece of paper in a high state of glee. "Governor, we've got 'em beat!" he chortled. "Here's a paper that's been carefully researched and is absolutely true, showing that Harding has Negro blood in him. The country'll never stand for that!"

The President calmly finished his glass of milk and set it down. "Even if that is so," he said, "it will never be used with my consent. . . . We must base our campaign on principles, not backstairs gossip. That's not only right, but it's good politics. Kill this thing!"

Harding won by a landslide. As the Wilsons read the bulletins coming by direct wire to the White House Edith's heart ached when she saw the bitter disappointment etching lines of anguish in her husband's face. Next to the night the Treaty was defeated it was the most unhappy; even Wilson knew this was the end.

His only known comment on the President-elect was made to Grayson. "How can he lead when he doesn't know where he is going?" Wilson asked.

Long before Election Day, life in the White House had settled down to a rather monotonous routine. As early as March, 1920, the President had been able to resume the automobile rides that he and Edith loved so much. Wilson usually wore a cape for the same reason that Franklin Roosevelt later did—because it was easier for a handicapped man to get into than an overcoat.

Little Gordon Grayson, aged two, often went along. The charming young son of the Admiral became a great delight to Edith and her husband.

The work of the Presidency occupied only the mornings now. When it was done, there was lunch, a short nap and then the ride. After that there was the long evening to be filled. The President played innumerable games of Canfield, the solitaire which Edith had taught him when they were first married. He kept a record of all his scores, thousands of which are preserved in the Congressional Library. They show that he was 50,000 mythical dollars ahead of the bank. In addition, Mrs. Wilson says, "I read innumerable books to Woodrow—everything from Bagehot to detective stories. I hate detective stories."

Almost every evening there was a moving picture. Ray Stannard Baker happened to be a guest when they showed what in the circumstances was the most tragic picture he had ever seen.

The screen was set up at one end of the almost empty East Room whose frivolous gold and white décor and splendid crystal chandeliers made the absence of furniture seem especially grim. At the other end was the big sputtering projector and in between was a forlorn huddle of chairs and an armchair for the President. As the lights went down and the screen began to flicker, Baker realized that this was the first showing of a documentary of Wilson's trip to Europe.

With a kind of horror the reporter, who loved the President so well, saw the splendid pageantry of the *George Washington*'s arrival in Brest recreated before his eyes. On her bridge stood a young, vibrant Woodrow Wilson, smiling gaily and waving his hat to the crowds, with his beautiful happy wife beside him. Relentlessly the film followed the Wilsons through all their triumphs— driving through the Arc de Triomphe amid the delirious French; the royal pomp and splendor of England; the frenzied ovation in Rome; right on up to the great day at Versailles with the fountains playing and the guns firing and the happy people lovingly mobbing the smiling statesman who had brought them peace at last. . . .

Then the screen went blank. Admiral Grayson half lifted the

President to his feet, and "He turned slowly and shuffled out of the doorway. . . ." His face was almost expressionless, but Edith, following him swiftly, was for once unable to erase the grief from her face.

One of the Wilsons' pleasantest occupations was planning the house to which they would retire. They had never had a home outside the White House and were free to choose any place in America in which to live. First they narrowed the hunt down to Baltimore, Washington, Richmond, Boston and New York. Then they made a game of rating those cities. Edith drew a chart on a piece of note paper and they scored the five urban centers on climate, friends, freedom, amusements and libraries. New York won, but they chose the second high scorer, Washington, because the Library of Congress had the best facilities for the book the President wanted to write on government and, as Edith put it, "It was home to me."

Unfortunately all that was ever written of the book was the beautiful dedication, "To E.B.W. . . . who has shown me the full meaning of life. Her heart is not only true but wise; her thoughts are not only free but touched with vision . . . her unconscious interpretation of faith and duty makes all the way clear; her power to comprehend makes work and thought alike easier and more near to what it seeks—Woodrow Wilson."

Now Edith began looking for a house in earnest. Her brother Wilmer Bolling, who had been in the real estate business, brought her all the prospects he could dig up. First the Wilsons looked at pieces of land on which they could build their dream house. Wilson enjoyed going through architectural magazines, cutting out especially beautiful details of doorways, moldings and so forth.

But when they got preliminary plans they found that the high cost of building prohibited the dream house, so Edith set up a schedule of house-hunting. Since she would never leave her husband when he might need her, she started out at eight o'clock every morning, while the President was shaving and bathing. In this way she saw dozens of houses, several of which appealed to her. Finally she found the perfect place: a lovely old house shaded by fine trees on twenty-six acres of land near the Bureau of Standards. It was offered at a price they could afford. When the President saw it, he agreed that it was wonderful. Then his unbendable conscience dashed his wife's hopes. "The Bureau of Standards is going to have to expand," he said. "And they will need this land some day. It would embarrass the government to condemn land owned by an ex-President and it would embarrass me to keep it when the government needed it. We'll have to look some more."

Finally, almost as an afterthought, the real estate agent showed Mrs. Wilson a charming house on S Street near Massachusetts Avenue. It was made of brick with marble trim in the colonial style; large enough for dignity, small enough for comfort. There was an attractive terraced garden behind it and the rooms were filled with sunshine. Edith knew they could be happy there.

There was, of course, a hitch. The owner was not especially anxious to sell. Edith told her husband how much she liked it, but by this time she had had so many disappointments that she had little hope and continued her search. Then one day the President suggested that she go to a Philharmonic concert. She had given up this pleasure since his illness, but he was so insistent that she went now.

When she got back to the White House, she found the President sitting before a fire in the Oval Room looking as pleased as Punch. He handed her an impressive legal document that she saw in wonder was the deed to the S Street house. "I bought it for you hoping it would make up for my obstinacy about that house you wanted so much," he said, boyishly.

Wilson had managed the whole thing quietly through her brother. It was the only important transaction that he ever kept secret from her.

After the first flush of gratitude Edith had terrible qualms. She had seen the house only once; her husband had never seen it. Suppose he hated it! She had a rather bad night. The next day, December 15, they drove together to look it over. As their car

stopped in the curve of its small driveway, the previously instructed
Secret Service man leaped out and dug a small piece of sod from
the lawn. He handed it to the President, who gave it and a key to
Edith. "The sod's for the land and the key for the house," Woodrow said smiling. "It's an old Scotch custom."

Then they went through the house, happily planning the use of
the rooms, and necessary alterations. Wilson was charmed by it.
Edith need not have worried; she should have known that by now
their minds were so attuned that anything which pleased her would
delight him.

Their last month in the White House was a frantic time for
Edith. Since she did not get possession until February 4, she had
exactly twenty-eight days to make the new house ready for her
husband, and she was determined that there should be the minimum dislocation of his life and habits. There were a million things
for her to oversee concerning the alterations, installation of an
elevator and building a garage. Then there was the furniture. The
President's possessions had been stored in Princeton for eight years,
hers in Washington nearly as long. They arrived in great van loads
and had to be piled in the middle of rooms while the painters and
plasterers worked around them.

The last week Edith went to the house every night at ten o'clock
and worked there until 2:00 A.M. or later. One of her hardest
tasks was arranging her husband's personal library of 9,000 vol-
umes. It was a working library with few examples of beautiful
bindings. Wilson said to her, "It's not the covers that count but
what's inside 'em."

Shortly before Inauguration Day, Mrs. Wilson invited Mrs.
Harding to tea to look over the White House. The lady arrived in
a costume that Edith considered anything but smart, and she proceeded to talk like a fountain. Edith took one of her whole-hearted
dislikes to her.

When she introduced Mrs. Jaffrey, the White House housekeeper
of whom she had grown very fond, to the new first lady, Mrs.

Harding put her nose glasses on over her veil and only acknowledged the introduction with a brief nod. This confirmed Mrs. Wilson's conviction that her successor would be a hard person to
please.

March 4, 1921, was a fine day for an inaugural. By nine o'clock
the White House was swarming with cabinet officers, senators, congressmen and their wives. Mrs. Wilson entertained them until she
heard the cars of the President-elect's party. Then she hurried
upstairs to get her husband. Edith was worried about how the
emotional strain of this day would affect him. But she found Woodrow already dressed in his cutaway looking very cheerful. For the
last time Brooks handed the President his high silk hat and gloves.
Then leaning heavily on his cane, with Edith beside him, Wilson
walked to the little elevator where they had met so many ages ago.

They reached the Blue Room just as the Hardings came in accompanied by the Vice-President-elect and Mrs. Coolidge. The
Hardings were bluff and hearty. Coolidge looked as unhappy as
the last time Edith had seen him that tumultuous day in Boston.

Then Wilson and Harding got into the first open car and Mrs.
Wilson preceded Mrs. Harding into the second. They drove slowly
out of the White House circle with Mrs. Harding shouting greetings to the newspapermen standing on the grass. "They're my
boys!" she explained, beaming happily.

Meanwhile, as the Presidential car drove through the cheers
down Pennsylvania Avenue, Harding was chattering exuberantly
to the President about his love of pets. "You know, I've always
wanted to own an elephant some day," he said.

"I hope it won't turn out to be a white elephant," said Wilson.

In those days it was the custom for the President and President-
elect to enter the Capitol by the cascade of steps in front. Since
Wilson obviously could not climb them, arrangements had been
made for him to enter on the ground floor under the stairway.
However, when the car reached the Capitol, Harding jumped out
and ran gaily up the steps, leaving the President to go in alone.

Mrs. Harding took off after her husband like a bighorn and Edith followed her steaming with rage.

As soon as she could, Edith joined her husband in the President's Room, where he was sitting at the desk surrounded by his Cabinet, signing last-minute documents, and greeting his friends in Congress who came to pay their respects. Edith sat down nearby wishing for his sake that it were all over; smiling a little as the President cracked jokes with Josephus Daniels.

Then there was an influx of other people. According to custom the Joint Committee of the House and Senate had come to report to the President. The accident of seniority made a moment of drama, for Senator Lodge was its spokesman. Edith saw the little senator's face stiff with hatred as he icily spoke the traditional words, "Mr. President, we have come as a Committee of the Senate to notify you that the Senate and House have finished their business and await your pleasure."

There was a quizzical half-smile on the President's face as looking into the eyes of his enemy he said almost gently, "Senator Lodge, I have no further communications to make. Thank you for your courtesy. Good morning."

It seemed only a moment more before the clock began to boom out the strokes of noon. As it struck, Woodrow Wilson removed from his tie the scarf pin of California gold with the presidential seal and slipped it into his pocket. Then he rose and moved slowly toward the door where Harding was waiting. Grasping his successor's hand he said, "Mr. President, I wish you all the luck in the world!"

Then quite suddenly the Wilsons were alone except for Admiral Grayson, Randolph Bolling and two Secret Service men. From the Capitol they drove to S Street in a White House car. The avenues were as empty as on "Sunday at church time." Apparently the whole world was gathered at the Capitol and along Pennsylvania Avenue to acclaim the new President.

Edith was still boiling at the thought of Harding leaving her husband and running up the front steps alone. She expressed her opinion of his "discourtesy" in very certain terms. Her husband just laughed at her. "Harding's a good fellow," he said. "He meant no harm. He was just eager. . . ."

When the car turned into Massachusetts Avenue and came to S Street they had a surprise. A crowd of at least 20,000 people filled the street in front of their new home from the avenue all the way up the hill. When they saw Wilson they began to cheer, not exultantly but with a sort of affection that was infinitely touching. He waved his hat to them smiling tenderly and Edith smiled and waved through sudden tears.

So as he entered his new home Woodrow Wilson realized at least one ambition he had always cherished. For here was proof that the people loved him.

CHAPTER XVIII

"WELL, I AM READY"

WHEN THE WILSONS ENTERED their new home Edith was amazed. She had left it forty-eight hours before in a state of chaos. Now every picture was hung, every chair in place and the sunny rooms were radiant with flowers sent by friends. The miracle had been achieved by her brother Wilmer and the combined efforts of their new staff and their old friends who had served them in the White House; none of them had slept that night.

Margaret Wilson joined the party for luncheon in the new dining room overlooking the gay, terraced garden which was enclosed by a brick wall. It was a carefree meal. Wilson was in high spirits and lingered at the table, cracking jokes. Finally Admiral Grayson said, "Mr. President . . ."

"Just Woodrow Wilson," said his host, smiling.

"Mr. Wilson," Grayson said, "it's been an exciting day. I think you should excuse yourself and get some rest."

So Edith and her husband went up to his room in the new automatic elevator. Miss Powderly, Wilson's favorite nurse on loan from the Navy, was his first pleasant surprise. Then she swung the door open, and Edith enjoyed the amazed delight on her husband's face as he surveyed the room.

Every piece of his personal furniture—chairs, footstools, writing table, pillows and lamps—was in the same relative position that it had occupied in his room in the White House when he left that morning. And looking immense, even in that big sunny room, stood an exact replica of the Lincoln bed her husband had liked so much. Edith had had the copy especially made as a surprise. The logistics of this quick transfer of goods and chattels from the White House had been worked out and supervised by Brooks and Ike Hoover as their final token of devotion to the President they had served so well.

The house on S Street became a happy home. Both Mrs. Wilson and her husband loved it. From the street level one entered a rather formal hall with a black and white marble floor from which a broad stairway mounted to the second floor. Facing the garden were the dining room, a pleasant library, and, between them, a delightful little solarium arranged as a study with French windows opening on the garden, which was almost at the second-floor level, due to rising ground. On the other side of the house was a long drawing room for formal entertaining.

The five bedrooms and baths were on the third floor, and on the ground floor, in addition to the hall, were the kitchen, a billiard room, powder rooms and an office called the "Dugout," where Randolph Bolling, who had become Mr. Wilson's secretary, sat, like an Indian chief in mufti, guarding the Wilsons' privacy and working with unselfish devotion on the great scrapbooks which recorded all the doings of the Wilsons from the day they announced their engagement. These are now in the Congressional Library.

Nearly every room in the house had a fireplace, and those 9,000 books overflowed into every corner. There were even great piles of them stacked at one end of the billiard room. Wilson once told his wife that though he had not read them all he thought he knew the contents of each and every one.

To take care of the house Mrs. Wilson hired a devoted Negro

couple named Isaac and Mary Scott, who remained with her for many years. Recently, toward the end of his life, Scott grew so feeble that virtually his only duty was locking the big front door at night. One evening Edith found him struggling into his white jacket for this ceremonial gesture. She held it for him, and after that she often managed to happen by just in time to give Scott a helping hand.

Both Mrs. Wilson and Admiral Grayson had worried for fear the change of scene would have a depressing effect on their beloved invalid. On the contrary, he bloomed in his new surroundings, seeming stronger every day. The only thing he missed was the chiming of the many clocks in the White House. So Edith had a tall mahogany grandfather clock with Westminster chimes made for him—at Galt's, of course.

A pleasant routine was soon established. The Wilsons got up about seven, and breakfasted together in dressing gowns, sometimes upstairs, or in the solarium on sunny days. Then they would go down to the Dugout and work with Randolph on the mail— great stacks of letters came nearly every day. After that Wilson would exercise by walking back and forth across the hall until he was tired. Incidentally, President Harding had thoughtfully ordered Admiral Grayson to duty in Washington so he could remain close to his famous patient.

Then Wilson went upstairs and shaved, a long difficult process which he insisted on performing himself. After that came lunch and an hour's rest. At three o'clock the Wilsons received visitors in the library until it was time to go for their afternoon ride. When the government turned in Wilson's favorite Pierce-Arrow touring car for a new one, Wilson bought the old car from the company and had it painted in Princeton colors—orange and black.

In the evening Wilson usually put on his dressing gown and had his dinner in front of the library fire. Mrs. Wilson says that he would not think of going into the dining room unless he was properly dressed. The evenings varied. Sometimes Edith read to her husband; sometimes they had a moving picture shown in the library, and occasionally members of the family or the Graysons came to dinner.

Saturday nights were special. They almost always went to Keith's Vaudeville House or the theater. Woodrow Wilson loved the theater too much to give it up even now, however difficult it was for him to attend a performance. The first time he went after his illness was on February 1, 1921, while he was still President. The play was John Drinkwater's *Abraham Lincoln,* at the National Theatre. The President, Mrs. Wilson and Randolph Bolling sat in the second box from the stage. As he limped into his seat, the President was greeted with cheers and hand-clapping, but that was nothing compared to the great ovation he received when the final curtain fell. Apparently the audience associated the tragic story on the stage with this President who had spent his strength and almost his life to serve them.

The Wilsons' appearances at Keith's were much more informal. Seats were always reserved for them at the rear, near a convenient side entrance. The audience always rose and clapped when he came in, but it was no novelty, for they were almost all regulars.

The last time the Wilsons went to the theater together was on December 24, 1923. Olsen and Johnson were playing in one of their rowdy slapstick revues which Wilson loved and Edith enjoyed for the pleasure of seeing her husband's belly laughs.

At the finale that Christmas Eve, the whole company was on stage in front of a huge fireplace surrounded by Christmas trees, mistletoe and holly. Over the fireplace was a large picture of Woodrow Wilson. As the curtain rose the audience burst into applause. Chick Johnson bounded onto the stage as a jolly, noisy Santa. Nan Halpern came to the front of the stage and wished the audience, "Merry Christmas to you, and you, and you . . ." Then turning toward the picture of Wilson she said, "And to you an abundance of Yuletide's blessing and a bountiful year," and kissed his pictured face, while show girls came down the aisle with armfuls of roses which they laid beside Mr. Wilson's wheelchair.

Olsen later said that after one chorus of "Auld Lang Syne" they had intended to wind up the show in their zany "hellzapoppin" style, but the audience took it away from them: "At the first notes of the song every last person in that house stood up and facing the former President began to sing with the orchestra—it wasn't ordinary singing either, but as though the audience sensed that this was to be Mr. Wilson's last Christmas on earth. They sang with such heartfelt emotion that Mr. Wilson bowed his head and covered his eyes with his right hand. . . .

"There was utter silence when it ended, that lasted and lasted until Chick stepped forward with his cheeks glistening with tears and said, 'Merry Christmas, Mr. President.'

"Woodrow Wilson looked up. In a voice that carried through that hushed house he said, 'Merry Christmas to you all, and God bless you!' "

Wilson's first public appearance after leaving the White House was at the burial of the Unknown Soldier in Arlington on Friday, November 11, 1921. When the rather stiffly worded invitation came, Edith, ever fearful of emotional strain for him, asked, "Do you think you had better undertake it?"

"I *must* go," said Woodrow Wilson. "Randolph, please call on the Secretary [of War] and make the arrangements. Tell him that I should prefer to go in an open carriage rather than a motor."

Fortunately November 11 was a fine sunny day. In a hired victoria with a Negro coachman and Scott, wearing a rather battered slouch hat, on the box, Mr. and Mrs. Wilson were at the east front of the capitol at 8:25 A.M. The procession was forming with considerable confusion and no official appeared to guide them to their assigned place, "immediately preceding the Associate Justices of the Supreme Court." The Supreme Court went on its way and still the former President seemed forgotten. Edith finally ordered the driver to wedge into line—"Crashing the gate," she called it.

The long cortege moved up Pennsylvania Avenue to slow solemn music between somber sorrowful crowds who stood in respectful silence as the body of the Unknown Soldier went by.

Then a strange and rather wonderful thing happened. Almost at the end of that procession of sorrowful pomp and high official mourning came what must have seemed like an apparition from the past—an old-fashioned open carriage in which rode an old-fashioned gentleman in a glistening high silk hat and beside him his lovely wife dressed in black. As they saw them the somber crowd broke into almost hysterical cheers. They surged through the police lines and surrounded the carriage. American Legion men in their old service uniforms quickly formed an impromptu cordon around the carriage as they had on that first Armistice Day. Then, guarded once more by his boys, the President continued to West Executive Avenue, where, according to the formal instructions of the Secretary of War, he left the procession. Wilson had wanted to go all the way to Arlington.

However, when Edith and Woodrow returned to their house they found more evidence that he was not forgotten. Once again S Street was crowded with people cheering for what one journalist called "The Known Soldier."

Nor had the rest of the world forgotten Wilson. In 1920, while he was still President, he was awarded the Nobel Peace Prize, and in 1922 Poland gave him the Order of the White Eagle, the only foreign decoration he ever accepted.

Mrs. Wilson says that he wore it just once, at a family dinner in honor of her mother's eightieth birthday. It was a fancy dress party with Edith costumed as a harem wife; Randolph as an Indian chief —out of mufti—Wilmer as a shiek, and the others in equally exotic costumes. Edith notes how handsome her husband looked in white tie and tails with the jeweled star of the order on a broad blue ribbon lying diagonally across his chest.

Almost all the "greats" who came to Washington called to pay their respects at S Street. Among them was Margot Asquith, gushing like a broken hydrant and doing a strip tease to show them how cleverly her dress was designed, much to Randolph's embarrassment.

Most welcome of all was the old Tiger of France. Mrs. Wilson says that he looked younger than before as he shed his fur-lined coat in the hall and fairly skipped up the stairs, ignoring the elevator. Clemenceau kissed his old antagonist on both cheeks, and they had a wonderful talk about old times and new problems. "How merry the old man was!" Mrs. Wilson commented.

But when he said goodbye to her downstairs, there were tears in the Tiger's eyes. "I was deeply touched," Mrs. Wilson says.

Late in July 1923, Mrs. Wilson gave Isaac and Mary Scott a well-deserved vacation of two weeks. Five days later on August 2, Scott appeared in his white jacket to serve lunch. In answer to her astonished query, "What are you doing here?" he said that he and Mary had decided that they had been away long enough.

But when she questioned him alone he said, "I went to bed last night with no thought of coming home, but I suddenly woke wide awake as though somebody called me and said, 'Mr. Wilson needs you. Go home!' "

So he and Mary had caught the 6:00 A.M. bus. "I really expected to find Mr. Wilson sick," he said, "but I'm mighty glad to see he isn't."

Edith was upset. She believed in Scott's extrasensory perception to the point that she had a feeling of doom hanging over them. All that afternoon she worried, and that evening she went uneasily to bed. Hardly had she reached her room when the excited voices of newsboys shouting "Wuxtra! Wuxtra!" echoed and reverberated back and forth on the quiet street. Through the unintelligible din one voice came clear: "Death of the President!"

Edith was both shocked and relieved. Scott's premonition of disaster was for Harding.

Woodrow Wilson was genuinely saddened by his successor's death. He had always regarded Harding as a good fellow with a kind heart. Never once had he voiced a criticism of the President, and when Admiral Grayson once said something derogatory about Harding, Wilson said, "No, Doctor. We mustn't criticize the President, because we don't know the facts as he knows them. . . . I have had enough experience of that kind of injustice to feel a sympathy for President Harding."

The funeral ceremony was held at the White House on August 8, 1923. With Admiral Grayson the Wilsons arrived promptly at the appointed hour. Because Mr. Wilson was so lame they did not go in, but sat in the car waiting for the procession to the Capitol where the President was to lie in state. As she sat beside her husband Edith thought how strange it was that they should be attending the funeral of the young, vigorous man who had run up the Capitol steps just a little over two years ago.

In that torrid sunny Washington day they sat waiting in the open car for nearly an hour. Young Marines in full panoply were keeling over to be dragged aside by their comrades, but to Edith's anxious eyes her husband seemed impervious to the heat.

It took a strange incident to ruffle him. As the procession was forming at last a frantic cavalry colonel galloped up and said to the former President, "May I ask you a question, sir?"

"Certainly, Colonel," was the answer.

"Do you know where I can find Senator Lodge?"

In a voice so chilly that it almost turned the colonel's sweat to icicles Woodrow Wilson said, "I am not Senator Lodge's keeper."

Then as their car moved slowly into its appointed place in line Wilson commented, "That colonel must be crazy."

Since early spring Woodrow Wilson had been made increasingly anxious by the signs of the times—the American rush to materialistic conservatism and the unease throughout the rest of the world. He decided to write an essay to guide his fellow countrymen. He had his old typewriter set up, but found that because of his useless left hand he could not use it, so Edith undertook to write at his dictation.

It was a long business, for Wilson was as meticulous about polishing and rephrasing every sentence as though he realized that it would be his last written message to the world. Mrs. Wilson says, "Woodrow always had a great big fire burning in his room all night long, and he did not always realize it was not daytime. Sometimes he'd call me at three or four o'clock in the morning. He'd dictate a single sentence. Then we would talk a little, and I would go back to bed. Sometimes he'd call me again at six for another sentence."

"The Road Away From Revolution" was an eloquent plea for the revival of enlightened liberalism to counteract the dangers that the Russian Revolution had made evident. The sum and pith of it lay in the sentence, "Our civilization cannot survive materially unless it be redeemed spiritually."

When the booklet was finished Edith very nearly was, too. She was so worn and nervous that Admiral Grayson urgently advised her to get away for a rest. So she went to stay for a week with her friends the Charles Sumner Hamlins, in their big, old-fashioned house at Mattapoisett on Buzzard's Bay. It was the longest time she was ever separated from her husband in all their married life.

When she came home early in September, the brief absence enabled her to see with "startling clarity" that Woodrow had begun to fail. Grayson was terribly worried. He writes that although Mr. Wilson appeared to improve up to the summer of 1923, "He had general arteriosclerosis which made final recovery impossible."

In the autumn of 1923, the symptoms increased alarmingly. Years before he became President, Wilson had lost most of the sight of one eye through a hemorrhage. Now, Grayson writes, "His good eye began to fail, there were minute hemorrhages in the retina. Though he kept his courage and was frequently as cheerful as he had ever been . . . he discovered that he had difficulty recognizing people on the street from his motor car, as well as great difficulty in reading . . . new glasses did not remedy the difficulty. This was a sign of progressive arteriosclerosis."

Grayson was too good a friend to try to fool Edith about her husband's condition; and she had too much courage to try to fool herself. Nor was Woodrow Wilson given to self-delusion. All of them knew that there was very little prospect for anything but a continued deterioration of his health.

In that heart-breaking time Edith never allowed herself to falter. With her husband, at least, she was as gay a companion as ever, and, except for brief periods of depression, he too kept up the game. In fact, by the strength of their minds and characters they were frequently able to shove the future into the background and enjoy many hours of real happiness.

And a great many people still came to S Street—in September the house was suddenly full of Sayres, and Wilson had a fine time with his grandchildren.

In October Mr. and Mrs. Lloyd George came for tea with their daughter Megan. Now that they were no longer antagonists Edith could say, "Mr. Lloyd George was always a charming companion. . . ."

A little later in the month came a really delightful break. Bernard Baruch's daughter, Belle, wrote that she and her friend Evangeline Johnson had a wonderful plan to promote interest in the League of Nations and would like to see Mr. Wilson. Not knowing these women, but well aware of how hard they had worked for the League, Edith invited them to dinner the following Saturday and then to go on to Keith's. Thus she met two of her greatest friends of later years.

"Those girls stand out like birds of brilliant plumage against a dark sky," she wrote. They were both in their early twenties and both were over six feet tall, a striking pair in their long velvet evening gowns from Paris and splendid jewels. But if they looked like birds they were not bird-brains. On the contrary, they both had what Wilson might have called "first-class minds," and rollicking senses of humor as well. Their great plan was for him to make a radio address about the League on the eve of Armistice Day. Ill as he was, Mr. Wilson embraced the idea with enthusiasm.

He had two weeks to prepare his speech. In the old days he

could have done this in a few hours, or, indeed, delivered a master-
piece impromptu. Now it was a terrible strain as he dictated
sentence by sentence, often in the middle of the night.

On November 10, the radio technicians wired the house for
sound. At eight-thirty that evening Woodrow Wilson was before
the microphone in the library. He stood in his dressing gown leaning on his cane, for he always said he could speak well only on his
feet. Edith stood beside him with a carbon copy of the speech
ready to prompt if he should falter. He did not falter.

Making a tremendous effort, he mustered, for those brief moments, his ancient oratorical power. Castigating America's with-
drawal into "a sullen and selfish isolation," he proclaimed that,
"The only way in which we can worthily give proof of our apprecia-
tion of Armistice Day is by resolving to put self-interest away, and
once more formulate and act upon the highest ideals and purposes
of international policy.

"Thus, and only thus, can we return to the true traditions of
America."

Listening to his voice go out to hundreds of thousands, perhaps
millions of listeners, Edith could only think of how their lives and,
indeed, the history of all the world might have been changed had
the radio been developed just four years earlier.

The speech cost Wilson heavily in strength and nervous exhaustion. The process of disintegration was quickened. But he
still had spirit for a few more gay days. One was the night at
Olsen and Johnson's. Then Margaret Wilson and Helen Bones
came for family Christmas. Wilson's sixty-eighth birthday was
December 28, 1923. When he and Edith came out for their afternoon ride that day he got a thrilling surprise. In front of the door
stood a superb Rolls Royce bought for him by friends and admirers. He was told it had interchangeable bodies, limousine and
touring car, and it was painted in the Princeton colors. The open
body was on it now. It was a very chilly winter day; nevertheless
he and Edith bundled up well and had a "lovely ride."

However, Wilson did not have long to enjoy his fine new car. On January 16 he received 125 members of the Democratic National Committee, with all of whom he shook hands. Afterward he seemed exhausted. Edith had a rare attack of grippe and for six days did not dare go close to him for fear he would catch it.

When she recovered, Admiral Grayson, who looked almost as exhausted as his patient, prepared to go to South Carolina for a week's shooting with Bernard Baruch. As he came to say goodbye Edith asked him fearfully, "Woodrow seems so weak, do you think there is any immediate danger?"

"No," Grayson said, pressing her hand reassuringly. "If I did I would not leave him. But if you want me to give up the trip I will."

Considerably comforted, Edith went up to her husband's room. He looked so depressed that she asked, "Are you feeling badly?"

"I always feel badly now, little girl," he answered. "Somehow I hate to see Grayson go."

"He's still downstairs," Edith said quickly. "Let me run and tell him. I know he'll stay."

Wilson caught her hand. "No," he said, "that would be a selfish thing to do. He needs the change. . . ."

On January 29 Woodrow Wilson could not sleep. He was so restless and hot that at 1:00 A.M. Edith said to Randolph, "Telegraph Grayson to come back."

The next morning Wilson dictated a few letters, but by evening he was so ill that Mrs. Wilson sent for Drs. Ruffin and Fowler. Early the next morning, January 31, Grayson arrived. He and Edith went into the bedroom where his patient lay. The former President smiled weakly at his little admiral and said, "I guess the old machine is worn out."

Then after a moment he added, "Well, I am ready."

When they left the room Grayson's face was chalk white under his black brows and hair; his eyes dark pits of misery. "There is very little hope," he told Edith. "You had better send for his daughters."

Grayson has noted his diagnosis of Mr. Wilson's condition: "On January 31, 1924, there came a sudden turn for the worse. His stomach ceased to function and the kidneys were involved. Contrary to popular impression, he did not have a second stroke of paralysis. . . ."

Margaret Wilson arrived that afternoon. Nell had started on her way from California but Jessie was with her husband in Siam. That night Margaret was reading to her father while Edith snatched a moment's rest in the next room. He seemed to lose consciousness and Margaret put down the book. His eyes were closed; his body, lying so quietly beneath the covers, seemed as small as a child's. In a dreamy voice he said, "Perhaps it is as well that the League failed."

At Margaret's startled gasp his eyes flew open and there was a familiar gleam of humor in them. "You think I'm wandering," he said quite strongly, "but I'm not. I meant what I said. If the Treaty had been ratified it would have been a great personal triumph for me. But the American people were not ready for it, and so in the end it would have failed. God did not will it that way. Some day, when the people are prepared, it will come about in the right way. . . ."

Through the next day and the next Woodrow Wilson in his great carved bed had fitful moments of consciousness. Edith sat beside him almost all the time thinking she knows not what, perhaps not thinking at all; it was better not to. Each time, after a brief absence, she returned to the room, her husband roused himself. "He would lift his hand and take mine. . . ."

On February 3, 1924, one of those unexpected bright spring days that light Washington's somber winter, while the church bells were calling the people to worship and thousands of men and women knelt praying outside the house on S Street, Woodrow Wilson died.

EPILOGUE

HER FAMILY AND HER FEW CLOSE FRIENDS who saw Edith Wilson the day that her husband died said to each other, "She is wonderful." She was not wonderful; she just felt that her life had ended, too, and was mercifully numbed to the ravages of emotion. The long, stringent discipline of the years of public life and the years of private sorrow enabled her to carry on automatically.

Only to Altrude Gordon Grayson, who came to see her that morning, did she make a momentary revelation. They talked for a few moments and then Mrs. Wilson took her into her husband's room. The President lay with his eyes closed as though asleep. His face was strong but gentle, for death had smoothed away the marks of care and passion, leaving only the lineaments of his great spirit. He looked so young that his hair seemed prematurely white.

Edith Wilson stood for a long time looking down at her beloved. Then in an expression of sorrow and pride and love and awe she said, "Oh, the majesty of death!"

Eighty-eight years is a long, long life, and eight years a short time to have lived fully. That is the way it has been with Edith Wilson.

Not that she retired into lachrymose widowhood. She was much too intelligent and forceful, and her spirit of gaiety was too strong for that. The things she did just did not seem important to her. When she was questioned about any incident that occurred during eighty years of the eighty-eight she invariably asked, "Why would anybody want to know about that?"

Yet she has enjoyed an unusually crowded and even glamorous life.

The President's funeral was Mrs. Wilson's last public appearance for over a year. Wilson had said to her at President Harding's funeral, "Don't let them give me a great public ceremony like this." Following his wish Edith arranged a small private service in the house on S Street. But the interment in the chapel of Washington's unfinished National Cathedral was solemnly ceremonious, with President Coolidge and nearly all the leaders of America present.

During the following year Edith remained in almost complete seclusion while she gradually came to life again. She was, however, kept extremely busy answering more than 8,000 telegrams and letters of condolence. Fortunately for her pocketbook as a presidential widow she had the customary privilege of franking her mail, but this meant that she had to sign the envelope of every letter. (Congress later passed an act permitting her to use a rubber stamp with a facsimile signature.) In addition Woodrow Wilson had made her executrix of his $250,000 estate.

After the year had passed she began to make public appearances, always in connection with ceremonies in her husband's memory or to further matters in which he believed. Altrude Gordon Grayson says, "Mrs. Wilson never went in for causes, except her great Cause. She always hesitated to use the name she bore for anything like raising money. She devoted a great deal of time to correspondence and contacts concerning the President."

And Mrs. Wilson herself says, "I never gave interviews. I have always felt that the wife of a former President should not speak in public."

However, she remained an ardent Democrat, for that, too, was part of the Cause.

Gradually Edith Wilson's irrepressible gaiety revived. Once again she indulged her love of travel. During the twenties and thirties she went to Europe seven times, once around the world, and twice to Japan. Her trips abroad were almost a royal progress, for the heads of many of the countries she visited sought to honor the late President by honoring her. On every trip Mrs. Wilson always attended at least one session of the League of Nations in Geneva.

Wilmer Bolling and Belle Baruch were her favorite traveling companions. When Belle was along she was sure of gaiety and amusing adventures. Twice Edith stayed in a supposedly haunted castle that Bernard Baruch had rented in Scotland. It reminded her of the peculiar construction of the Bolling house in Virginia, because each room had a separate staircase. The first night, she carried a candle up the winding vaulted stairway to her room and nervously closed the heavy wooden door, which had no lock. Then the haunts began. Such moans and groans and rattles sounded through the door that Edith with the strength of terror pushed a big armoire against the door. To this day no one can convince her that castle was not full of ghosts.

After leaving Scotland she motored with Belle and Wilmer through Czechoslovakia to Prague. There President Masaryk insisted they stay at the palace. He escorted Edith to her suite of five enormous rooms. "If you hear people walking through the rooms do not be alarmed," the President said. "The guards patrol all the rooms all night long."

Edith discovered a bathtub in "a sort of cubbyhole," and immediately decided to wash away the grime from her long dusty drive. No sooner was she relaxed in hot water than she heard the outer door open. Thinking it was the guard, she says, "I slid completely under water. It was so dirty by that time that he could not have seen a thing."

However, the intruder turned out to be a woman, "who looked nine feet tall." She was only bringing her the pictures taken of their arrival.

In 1929 Edith went around the world to Japan with her cousin, Dr. Rudolph Teusler, his wife, son and two teen-age daughters. Dr. Teusler, who was the son of her Aunt Jeff's romantic marriage to the wounded German-Confederate soldier, had founded St. Luke's International Hospital in Tokyo. It was completely destroyed by the earthquake of 1923, but he raised funds in America and Europe to rebuild it in what was dazzling modern style for Japan in that era.

After visiting Paris and Geneva, the party sailed east from Marsailles in the Japanese ship *Harauna Maru.* Somewhat ironically, Edith occupied the "Kaiser's Suite." En route she visited Cairo, Colombo, Singapore and Hong Kong, landing at Shanghai after a five weeks' voyage. From there they went to Peking by train. "Peking is the most fascinating city I have ever seen," Mrs. Wilson says.

Her room, high in the southwest corner of the hotel, commanded a magnificent view of the Forbidden City about whose curving, blue-tiled roofs and dragon-guarded gardens she wrote lyrical letters to Randolph. In addition she was kept busy attending twenty-course banquets given in her honor by the rich Chinese and the Diplomatic Corps.

From Peking they went by train to Mukden in Manchuria and then across the Sea of Japan to Tokyo, where the Japanese government did great honor to the widow of President Wilson. She could pay for nothing. Passes were given to her on all railroads, bus lines and every government-owned building.

One night the Emperor's brother, Prince Chichibu, gave a Western-style dinner in her honor. At dinner Mrs. Wilson sat on Prince Chichibu's right. At one point she thought he asked her if she liked "rare fish."

"I don't know, Your Highness," Edith said.

So the Prince clapped his hands and servants produced *raw* fish running with blood. Edith says, "I had to tell him I couldn't go it."

She had much more fun at the pearl farms of Mr. Mikimoto, who made a great fortune by discovering how to annoy an oyster into producing a pearl. With her aged, wispy little host she sailed out to view the beds in a high-sided open boat of ancient design. It was rowed by stalwart Japanese with long-handled sweeps; they were rather like galley slaves except that they were grinning as happily as oysters at high tide.

There is a wonderful picture of Edith and her host fishing in the rain from a bow-shaped Japanese bridge. She is wearing a picture hat and a rather long afternoon dress. Mr. Mikimoto is in sandals, a black kimono and a derby hat. The top of his hat is just level with Edith's broad shoulders.

Mrs. Wilson arrived home late in December 1929. On June 17, 1931, she was off again in the *Leviathan* to attend the unveiling of a statue of Woodrow Wilson in Poznan at the invitation of the President of Poland. The Poles, who attributed their independence to Woodrow Wilson, gave her a tremendous reception as she drove through Warsaw in the presidential cars paneled with the white eagles of Poland.

At Poznan she stayed in a great gloomy palace built by Kaiser Wilhelm II. There was a clamorous crowd in the square around Gutzon Borglum's statue of Woodrow Wilson, which was hidden under a mass of Polish and American flags. After cascades of oratory worthy of the Fourth of July (which, incidentally, it was), the President of Poland pulled the cords that dropped flags and revealed the statue. Edith gasped.

She wrote to Randolph, "The monument as a portrait is the worst thing I have ever seen. It is all out of drawing and there is no resemblance.

"Borglum and his wife and son were there, and when she asked me if I thought it good, I told her 'N-O.' "

At home Edith was heavily engaged in her Cause. There was nothing she would not do to further the ideals of Woodrow Wilson or honor his memory. She played a very active role as a director of the Woodrow Wilson Foundation, founded to promote international co-operation. Indeed, she practically ran the meetings of the board even while Franklin Roosevelt was its titular head.

She was active in making Wilson's birthplace, the Manse at Staunton, Virginia, a national shrine, and gave it most of the furnishings. In 1946 she presented the $50,000 she received from the motion picture *Woodrow Wilson* to the Staunton Foundation, of which she is still honorary president. At the age of eighty-five she served actively as a member of the Woodrow Wilson Centennial Commission, and attended all the ceremonies.

In addition to work on these foundations and commissions, she accepted every invitation and traveled to any place, no matter how small, where her husband's memory was to be honored.

Since the fortunes of the Democratic party were part of the Cause, Edith Wilson was always a militant Democrat, though as a President's widow she refused to play politics. She hardly ever made a political speech. One time that she did was at the Democratic Convention of 1928, in Houston, Texas.

She went there with former Ambassador to France Hugh Wallace and Mrs. Wallace in their private car. Bernard Baruch and Governor Ritchie of Maryland had also invited her to ride in their cars —those really were the good old days. In Houston Edith stayed with that financial giant of Texas, Jesse Jones. One night when the convention was in session, Mrs. Wilson says, "Mr. Jones took me up on the platform. Then without any warning to me at all he stepped on to the rostrum and announced to the delegates, 'Mrs. Woodrow Wilson will now address you.' "

As the cheers thundered around her head Edith saw she had no choice. When they died away, she stepped forward and addressed the Convention. As many a practiced feminine orator forgets to do, she pitched her voice as low and resonant as possible so that Permanent Chairman Claude Bowers, who happened to be at the rear of the hall, said that he heard every word.

But what those words were is lost to memory. When asked about her speech, Mrs. Wilson answered simply, "I said what I could."

The Convention nominated Governor Al Smith of New York. During the campaign former Ambassador Norman Davis took Mrs. Wilson over to Baltimore to hear him speak. "We had dinner together beforehand," she says, "and Al ate two dozen Lynhaven oysters. I said, 'I'm surprised you can eat before you speak. Mr. Wilson never could.'

"Said Al, 'I couldn't speak unless I ate.' "

Summing him up, Edith thinks that "Al Smith was a little crude, but a very nice man."

She went to the Chicago Convention of 1932 as the guest of Bernard Baruch. Also in his box were the Condé Nasts, Nell McAdoo and a beautiful young woman named Clare Booth Brokaw. For the famous all-night session which nominated Franklin Roosevelt, Mrs. Wilson arrived at the Convention Hall at 9:00 P.M. There is a picture of her taken at nine the following morning looking as fresh as though she had just bathed and dressed after a good night's sleep.

Edith was so enthusiastic about Roosevelt that she actually campaigned for him. After he was elected she was a frequent guest at the White House. On one occasion when she was at a small dinner there, President Roosevelt said, "How do you like these wine glasses, Mrs. Wilson? I got them off the *George Washington* for five cents apiece."

Edith duly admired them. Then she told Roosevelt that when the *George Washington* was being broken up, Secretary Daniels had offered her husband the beautiful desk he had used on the crossings. "I can't take it," Wilson said. "It belongs to the government."

"No it doesn't," Daniels corrected. "It was a personal gift to you from Rodman Wanamaker."

Wilson said that being the case he would like it very much. A few days later Daniels called back very red in the face to say the desk had disappeared. "We never found out what happened to it," Edith concluded.

President Roosevelt laughed in glee. "I can tell you," he said. "I have it. And what's more, you're not going to get it away from me."

Edith looked the President of the United States straight in the eye and said, "You're nothing but a common thief."

However, this exchange did not break their friendship. Edith realized that Franklin Roosevelt's desire for the desk stemmed from his great admiration for her husband. But in Galileian fashion she says, "All the same, it's my desk."

Age has not dimmed Mrs. Wilson's dedication to the Democratic party. During the campaign of 1960 she refused to go to the Manse at Staunton when President Eisenhower spoke there; not because she did not like him—she liked Ike very much—but because she felt her presence might be publicly construed as support for his party.

During the same election an unfortunate gentleman who was calling on her had a Nixon-Lodge sticker on his car. When she saw it Mrs. Wilson's eyes lighted with a fire that made her guest tremble. "Don't you ever park a car with that thing on it in *my* driveway again!" she said.

During the twenties and thirties several of Wilson's former associates and opponents published their memoirs, among them Tumulty, Lansing, Lodge and Colonel House.

Mrs. Wilson's own book, *My Memoir,* was published in 1939. "I wrote the first part of my book on the train," she says. "I was so mad after reading Colonel House's book that I just started to write furiously. Then I continued to write at home. But I never expected to publish it. I was writing the truth for my own satisfaction."

Then Bernard Baruch came to stay at S Street. After reading the manuscript he said, "You must publish this book."

"It's not good enough," Edith replied. "I don't know how to write."

"It is good enough to have kept me up until one o'clock this morning," Baruch said. "Mark James has been helping me with a book. I'll send him to you."

"I don't think he can help," Edith said stubbornly. "I can't publish it."

"I command you to," said Bernard Baruch.

In due course Marquis James came to stay at S Street. Twice winner of the Pulitzer Prize for biography, James was a wise and humorous gentleman whose seamed and craggy face showed his Cherokee blood. After studying Mrs. Wilson's manuscript he said, "I can't change it. It's yours and I would spoil it. Just leave out a few of the nasty remarks you made about Colonel House and some of the others."

So it was done. In it you will find little about Edith's life before she married Woodrow Wilson, and the book ends with his death. Her other memories did not seem to her worth recording.

The success of *My Memoir* amazed Mrs. Wilson. The *Saturday Evening Post* paid her $40,000 for the first serial rights, which she gave to her brother Randolph. He invested it and when he died in 1951, left it to her in his will; it had tripled in value.

When the book itself came out the reviews were generally highly favorable. In the *Saturday Review* William Allen White wrote, "She has told her story unselfconsciously out of her heart. . . ." On the first page of the *New York Times* Book Review it was called "A book that humanizes the President without detracting from his dignity," and the review added, "Curiously enough it is the first volume of memoirs ever written by the wife of an American President."

Anyone who writes anything important must expect some mudslinging from the unsympathetic. Old Admiral Hugh Rodman got in a terrible temper over Mrs. Wilson's description of the inept seamanship that nearly capsized the President's launch the day he reviewed the fleet in Seattle. And one Washington columnist made the astounding statement that "The mind of Edith Bolling Wilson

looks like a smudge pot beside Eleanor Roosevelt as she reveals
herself in her biography [*sic*] of Woodrow Wilson."

But in *My Day,* Mrs. Roosevelt herself wrote in praise of it.

The publicity attendant on publishing the book also brought
Edith a great new flood of odd letters. The following is a spirited
example:

ANDOVER, CONNECTICUT, RFD 2

DEAR MADAME:

Kindly give me a good 300 acre farm promptly.
Kindly attend to this matter promptly.
I hope to hear from you favorably promptly.

Truly yours,
GEORGE E. WHITE

To all who live beyond the normal span sorrow and loss and
loneliness are bound to come. Edith Wilson has watched almost
all the people dearest to her go. First her mother, and then in
1933, Alexander Galt, at whose home she had met her first husband. Bertha Bolling died in her old apartment at the Powhatan
Hotel in 1935. Admiral Grayson died suddenly in 1938 when he
was only fifty-nine, after further distinguishing himself during
Franklin Roosevelt's administration as head of the Red Cross.

Finally in 1951, both Wilmer Bolling and faithful Randolph
died. Of her own contemporaries there is left only Miss Benham,
who is the widow of Admiral James M. Helm, and Altrude Gordon
Grayson, now Mrs. George L. Harrison.

Of Mrs. Wilson's own generation of Bollings, the rugged sur-
vivor was her sister Gertrude (Mrs. Alexander Galt) who, aged
ninety-eight, lived with her on S Street.

But even such shocks as these could not quench Edith Wilson's
spirit. Her relatives and old friends say she has mellowed through
the years, but not so much as to lose the sharp tang of wit in her
speech, nor to damp the frightening fire in her eyes if anyone so
much as faintly implies that her beloved was not perfect.

At eighty-eight she is still ready to go anywhere that promises gaiety or service to her Cause. She plays a rousing game of bridge and is willing to continue all night or until her guests fall fainting at the table. The first nights of new plays at the National Theatre usually find her among the audience.

She showed an example of her determination and unquenchable gaiety at President John F. Kennedy's inaugural. The night before, when Washington was immobilized by a blizzard, Mrs. Wilson was to dine with Mrs. Gilbert Hitchcock, the widow of her husband's staunchest supporter in the Senate. She was a little late for dinner because it took her car an hour and ten minutes to negotiate six blocks. After dinner she went undaunted to the Inaugural Concert. It took her over two hours to reach Constitution Hall, but she arrived.

Bright and early the next morning, Inauguration Day, Mrs. Edith Wilson and her dear friend and companion, Mrs. Margaret Cherrix Brown, rode to the Capitol behind howling motorcycles thoughtfully provided by the incoming President, with whom she is on very friendly terms. In the brilliant sunshine and arctic cold—16°—she sat through the long ceremony in her high place almost immediately behind President Kennedy. However, she had taken the precaution of putting same small flasks of bourbon in her pockets and managed to keep warm.

After the inaugural she went to the lunch in the Capitol where she exchanged quips with former President Truman and ate large quantities of lobster Newburg, of which she is very fond.

Then came the ride up Pennsylvania Avenue in an open car near the head of the Inaugural Parade. When the car finally turned out of the line of march beyond the White House, the shivering driver suggested, "I think we could put the top up now."

Three minutes later Edith Wilson said, "Open all the windows. I'm stifling."

An indomitable woman!

INDEX

277

Pichon, French Foreign Minister, 157
Plantation, The, 42-44
Pocahontas, 35, 42, 118
Poincaré, Madame, 133, 135
Poincaré, Raymond, 55, 133, 135, 139
Powderly, Miss, 252
Powell's School (Richmond, Va.), 48
Preston, Mayor, 119
Princeton, New Jersey, 85
Princeton University, 30, 58
Pullman, Major, 122

Quirinale Palace, 150-152

Raleigh *Observer,* quoted, 169
Reading, Lady, 145, 147
Reed, James A., 198, 206
Richmond, Virginia, 48
Ritchie, Governor, 270
Robinson (chauffeur), 14, 24, 80, 196
Rodman, Admiral Hugh, 208, 273
Rolfe, Jane, *see* Bolling, Mrs. Robert
Rolfe, John, 42
Rome, Wilsons' visit to, 150-153
Roosevelt, Franklin D., 167, 243, 244, 270, 271-272, 274
Roosevelt, Mrs. Franklin D., 167, 274
Roosevelt, Theodore, 68, 77, 84, 92, 129, 220
Root, Elihu, 172
Ruffin, Dr. Sterling, 219, 220, 229
Russia, 97, 116

Sargent, John Singer, 113-115
Saturday Evening Post, 273
Sayre, Francis, 26, 85, 88, 93
Sayre, Mrs. Francis (Jessie), 26, 88, 93, 110, 113
Schiff, Jacob, 82

Scott, Isaac, 254, 256, 258
Scott, Mary, 254, 258
Scott, Sir Walter, 46
Shadow Lawn, 77-78, 80, 81, 82, 85
Smith, Al, 83, 196, 271
Smithers, Edward, 202
Smith, Dr. Herbert Scott, 39, 41
Sonnino, Sidney, 152
Spring Lake, New Jersey, 77
Standards, U. S. Bureau of, 247
Starling (Secret Service man), 41, 103, 130
State Department, U. S., 19, 20, 72, 94, 123, 227, 240-241
Statue of Liberty, first lighting of the, 91
Staunton Foundation, 270
Stitt, E. R., 219, 220
Sullivan, Mark, 90, 206
Susan (Negro maid), 64-65, 130
Swem, Charles, 64, 82, 130, 200, 223
Sylph (ship), 111

Taft, William Howard, 172
Tardieu, André, 157
Taylor, Dr. James H., 39, 41
Teapot Dome scandal, 233, 241
Terry, General William, 44
Teusler, Rudolph, 43, 268
Teusler, Mrs. Rudolph (Mary), 43, 268
Texas (battleship), 133
Thompson, Charles Willis, 219
Trotsky, Leon, 116
Truman, Harry S., 275
Tumulty, Joseph, 19, 27, 33, 34, 59, 65, 74, 77, 80, 87, 102, 130, 158, 201-202, 207, 214, 215, 216, 224, 227, 228, 231, 242, 244, 272
Twain, Mark, 66

Utah (battleship), 133